Behold! The Second Coming of Jesus Christ Is Near

He Wants Us to Be Prepared For His Arrival

Behold, He is coming with clouds, and every eye will see Him.
—Revelation 1:7

Watch, therefore, for you do not know
the hour your Lord is coming.
—Matthew 24:42

Sarah A. Jones

WESTBOW
PRESS®
A DIVISION OF THOMAS NELSON
& ZONDERVAN

WestBow Press books may be ordered through booksellers or by contacting:

WestBow Press
A Division of Thomas Nelson & Zondervan
1663 Liberty Drive
Bloomington, IN 47403
www.westbowpress.com
1 (866) 928-1240

Scripture taken from the New King James Version®. Copyright © 1982 by Thomas Nelson. Used by permission. All rights reserved.

Scripture marked (KJV) taken from the King James Version of the Bible.

ISBN: 978-1-9736-6665-3 (sc)
ISBN: 978-1-9736-6666-0 (hc)
ISBN: 978-1-9736-6664-6 (e)

Library of Congress Control Number: 2019908307

Print information available on the last page.

WestBow Press rev. date: 7/10/2019

Dear people, surely you can see that this world
as we know it is passing away.

And knowing this, it is now high time to awake out of sleep;
for now is our salvation nearer than when we first believed.
—Romans 13:11

And the world is passing away, and the lust of it; but
he who does the will of God abides forever.
—1 John 2:17

God, who made the world and everything in it, since He is Lord
of heaven and earth, does not dwell in temples made with hands.
Nor is He worshiped with men's hands, as though He needed
anything, since He gives to all life, breath, and all things. And He
has made from one blood every nation of men to dwell on all the
face of the earth, and has determined their pre-appointed times
and the boundaries of their dwellings, so that they should seek the
Lord, in the hope that they might grope for Him and find Him,
though He is not far from each one of us; for in Him we live and
move and have our being. ... For we are also His offspring.
—Acts 17:24–28

Therefore, since we are the offspring of God, we ought not to think
that the Divine Nature is like gold or silver or stone, something
shaped by art and man's devising. Truly, times of ignorance God
overlooked, but now commands all men everywhere to repent,
because He has appointed a day on which He will judge the world in
righteousness by the Man [Jesus Christ] who He has ordained. He
has given assurance of this to all by raising Him from the dead.
—Acts 17:29–31

For the grace of God that brings salvation has appeared to all
men, teaching us that, denying ungodliness and worldly lusts,
we should live soberly, righteously, and godly in the present
age, looking for the blessed hope and glorious appearing of our
great God and Savior Jesus Christ, who gave Himself for us,

that He might redeem us from every lawless deed and purify for Himself His own special people, zealous for good works.
—Titus 2:11–14

Are you prepared for the Second Coming of Jesus Christ? It doesn't matter if you believe it or not; God's Word, plan, and purpose *must* and *will* be fulfilled. Be prepared because Jesus Christ is coming soon!

Contents

Preface

And this gospel of the kingdom shall be preached in all the world
for a witness unto all nations; and then shall the end come.
—Matthew 24:14 (KJV)

This book is about the Second Coming of Jesus Christ and about what we can do according to the Word of God to be prepared for His return. It also tells us according to God's Word what will happen to those who believe in Jesus Christ and those who do not believe in Him and reject Him as God's Son, Lord, and Savior of the world. Jesus told us in John 14:2–3 that He would go and prepare a place for us (to live with Him forever), that He would come back for us and take us to this place and live with Him, and that wherever He is, we will also be with Him. When Jesus came to earth the first time over two thousand years ago, He came as a baby born in a manger located in a stable in the town of Bethlehem. Only perhaps a handful of people knew of His arrival. He came to die so that we could live. Jesus died on a cross for the sins of the world, and God raised Him up on the third day for our justification. He redeemed us, purchased our salvation, and reconciled us to God the Father. He has given us the gift of eternal life.

When Jesus Christ returns to earth at His glorious appearing, He will come as Lord of Lords and King of Kings. Every eye shall see Him coming in the clouds with great power and glory along with His children (saints) and angels. He will reward everyone according to their deeds and will send us to our eternal home, which is either in His kingdom, where we will forever live happily in His presence, or the lake of fire, where we will be in torment, burning forever with brimstone and enduring absolute separation from God for eternity.

In this book I speak about what is going on in the world today as it affects everyone in one way or the other. No one is exempt from the ups and downs in life, nor from the economy, crimes, racial tension, the threat of nuclear war threat, terrorist attacks, hate crimes based on race and gender, world disasters and catastrophes, climate change, occurrences in the political arena, and so on. We are indeed living in perilous times in these last days. This world is in bad condition, and it is going to get worse.

However, God will intervene before humankind totally destroys itself. As for His people who believe in Him and have surrendered our lives to Him, Jesus will return and save us from humankind and its wickedness. He will come take us home. The next event to follow will be the righteous judgment of God. It is here at the judgment seat of God where everyone will be judged according to their works and deeds, the lives they lived, their belief and faith in Jesus Christ, their every spoken and unspoken word, and their love for one another and love for God. All will be judged and sent to their eternal home.

In this book you will find prayers and also answers to questions that you may have relating to Jesus Christ's return. I have provided numerous scriptures from the Bible, God's Holy Word. There are many people who will read any other book before they will read a Bible.

I will talk to you about the branch of theology known as eschatology, which has to do with the judgment of God, the final destiny of the souls of humankind (human beings), eternal death, the end of this age (the world as we know it), and some of the signs and final events that will take place on this earth before Jesus Christ returns. Everything is Bible based; I have made up nothing. Truly I believe, without a shadow of doubt, that we are living in the last days and that the end of this age is approaching quickly. And whether you believe it or not (it doesn't really matter), Jesus Christ is coming; He will soon arrive at the time God chooses. All that He has said in His Word will happen before He comes again to this earth has happened, is happening, or will happen. God loves us and wants us to be prepared for the Second Coming of His Son Jesus Christ.

However, until He comes, we are to share the love and gospel of Jesus Christ; preach the Word of God; live our lives according to God's Word; love our family, our neighbors, and all people; and be prepared at all times for Jesus's return. As true born-again Christians, we are ambassadors for Him. We are to convince, compel, rebuke, and exhort with all long-suffering, teaching and preaching God's Word to all people in love and without prejudice. For God sees only a person's heart, not the color of his or her skin or his or her nationality. We, as His children, are to do the same and be more like Him according to His Word. Remember, He knows those who are His.

We must see each individual for who they are as a person, not the color of their skin or their gender. We must be kind and compassionate to others. We must genuinely love and sincerely pray for one another. We must build up one another with words of encouragement and not tear down one another with our words. We must speak the truth in love. We must be truthful and not lie to or about one another. We must lend a helping hand to those who need it. We must share our riches or what we have with others who do not have. We must do all we can to feed the hungry, clothe the naked, find housing for the homeless, and provide medical assistance for those who really need it—physically and mentally.

We must visit the sick, the homebound, the elderly, and those in prisons, and we must pray for, encourage, and comfort them. We must stick together like strong glue as a people and pray together for one another now—like never before in church history. We must use our God-given gifts to aid in equipping our brothers and sisters for the work of the ministry and for edifying the body of Jesus Christ. We must stand up for justice, truth, and the gospel of Jesus Christ and not be ashamed or afraid.

We *must* stop the hatred and violence among races (induced by Satan himself) before we completely destroy one another. For this is Satan's purpose and goal, to kill, steal, and destroy you and your eternal life with God. You are neither better nor any more righteous than the person of another race or color. God made us with one blood and in His likeness. We all have sinned. We have no righteousness of our own. There is none good—not one person. The soul that sins will surely die (physically and spiritually).

God doesn't love you any more than He loves me, nor does He love me any more than He loves you. He sent His Son Jesus Christ to die on the cross and rise from the dead for all humankind. But He does look deep inside the heart of a person, which only He can do, and He judges that person based on their character, motives, and sincerity of heart. Whoever will believe in Him and in Jesus Christ His Son; ask for forgiveness of their sins and repent; accept Jesus as their Lord and Savior; and live according to His Word will become His child (born again by His Spirit), will be saved, and will obtain the gift of eternal life. You are destined to live forever with Him.

We must tell Satan that he is a liar, the father of lies, and give him no place in our lives. We must resist him and stop allowing him to use us. We must stop listening to him in our minds and through the voices of others who are being used by him.

We must tell the world that Jesus Christ, Son of the living God, is coming and to get their lives and houses in order now, as we must do ourselves. We must tell them to be prepared for His long-awaited return, when He will take His people home to a place that He prepared for us over two thousand years ago. We must tell them about the love, mercy, and grace of God, *but* we must also tell them about the wrath and judgment of God upon the unrighteous, the wicked, evildoers, and all who have not believed and do not have faith in His Son Jesus Christ and who have not accepted Him as their Lord and Savior so they might be saved.

We as Christians are called to be the salt of the earth. Where is your flavor? We must let our light shine so that others can see God in us and will desire to have a relationship with Him.

Acknowledgments

Foremost, I thank Almighty God, my heavenly Father, and Jesus Christ, my Lord and Savior, for choosing me for such a time as this and for entrusting me to deliver this message. I thank Him for His love, for His grace, and for His mercy which is new to me every day. This book is dedicated to God the Father, Jesus Christ His Son, the Holy Spirit, and all who will believe, receive God's Word, and accept Jesus Christ as Lord and Savior.

To Jessie, my only sister, whom I love dearly and who is always in my prayers. Trina, my beautiful niece who's like a daughter, thank you for your love, your respect, and all you do for me. May God continue to keep and bless you. To my beautiful daughters whom I am so very proud of and who have shown their love for me: Rhonda, Ursula, and Tameeka. Thank you for loving, protecting, and respecting me. May God's blessings continue to rest upon you. Ricardo (Tameeka's spouse), my son-in-law: I am very proud of the man, husband, father, and person that you are. Your love, support, and kindness shown to me will always be remembered. God's blessings to you always. To my beautiful grandchildren: Elisa, Ricardo III, and baby Tyler. You are the love and joy of my life, and I adore you all with all my heart. I truly thank God for you, and I treasure every moment that He allows us to spend together. You give me the best medicine in the world—which is your pure love and laughter. May God continue to keep you all as the apple of His eye, hide and protect you under His almighty wings, and embrace you with His love. May His blessings, amazing grace, and mercy be with you always. May the Holy Spirit abide in you and guide you.

To my friends who are like family, Michelle (whom I call my little sister), Xiomara, and Anita (who are like sisters), who are always there for me. I'm so grateful for your love and prayers and for the thoughtfulness and kindness you have always shown me. I will never forget, and neither will God. May He always bless you.

Thank all of you for being such a blessing to me. I am so thankful to God that you all are a part of my life. My love will always be with you. I pray in the almighty and glorious name of Jesus that you all grow in the grace and knowledge of our Lord and Savior Jesus Christ. May His love, grace, and mercy be with you all both now and forever. I pray that we all will be found worthy to go back with Him when He comes. Jesus is coming soon! I pray that you will prepare so that you will be ready for that great and awesome day. I also pray that I will see you all in our eternal home in the New Jerusalem (God's kingdom). Please be there! Pray for me also.

Introduction

I am blowing the trumpet and sounding the alarm: Jesus Christ is coming! It doesn't matter whether you believe it or not, receive this message or not, or prepare yourself or not: the return of Jesus Christ is near. He loves you and desires that all be prepared for His arrival.

Are you certain that you are prepared for His coming? On March 25, 2006, I heard a voice in my dream say: "Let your testimony be: 'Jesus is coming!' The people must be told so that they can be prepared for His return." Therefore, I have written this book to inform you, warn you, encourage you, build your faith, and draw you nearer to God in the hope that you will change your life and your thinking, so that you will be prepared upon His arrival.

To prepare for something or someone, according to the *Merriam-Webster Dictionary*, is to make ready beforehand for a specific or special purpose, occasion, or event or something that you expect to happen at some point in time. You're not quite sure when it will happen, but you're confident in the knowledge that it is going to happen—sooner or later. The *American Heritage Dictionary* tells us that *prepare* means to establish, to fix. It conveys the idea of deliberate effort over a prolonged period of time. *Fixed* means not subject to change or variation, constant, held firmly in mind.

Dear brothers and sisters, we must stay in a prepared state for Jesus's return at all times—spiritually, emotionally, and mentally. We must be watchful, sober, and prayerful and keep on the full armor of God. We must ask God to help us to prepare our hearts and minds. For if we are prepared, then we have gotten ready in advance. We don't know the day or the hour (only God knows), but when it does happen, God the Father wants us to be prepared for this glorious destined event of the return of Jesus Christ.

I believe that there are many Christians who say and believe that they are ready, but they are not fully prepared. For many are still living worldly lives; they do not have a personal relationship with God and have no true expectation of Jesus's return. They use all the theatrical signs and acts like they are Christians, but it's only an act, only a display of godliness. If you say you are a Christian, a born-again believer in Jesus Christ, yet you consciously and continually live in sin, living your own way and not God's way according to His Word, then you are not prepared for His return. If you haven't truly repented of your sins, then you are not prepared for His return. If you haven't asked Jesus to forgive you of your sins and invited Him into your heart, then you are not prepared for His return.

If you do not confess with your mouth and believe in your heart that Jesus Christ is the Son of God, that He died on the cross for our sins, and that God raised Him on the third day, then you are not prepared for His return. If you haven't been spiritually born again, then you are not prepared for His return. If you do not have love in your heart for God, for Jesus, and for everyone regardless of the color of their skin or their race, gender, or religion, then you are not prepared for His return. If you do not believe that Jesus Christ is coming again, then you are *not* prepared for His return. My friends, to help prepare us for Jesus Christ's return, let us strive to have a deeper personal loving relationship with Him.

Ask Jesus to forgive you of your sins and come into your life. Ask Him to change your heart of stone to a heart of flesh. Ask Him to wash you in His blood. Ask Him to baptize you with the Holy Spirit to help you live a holy life, to lead you and direct you, teaching you to witness to others and do all that He has called you to do. Ask Him to help you to prepare for His return so that you will be called to spend eternity in God's kingdom.

Jesus wants us to be prepared for His coming. He wants us all to be found worthy to go back with Him and therefore have a smooth and glorious transition. But the *choice* is yours.

I pray that your faith be broadened, strengthened, and edified in God our heavenly Father and Jesus Christ our Lord and Savior. I pray that your eyes, ears, and heart will be opened spiritually to enable you to see, hear, and receive God's Word.

The clock is ticking. Time is running out. Prepare today to meet and stand before the one true and living God. It is a fact: Jesus Christ's Second

Coming is near. Are you prepared for your final and eternal destination? Are you prepared to be judged and rewarded according to your works (in words and deeds)? Jesus wants you, me, and everyone to be prepared for that great day when He comes back to planet Earth and for Judgment Day.

I did not choose to deliver this message; God chose me and told me to tell you that Jesus is coming. That was thirteen years ago, and those words still burn within me, now more than ever before. Only now the clock is ticking on my behalf; my eternal life is at risk more so than yours. It is not a good feeling when you know that you haven't done all that God has told you to do.

I must sound the alarm, I must blow the trumpet, and I must warn the people, or else God will hold me responsible for being disobedient. So, whether you hear and listen or not, whether you believe or not, Jesus Christ is still coming. Therefore, ultimately it is your choice and yours alone. No one else can make it for you. But remember, the choice you make now will determine where you will spend your eternal life.

You are a spirit, and you live in a body. One day when you die in this life on earth, your body will return to dust. Your spirit, which will never die, will return to God, who gave it (Ecclesiastes 12:7). He appoints a temporary place for the believers in Jesus Christ and for the unbelievers, until all are judged on that great day when their eternal residing place will be determined based on their faith in Jesus Christ and according to their works. Then God's mysterious and wonderful plan will be fulfilled.

Jesus Christ is coming! Although no one but God the Father knows the day or hour, it is a truth—He is coming again. The Bible (Word of God) tells us about events, signs, conditions, and things that will happen or take place on planet Earth before His return and also alerts us to prepare for this inevitable event: *the Second Coming of Jesus Christ*. You and I have heard about this countless times and for many years, and Jesus has yet to arrive. Therefore, you probably think that what I have to say is no different from what you have already read or heard and that there is no truth in such a saying. However, remember that one thousand years is like one day for God, and therefore He could appear at any time. God is full of mercy and is long-suffering. He doesn't want anyone to perish. He has patiently given us more time than we deserve to get our souls right with Him and to prepare for His return.

I am not delivering this message or writing this book for popularity or financial gain. I am doing what God has commanded me to do, lest I become a castaway. And I don't want your blood on my hands or to have my soul be eternally lost for being disobedient to God. I now feel a very heavy burden to get this message out to you in the fastest way possible, for *time* (yours and mine) is short. Dear friends, if there is a place called hell (and the Bible confirms that there is), I am not going, and I do not want you to go, to that awful place of eternal torment. I have a responsibility to God and to you the people. My eternal life depends upon my obedience to His Word and trusting and believing in His Son Jesus Christ and His finished work on Calvary.

I realize that many of you will not like what is said in this message because you do not believe; nevertheless, it must be said, and I will not apologize for it. My will is to do the will of Him who created me, called me, and ordained and appointed me to finish the work He has given me to do here on earth before the return of Christ. I must obey God my Father and Jesus Christ my Lord and Savior. So, if you have a problem with this message or with me, then talk to God about it. For, He has made it very clear that for the sake of your eternal life and my eternal life, I must deliver this testimony and message to you now, while you are alive on this earth to hear it and while I am alive on this earth to tell it.

There is no other choice for me but to obey God my heavenly Father and Jesus Christ His Son. I cannot worry myself with how you feel about this message or whether you believe it or not. That is not my primary concern, although I do pray that you will believe. I seek to please God and not humankind. What I have been told, shown, and taught came from God through the revelation of Jesus Christ. If I say, write, teach, or preach anything contrary to what is written in His Word or to what He has told me to tell you (through dreams, visions, and the Holy Spirit), then let God deal with me as He will. For we all will be judged and rewarded according to our works, whether good or bad, whether based on a lie or on the truth. I am no exception.

I must answer this call of God on my life because my eternal life depends upon it. I have already lost too much time. I thank God for His mercy and long-suffering shown to me. My assignment from God is to warn you, inform you, and increase your awareness, to impact lives with the truth according to the Word of God so that you can prepare for the Second Coming of Jesus Christ (the Son of God, Lord, Savior, High Priest, and King).

I have had many dreams since I was sixteen years old about the world (age) coming to an end and Jesus returning to this earth, and my response was always, "I'm not ready yet." For too long I have not taken heed of the voice of God telling me to warn the people and to preach the gospel of Jesus Christ. I was told to testify that Jesus is coming and to teach and preach many other messages He has given me over the years, but I have not fully done so because I have feared what people might say or think about me. Also, I felt that I could not speak or articulate well enough. I had a fear of failure and was slothful and procrastinating, among many other things, but my biggest problem or hindrance was my fear of speaking in public.

Truly I have been hardheaded and disobedient. I have asked God to forgive me, and He has done so. Now I also ask you to forgive me for not getting this testimony and message to you sooner as God had ordained, as He, having chosen me, called and told me to do. I thank God for those men and women of God who preach and teach about the coming of Jesus Christ. He will always find someone who is willing to obey Him, to be used by Him, and to get His Word out to all people.

God loves us so much and wants us to be prepared to go back with His Son Jesus Christ when He returns to this earth. He wants to give us eternal life and live with Him forever just as He planned from the beginning, before Adam and Eve disobeyed Him in the Garden of Eden. Through His Son Jesus Christ, God has given us another chance to reign with Him once our earthly bodies leave this present life. For when we are absent from the body (or die), our spirits are immediately in the presence of the Lord if we are saved and have given our hearts to Him (1 Corinthians 5:3).

"For God so loved the world that He gave His only begotten Son, that whoever believes in Him should not perish, but have everlasting life. For God did not send His Son into the world to condemn the world, but that the world through Him might be saved" (John 3:16).

Jesus was obedient to the Father, even to His death on the cross. He gave His life on the cross, shed His precious blood, suffered much shame and unimaginable torture, and died for our sins so that He could deliver us from this evil world (age) and give eternal life to all who would believe in Him according to the will of God the Father. He loved us and died for us while we were still in our sin.

God raised Jesus from the grave on the third day for our justification with all power in His hands so that we could once again be in right standing and fellowship with Him. We have been reconciled to God; we can once again communicate with Him, and He with us. We can now pray and come boldly to the throne of grace so that we may obtain mercy and find grace to help in our time of need (Hebrews 4:16). We have been redeemed by the blood of Jesus Christ (the blameless and spotless Lamb of God), who is now seated in heaven at the right hand of God the Father, making intercession and pleading on our behalf.

Jesus Christ is the Son of God the Father, Savior of the world, Lord of Lords, King of Kings, the Bread of Life, Almighty God, Everlasting Father, Prince of Peace, Commander in Chief, Miracle Worker, Redeemer, Holy and Righteous One, Lamb of God, Overseer, Light of the World, High Priest, High Judge, Chief Shepherd, Alpha and Omega, Promise Keeper, Author and Finisher of our Faith, and the Breath of Life.

He is the way, the truth, and the life; the Vine; the Bright and Morning Star; the Lily of the Valley; the Rock of our salvation; and the sun of righteousness. He is a comforter; a wonderful counselor, an advocate; a mediator; our liaison; our intercessor; the bishop of our souls; the apostle and high priest of our confession; the author of eternal salvation; a mind keeper and regulator; our burden bearer; our sustainer; our waymaker; our healer; our provider; our shield and buckler; our protector; our best friend; our caregiver; the lifter of our heads; and everything else that we need for Him to be for us.

Jesus is our only hope. He has promised to give us eternal life and a home with Him if we repent of our sins; believe, trust, obey, have faith in, and abide in His Word; and do His will. He promised to abide in us and never to leave us or forsake us. In Him, we live, move, and have our being. Without Him we can't do anything, and we are nothing.

Sad to say, not everyone will be receptive or believing the authenticity of this message. Not everyone will be saved because they choose not to believe in Jesus Christ.

"And some were persuaded by the things which were spoken, and some disbelieved" (Acts 28:24). For what if some did not believe? Will their unbelief make the faithfulness of God without effect? Certainly not! Indeed, let God be true but every man [person] a liar. As it is written: "That You may be justified in Your words and may overcome when You are judged" (Romans 3:3–4).

Therefore, whether you listen or not, whether you like this message or not, whether you like me or not, whether you believe and accept this message or not, whether you believe in God and in Jesus Christ His Son or not, whether you are a Christian or not; whether you are anti-God, whether you are rich or poor, and whether you are famous or not; and regardless of your race, the color of your skin, your gender, where you were born, where you reside, or what your religion or denomination is, the truth is this: Jesus Christ is coming!

Our Savior is about to make His return to this earth, and we will all stand before Him to be judged. Christ loves us so much and wants us (whosoever will) to be prepared to meet Him and spend eternity with Him. This is the family reunion that God and His people have longed for, talked about, hoped for, watched for, waited for, and prayed for. It is our blessed hope. God is not prejudiced; He looks at the heart, not the color of a person's skin, for He made all of us in His image with the same blood types, biological structure, and body parts, with all of these functioning in the same way.

It is my prayer and my hope that you will smell the aroma of the life that leads to everlasting life as you read and hear this message with your whole heart. I pray that you will be receptive and that the Holy Spirit will open your eyes spiritually so that you can see; open your ears so you can hear; and take away your heart of stone and give you a heart of flesh so that you can believe and receive God's Word. I pray that the Holy Spirit will draw you nearer to God as He draws nearer to you. And if you hear His voice in your heart, do not be stubborn; please listen and obey.

What I'm about to say to you is no different from what you likely have already heard from preachers, teachers, a loved one, a friend, or people in general. Perhaps you have read about it in books or even seen movies on television bearing this message. The only thing that I ask of you is that you please hear me out. This is your time, and it may very well be your last chance to make things right with God before Jesus comes or before your life ends on this earth (which would then be too late).

Some will hear and believe and ask the question "How can I be prepared for Jesus's return?" and some will not. Some will ask, "What must I do to be saved, because I want to be prepared when Jesus comes?" and some will not. Some will repent and ask Jesus to forgive them of their sins and come into their lives. These people will accept Him as their Lord and Savior. Their lives will change, and they will be born again and become a new creation in Christ. And some will not do these things.

Some backsliders will forsake their wicked ways and return to God as He restores them and rebuilds their relationship so that they can be prepared when Jesus returns, and some will not. Some people who confess that they are born-again Christians will examine and reevaluate themselves; take inventory of their lives as they take a good long look in the mirror; and have a face-to-face conversation with themselves about true holiness, faith, righteousness, integrity, love, honor, and obedience to God. And some will not.

"But they refused to heed, shrugged their shoulders, and stopped their ears so that they could not hear. Yes, they made their hearts like flint, refusing to hear the law and the words which the Lord of hosts had sent by His Spirit the former prophets. Thus great wrath came from the Lord of hosts" (Zechariah 7:11–12).

Dear friends, it is high time to stop playing church, high time to stop having just a form of godliness but denying the power of God, high time to stop professing and claiming to know God, but in your actions, words, and works you act otherwise and deny Him. It is high time to stop wearing masks—it's time for you to take the mask off and reveal the real you. You speak an entirely different language, being dishonest, greedy, selfish, and disobedient to God. Who do you think you're fooling other than yourself? You're certainly not fooling God your Creator.

It is high time to stop lying, misleading, and taking advantage of the people of God, and high time to cease robbing God and His people. Repent and change your evil ways, or you will be left behind when Jesus comes, and your final destination will be hell. Remember that God knows your heart and your every thought, He sees all and hears all. You may be able to fool some people, but you can't fool God, no matter how hard you try to cover up your lies and evil works.

"Wherefore the Lord said, Forasmuch as this people draw near with their mouth, and with their lips do honour me, but have removed their heart far from me, and their fear toward me is taught by the precept of men" (Isaiah 29:13 KJV).

"And all the churches shall know that I am he who searcheth the reins [minds] and hearts: and I will give unto every one of you according to your works" (Revelation 2:23 KJV).

It is high time to stop murdering (taking innocent lives senselessly. Know that if you murder, you will pay with your own life); robbing hardworking people (go get an honest job); raping little children and women (you are a wicked and evil demon); hurting elderly people who are too frail to fight back (you are disgusting and such a coward); and doing all kinds of inhuman and devilish acts typical of those committed by the people who belong to Satan. It's high time that all the wicked and unrighteous people get their just and eternal reward, which is eternal damnation in the lake of unquenchable fire and total separation from God. *Stop* the madness and your evil, wicked ways right now. What kind of person are you? Do you have you a conscience? Do you have any decency, morals, self-respect, or respect for others? Would you like to be treated the same way you treat others? Would you want your child, spouse, mother, father, sister, brother, grandmother, grandfather, and other loved ones and friends to be treated the way that you treat others?

Don't get it twisted, and do not be deceived, for God is not mocked. You will reap whatever you sow, and you can be certain of that (Galatians 6:7). No one will get away with anything. God sees and hears all and will judge you, me, and everyone else according to what we do and say. So, repent and get right with God before it is too late so that your covenant with death will be annulled and your agreement with Sheol will not stand (Isaiah 28:18).

Don't let Satan trick you out of everlasting life with Jesus Christ. In the end, you will see that nothing and no one was worth the fame, money, fancy cars, big houses, yachts, jets, airplanes, big job titles, education, immoral and riotous living, guns, gangs, killings, hatred, stealing, hurting of others, and unnecessary material things. For what does it profit a person to gain the whole world and yet lose his or her soul and suffer for eternity in pain and torment, in fire and brimstone that will burn forever and ever?

Dear friends, it is for certain: Satan doesn't want you to hear, believe, and receive this message, which is why he has fought against me so hard and so long. He has told me so many lies to hinder me from getting this word to you, and the biggest one he told me was based on fear. But Satan is a liar and is the father of lies (John 8:44). He couldn't tell the truth even if he wanted to.

I know that God has not given me a spirit of fear. But He has given me a spirit of love, power, and a sound mind (2 Timothy 1:7). I do not fear humankind or what they can do to me, because humans are limited and can only temporarily hurt or destroy my physical body. I fear only God, who can destroy both my physical body and my spirit eternally (Matthew 10:28). Only God can put me in heaven (a place with Him where there is beauty, peace, happiness, love, and joy) or in hell (a place with Satan in darkness, fire, and torment) to dwell forever. And I am determined not to go to hell for anyone. I am going to spend my eternal life with God the Father; Jesus Christ my Lord, Savior, and King; and the family of God.

You may say, "I'm not sure if hell is a real place of eternal torment; if Satan is real; or if there is a lake that burns with unquenchable fire and brimstone as the Bible states." Well, my response to you is: "Are you willing to take a chance with your eternal life?" I'm not. I'd rather play it safe. For what does it profit you to gain the entire world, having everything money can buy, and yet after dying in this life (without Jesus Christ in your life), being able to take only the clothes someone else put on your body and the coffin that will go in the ground, and maybe a headstone, with you? You will lose your soul, and you (your spirit) will live forever in unbelievable darkness, torment, and separation from God. Are you sure you want to take a chance with your eternal life?

My friends, life is not over when it's over on this earth. No, your life—eternal life—is just beginning, and you will now live forever in another place. For your spirit will never die, but it will live for eternity, either in heaven or paradise with God or in hell with Satan. And that is a true fact—the Bible says so. God our Father and Jesus Christ His Son, our Lord and Savior, love us so very much, and They have given us the gift of eternal life, if we so desire and choose. They have also given us the freedom of choice. You have an option as to where you will spend your eternal life, and only you can choose life or death, blessing and cursing. Therefore, you can't blame anyone else for the choice that you make. I pray that you choose life—eternal life. Jesus Christ is coming back to this earth, and He wants us to be prepared before it's too late.

One may ask the question "What must I do to be prepared for His return?"

Well, you must repent, admit that you are a sinner, and ask Jesus to forgive you of your sins. You must confess with your mouth that Jesus Christ is the Son of God and that He came and died on the cross for your sins. You must believe in your heart that God raised Him from the grave on the third day (Romans 10:9). Ask God to fill you with the Holy Spirit and live within you and reign in and over your life. You must live a holy and obedient life before God.

"'Sirs, what must I do to be saved?' And they said, 'Believe on the Lord Jesus Christ, and thou shalt be saved, and thy house'" (Acts 16:30–31 KJV).

"Repent, and be baptized every one of you in the name of Jesus Christ for the remission of sins; and ye shall receive the gift of the Holy Ghost. For the promise is unto you, and to your children, and to all who are afar off, even as many as the Lord our God shall call" (Acts 2:38–39 KJV).

It makes no difference whether or not one believes that Jesus will come a second time. The fact is that Jesus Christ, God's Son, Savior of the world, will come to this earth a second time any day. The question is: will you be prepared for His arrival? I pray to God that we all will be prepared.

> Therefore, be ye also ready; for in such an hour as you think not the Son of Man cometh. (Matthew 24:44 KJV)

> Behold, he cometh with clouds; and every eye shall see him, and they also which pierced him; and all kindreds of the earth shall wail because of him. Even so, Amen. (Revelation 1:7 KJV)

> Jesus is revealed from heaven with His mighty angels, in flaming fire taking vengeance on those who do not know God, and on those who do not obey the gospel of our Lord Jesus Christ. These shall be punished with everlasting destruction from the presence of the Lord and from the glory of His power, when He comes in that Day, to be glorified in His saints, and to be admired among all those who believe, because our testimony among you was believed. (2 Thessalonians 1:7–10)

Behold, the day of the Lord is coming. For I will gather all nations to battle against Jerusalem; The Lord will go forth and fight against those nations, as He fights in the day of battle. And in that day His feet will stand on the Mount of Olives, which faces Jerusalem on the east. And the Mount of Olives shall be split in two, from east to west. (Zechariah 14:1–4)

And the Lord my God shall come, and all the saints with thee. (Zechariah 14:5 KJV)

And it shall come to pass in that day, that the light shall not be clear, nor dark; but it shall be one day which shall be known to the Lord, not day, nor night: but it shall come to pass, that at evening time it shall be light. And it shall be in that day that living waters shall go out from Jerusalem; half of them toward the former sea, and half of them toward the hinder sea: in summer and in winter shall it be. And the LORD shall be King over all the earth; in that day shall there be one LORD, and his name one. And men shall dwell in it, and there shall be no more utter destruction; but Jerusalem shall be safely inhabited. (Zechariah 14:6–9, 11 KJV)

Jesus loves us very much and wants us to be happy. He wants what is best for us. He wants us to be obedient to Him and to live in His will so that we can live in His peace and have a successful good life. He wants us to have eternal life with Him and not with Satan. It is a fact that your spirit, and my spirit, will live forever (it cannot die) either with God our Father and our Lord and Savior Jesus Christ or with Satan, demons, and the wicked. There is no in between; it is heaven or hell. And guess what? You get to choose where you will spend eternity.

Repent! For the kingdom of God is at hand. It's time to seek God with all your heart, with all your soul, and with all your might. Believe and have faith in Him; trust Him; allow Him to lead you and guide your footsteps to His truths.

Jesus is coming! Believe it or not, and whether you are ready or not, you must be prepared for His return, which will be soon.

Blowing the Trumpet and Sounding the Alarm: Jesus Christ Is Coming!

O my soul, my soul! I am pained in my very heart! My heart makes
a noise in me; I cannot hold my peace, because you have heard, O
my soul, the sound of the trumpet, the alarm of war. Destruction
upon destruction is cried, for the whole land is plundered. … How
long will I see the standard, and hear the sound of the trumpet?
—Jeremiah 4:19–21

Blow the trumpet in Zion and sound an alarm in My holy
mountain! Let all the inhabitants of the land tremble; for the
day of the Lord is coming, for it is at hand. For the day of
the Lord is great and very terrible; who can endure it?
—Joel 2:1, 11

Also, I set watchmen over you, saying, "Listen to the sound
of the trumpet!" But they said, "We will not listen."
—Jeremiah 6:17

Thus, says the Lord God: "A disaster, a singular disaster; behold, it has
come! An end has come, the end has come; it has dawn for you; behold,
it has come! Doom has come to you who dwell in the land; the time has
come. A day of trouble is near, and not of rejoicing in the mountains.
Now upon you I will soon pour out my fury and spend My anger upon
you; I will judge you according to your ways, and I will repay you for
all your abominations. My eye will not spare, nor will I have pity; I

will repay you according to your ways, and your abominations will be in your midst then you shall know that I am the Lord who strikes."
—Ezekiel 7:5–9

They have blown the trumpet and made everyone ready; but no one goes to battle; For My wrath is on all their multitude.
—Ezekiel 7:14

To whom shall I speak and give warning, that they may hear? Indeed, their ear is uncircumcised, and they cannot give heed. Behold, the word of the Lord is a reproach to them; they have no delight in it. Therefore, I am full of the fury of the Lord. I am weary of holding it in. I will pour it out. … "For I will stretch out My hand against the inhabitants of the land," says the Lord.
—Jeremiah 6:10–12

Son of man, I have made you a watchman … therefore hear a word from My mouth, and give them warning from Me: When I say to the wicked, "You shall surely die," and you give him no warning, nor speak to warn the wicked from his wicked way, to save his life, that same wicked man shall die in his iniquity; but his blood I will require at your hand.
—Ezekiel 3:16–18; also see 33:7-9

Yet, if you warn the wicked, and he does not turn from his wickedness, nor from his wicked way, he shall die in his iniquity; but you have delivered your soul. Again, when a righteous man turns from his righteousness and commits iniquity, and I lay a stumbling block before him, he shall die; because you did not give him warning, he shall die in his sin, and his righteousness which he has done shall not be remembered; but his blood I will require at your hand. Nevertheless, if you warn the righteous man that the righteous should not sin, and he does not sin, he shall surely live because he took warning; also, you will have delivered your soul.
—Ezekiel 3:19–21

Again, the word of the Lord came to me, saying, "Son of man, speak to the children of your people and say to them: 'When I bring the

sword upon a land, and the people of the land take a man from their territory and make him their watchman, when he sees the sword coming upon the land, if he blows the trumpet and warns the people, then whoever hears the sound of the trumpet and does not take warning, if the sword comes and takes him away, his blood shall be on his own head. He heard the sound of the trumpet, but he did not take warning; his blood shall be upon himself. But he who takes warning will save his life. But if the watchman sees the sword coming and does not blow the trumpet, and the people are not warned, and the sword comes and takes any person from among them, he is taken away in his iniquity; but his blood I will require at the watchman's hand.'"
—Ezekiel 33:1–6

Say unto them, As I live, saith the Lord God, I have no pleasure in the death of the wicked; but that the wicked turn from his way and live: turn ye, turn ye from your evil ways; for why will you die?
—Ezekiel 33:11 (KJV)

But when I speak with you, I will open your mouth, and you shall say to them, "Thus says the Lord God." He who hears, let him hear; and he who refuses, let him refuse; for they are a rebellious house.
—Ezekiel 3:27

Be not afraid, but speak, and hold not thy peace: For I am with thee, and no man shall set on thee: for I have many people in this city.
—Acts 18:9 (KJV)

But who may abide the day of His coming? and who shall stand when He appeareth? for He is like a refiner's fire, and like fullers' soap.
—Malachi 3:2 (KJV)

Dear friends, God's heart longs for all to be saved; however, He cannot and will not force anyone to choose Him and surrender his or her heart to Him. It must be of one's own free will and choice. Please stop for moment and seriously think about what you're doing with the life that He gave you. Do you think that it pleases God? Have you asked Jesus to forgive you of your sins and invited Him into your life? What are you doing for Him? If

He returns right this moment, what will He find you doing, something good or something evil and wicked? Are you prepared to go back with Him upon His return? Are you prepared to stand before Him on Judgment Day to be judged for all you have done and said (good or bad)?

Dear friends, please consider your ways; think about what you are doing. If it's not a life of obedience to God and of pleasing Him, if you are not living a holy life according to His Word, then you are not prepared for Jesus's return. Repent of your sins, believe in the gospel of Jesus Christ, and accept Him as Lord and Savior. As sure as you are born and as sure as you will die in this life, Jesus is coming! The judgment and kingdom of God are at hand.

> See, I have set before you today life and good, death and evil, in that I command you today to love the Lord your God, to walk in His ways, and to keep His commandments, His statutes, and His judgments, that you may live and multiply; and the Lord your God will bless you in the land which you go to possess… But if your heart turns away so that you do not hear and are drawn away and worship other gods and serve them, I announce to you today that you shall surely perish; and you shall not prolong your days in the land. … I call heaven and earth as witnesses today against you, that I have set before you, life and death, blessing and cursing; therefore chose life, that both you and your descendants may live; that you may love the Lord your God, that you may obey His voice, and that you may cling to Him, for He is your life and the length of your days. (Deuteronomy 30:15–20)

Let those who have ears hear what the Spirit of God says. Choose eternal life.

Stop! Look! Listen!

Just stop for a moment, look around, listen, and see what is going on in this world. We are indeed living in perilous times and in the last days as written in the Bible (God's Word). Humans are doing the most inhuman, horrible, disgusting, heartless, and unthinkable things, and God must respond. He must hold us accountable for our actions and the things that we say. Our God is holy, righteous, and just. He *will not* and *cannot* allow the wicked and unrighteous to go unpunished for the evil deeds that they have done, the acts they continuously commit without shame or remorse. You evildoers are about to reap what you have sown, and there will be no exceptions. Nor will there be any pity for anyone.

The world's economic crisis grows worse; the cost of living is outrageous; the cost to rent an apartment or purchase a home in many states is unreal and what I consider robbery; major and small companies are going out of business; people are losing their jobs; there are few or no salary increases; and the cost of a college education has tripled in the last couple of years. The cost of health care is off the chain. It is shameful that our government has allowed this to happen to the American people.

Many have worked hard and long for very little and have contributed much to society, yet the government will choose to aid those from other countries before helping its own citizens who were born, were raised, have worked, and have paid taxes here, such as FICA, which is automatically deducted from our paychecks; we have no choice in the matter. That's wrong, and those in charge will have to give an account to God one day for their decisions and actions. I don't believe that social security and Medicare benefits will be here for my children (even though they have contributed).

There's so much hate in the hearts of people, as well as fear, distrust, and darkness in the world today. Yet there's little or no fear of God. People are calling on the name of Satan rather than on the name of Jesus, who is above every *name* and has all power. Satan is getting very bold and is stirring up a lot of trouble around the world because he knows that his time is just about up for deceiving, lying, destroying, and using the weak and wicked.

We could enter World War III (it may be nuclear in the end) at any time. History seems like it's trying to repeat itself. Racial tensions—hatred among races—is high, and the love of many has waxed cold. The people of one race think that they are superior to those of another race because of the color of their skin, not realizing that God made us all in His image and with the same blood and body parts. God is no respecter of persons. He made us all with different skin color and different hair color and texture. He wanted us to be different in this respect for whatever His reason. One day you will have a chance to ask Him, though I very much doubt that it will matter.

The crime rate continues to rise, and the use of firearms is totally out of control, causing thousands of senseless and untimely deaths each year. It seems like everybody has gone mad and has a gun. In some states, by law, a person can even carry a gun in public and shoot to kill anyone if they feel that their life is threatened. This is dead wrong! God is not pleased and will soon do something about it.

There are many people who abuse this law and use it as an excuse and opportunity to kill and then say that the killing was justifiable, that they were only standing their ground. I personally believe that all guns, except for those used for *some* law enforcement purposes, and of course those used for military purposes, should be banned. Seemingly everybody has guns, the good and the bad people, and they all have guns for different reasons. If all guns were banned for everyone (other than law enforcement and military), then there would be no need for anyone else to have a gun.

Believe this: those people who use guns unlawfully will one day stand before God and pay with their eternal souls in hellfire for the life (or lives) they took because they were trigger-happy or seeking personal revenge; because they shot senselessly; because of their hatred or prejudice; because they committed a robbery; because they were cold-blooded and committed murder; because they were involved with drugs or a gang; or for any reason other than to protect and save their own life, the lives of their family members, or the lives of others. Put away your guns! Those who live by the sword will die by it.

With the help of Satan, human beings are doing a very good job of destroying themselves. You are doing just what the devil wants you to do. Why don't you use common sense? Stop being a fool and a pawn for Satan. The only reward he has for you is torment, burning in a lake of unquenchable fire with brimstone, for eternity. And that's a long time, a time that has no end.

Remember, God sees everything you do. He knows your heart; He knows what you did and why you did it; and He knows why you shot and killed that person (man, woman, or child). Woe unto you! Believe me, one day soon you will pay with your own life with eternal indescribable suffering in the lake of unquenchable fire, unless you truly repent and ask God to forgive you of your sins.

Famines are occurring worldwide. There is pestilence, all kinds of disease, wars in diverse places, strange weather (the seasons seem to be out of whack), massive earthquakes, mudslides, floods, tsunamis, hurricanes, tornados, and wildfires. Families have risen up against each other; there is hatred and prejudice; there are murders, shootings, robberies, and kidnappings; there is human trafficking, slavery, and domestic violence; and no one cares for anyone other than themselves. And because many have become so evil, allowing Satan to use them, both men and women, young and old, are senselessly killing each other at the blink of an eye just for foolishness or because of hatred based on race or gender. The suicide rate is staggering. People of all ages (even young children) are taking their lives because they feel (and Satan is telling them) that suicide is the only way *out* for them. Our children cannot go to school to get an education without the fear of some disturbed, evil, and demonically influenced person going on a shooting and killing spree. This has got to stop!

People have no morals or respect for themselves. People have no love or respect for each other. Children are disobedient and have no respect for their parents or the seniors. But then some parents have no respect for their children, nor do they show respect for seniors. People of all ages use profanity (and take God's name in vain) as they stand or sit right in front or beside you (that is, if they're not cussing at you). People act like they are inhuman, like they're wild beasts. They are barbaric, vicious, cruel, sadistic, and brutish and just don't care about anyone—not even themselves. Woe unto you! For your day of judgment is coming—very soon.

People have no fear or respect for God and no respect for human life. They will kill, rape, and abuse anyone (man, woman, or child) and have no guilty conscience, and they won't lose any sleep at night. They are worse than monsters or wild beasts and are not fit to be compared to a human being. They are despicable and should have no place on earth. They will reap worse than what they have sown.

Many churchgoers have no respect for the house of God. They eat, drink, gossip, text, and talk on their cell phones in the main sanctuary, even during the service. They have little to no respect for the house of God. People will allow their children to run and play in the church as if it were a playground. It's a disgrace!

And although I don't blame everything on the devil (because some people are just plain wicked and evil by nature; it's their personal choice, and they do not want to change), it remains true that the devil will use anyone who will allow him to use them. Satan only wants to separate you from God and destroy your eternal soul in hellfire with him. Woe to all those individuals, for soon you will stand in judgment before Almighty God and be rewarded according to your deeds.

Parents

Parents are mistreating, neglecting, physically abusing, emotionally abusing, sexually abusing, verbally abusing, and/or selling and prostituting their children for money and drugs. Some are killing their own children. This is unthinkable! It is a nightmare for those children. Many even use profanity toward their little babies and young children as they would toward an adult. Many intimidate and threaten their children, causing them to live in fear. Many belittle their children, telling them that they are nothing and will never be anything, saying they are stupid, ugly, too fat, too skinny, too black, too light, and whatever else. This is very unfair to those children who did not ask to be born. Who are you? What are you? You're certainly not a civilized human being.

Why didn't you give the child up for adoption, in the hope that a loving person would take care of the child? Why did you lie down and have sex, especially unprotected sex, fully knowing the consequences, if you didn't want to have children or the responsibility of raising children? You knew that you could get pregnant; surely you're not that ignorant.

Then there are those so-called mothers who allow their boyfriends to abuse and rape their children and beat them to death. How sick is that? How can you put a man before your own child? You are an idiot, a sick horrible person, and you will spend your eternal life in hell in torment and burn in everlasting unquenchable fire. And you will remember all your evil works done to every one of God's children you harmed, hurt, abused, caused to live in fear, or killed. One day (in God's time) you will pay severely with your life in the worst way possible: by spending forever in hell.

Listen, do you really believe that you're getting away with your evil and wicked ways just because you haven't yet gotten caught by anyone, including the law, for what you have done and/or are doing to these children? Do you really think that God doesn't know or see everything? Your day of reckoning with God Almighty is coming. Woe unto you if you don't wholeheartedly repent and ask God to forgive you of your sins right now. (Also ask your children whom you harmed to forgive you.) And remember, God knows your heart and sees what you are doing. Sin has a costly price tag, and one pays for it with one's eternal life. Don't let this happen to you. God loves you—yes, even you! He wants you to be saved. He is a merciful and forgiving God, and He's full of grace.

Repent! Change your carnal mind and sinful way of living; turn away from your old lifestyle; and turn to Jesus Christ. Ask Him to forgive you of your sins, and invite Him into your heart and life. He will make you a new creation in Him and give you a new life and way of living. He died and rose again to give you a brand-new life, an eternal life of indescribable joy, peace, and happiness in His presence forever.

God sees everything that we do; nothing is hidden from Him. He knows what we are thinking before we even think it. He knows and searches the heart. We can't run and can't hide from Him.

"For there is nothing covered that shall not be revealed; and hid, that shall not be known" (Matthew 10:26 KJV).

Have genuine love and respect for your children. Protect them with your life. Your child did not have a choice in the matter as far as being born or who his or her parents would be. No, this was all your doing, your choice. Now, be a real woman and deal with it. Be the best mother that you can be to your child, and strive to be better than your mother and all the other mothers. The same applies to the dads be a real man, not a deadbeat, useless dad and man. Be a father, the best that you can be, and strive to be a better man and father than your dad and all the other fathers.

Believe me, you as their parents will be held responsible for how you cared for your children (until they became adults). You will have to give an account to God when you stand before Him on Judgment Day. And that day is coming sooner than you think.

Men and Women

Yes, you who rape, kill, kidnap, sell, hurt, abuse, terrorize, and cause harm to children—*you* will pay with your eternal life in the lake of unquenchable fire! What kind of creature are you? How can you live with yourself with no conscience to bother you about what you have done and are still doing? You belong to the devil, and you will burn in hellfire forever for your horrible deeds and for hurting God's precious children. Jesus said that it would be better for you to tie a millstone around your neck and be cast into the sea than to hurt one of His little children (Matthew 18:6). You will reap what you sow. You will pay with your life for eternity in a lake that burns with sulfur, brimstone, and fire that cannot be quenched. You will be in indescribable pain and torment forever and ever.

You will spend every moment remembering what you did to those children and anyone else you have killed or hurt in any way, fashion, or form. You will pay for all your evil and wicked ways forever. Remember, your flesh will die, but your spirit will live forever. Let me ask you this question: where do you want to spend your eternal life, in heaven or in hell? There is no in between. You think about it! It is your choice.

There are innumerable children in God's kingdom. He loves and cares about all children. And unless we all are converted (born again in the spirit and changed in character, heart, and mind, having become a new creation) and become as little children (full of love and innocence and being trusting and joyful), we will not enter God's kingdom (Matthew 18:3).

However, because God is full of grace, He is a merciful, loving, kind, and forgiving God—yes, he will even forgive you for the evil and wicked things that you have done. If you are sincerely sorry, then repent, stop your madness, forsake your wickedness right now, and ask Jesus to forgive you of your sins. You will then be saved from spending eternity in hellfire. No matter how I feel or what I think (and no matter what anyone else thinks or feels), Jesus Christ died on the cross for your sins and rose for your justification just as He did for me and everyone. He loves us and has given us all the same chance to live with Him for eternity.

Children, Teenagers, and Young Adults

Many young people today use profanity and have no shame. They are rude; they have no respect for their parents or their elders; and they have no self-respect and no sense of self-worth (I say this based on the way they act, talk, and dress). I have heard children as young as six years old cuss like an adult with no shame. Children ages eight and up use vulgarity, sell and use drugs, carry weapons, steal, hurt others, and even commit murder. This is crazy and sad. Where are the parents or guardians of these misled and misguided children? What have they seen and heard from those around them that makes them feel that they have to say and do these horrible things, to emulate these actions, or to protect themselves? These things make them feel vulnerable, unloved, worthless, and afraid. Believe me, you as the parent or guardian, or as some other individual who caused harm and mistreated these children, will be held responsible by God, and you will pay.

Children, teenagers, and young adults, you who know right from wrong, and if you choose to do evil, you will be held accountable for your actions and choices. You will suffer the consequences of your wrongdoings. God hears, knows, and sees everything that you do and say. You can't hide anything from Him. Stop! Don't let Satan talk you into doing these wicked things; he will destroy your life before it really begins.

However, if you are in trouble or afraid, if someone is mistreating, abusing, and hurting you or making you do illegal things against your will, you *must* tell someone (no matter what the enemy or the person who is hurting you tells you). Don't be afraid. Tell your parents or guardians (if it's not them), your schoolteacher or principal, the police, a friend, a family member, or the pastor of a church. I know that it may be hard for you to trust, but you have got to trust someone so you can get help.

There is a way out; there is a better way for you even though you may not feel like there is or it may not seem there is. God loves you, and He will deliver you. But you have got to speak up and tell someone what is happening to you. Be strong and be brave. Don't feel embarrassed or ashamed, because you have done nothing wrong. You are the victim now, but you will be the victor in Jesus. And those devils who hurt you will be punished by the law and by God.

Young girls and women advertise their body parts and wear short shorts, minidresses, skintight pants, and tops that show most of their breasts, leaving nothing to the imagination. And you expect someone to respect you? I think not; you're only attracting the eyes of Satan and opening doors for him to attack you. (*Note:* Regardless of how you dress, no one—man or woman—has the right to violate or attack you.) No young man or older man respects or wants a loose woman for a wife. He wants a young woman or a woman with intellect, morals, values, and respect for herself. He wants a wife he can trust, respect, and be proud of. He will use you for his pleasure, but he will not marry you. He will seek, love, and marry a virtuous woman.

What is wrong with you? Don't you value yourself any more highly than that? Must you flaunt your body or put your body on display just to get attention? to get a job? Don't you believe that you are better than what some people may think of you or than that which you portray? Don't you love and respect yourself? Can't you think for yourself? Must you follow others in their wrongdoings? Don't you have any intelligence? Don't you know that you are now old enough to be held accountable for your sins? Don't you know that when you die in this life, if you have not given your life to Jesus Christ and repented of your sins, you will spend your eternal life in a place called hell? Wake up! Open your eyes and see; open your ears and hear.

Young boys and men of all ages are disrespectful to their parents, young girls and women, and the elderly. They wear their pants halfway down to their bottoms with their dirty underwear showing. This looks tacky, trashy, tasteless, unprofessional, and just plain dirty and nasty. What are you thinking? Do you really think you look nice dressed this way? Who told you such a lie? Who convinced you to do such a thing? Why do you follow others who look silly and say silly things, demonstrating a lack of intelligence and common sense? Why can't you be your own man? How do you see yourself? How do you think others see you? Who are you trying to impress? What are you trying to prove, and to whom? What are your goals and purpose in life?

Pull up your pants, put a belt on if one is needed, and look decent and neat. Talk, walk, stand, dress, and act like the intelligent man God created you to be. Have respect for yourself and others. Don't be rude and distasteful. Stop using obscenities and vulgarity, and stop taking God's name in vain. You look and sound foolish when you do. Don't follow or talk like someone else; be your own person. Most young women who respect themselves are looking for real men and husbands who are well-dressed, decent-looking, educated (at least some education), well-spoken, employed, and intelligent and who act like they have common sense.

Get yourself together before it is too late. You are so much better than what you portray yourself to be. Prove it to yourself—and to everyone else. You are somebody special, so act like it, talk like it, and dress like it. Believe in yourself and be the best *you* that you can be. Be a great leader and not a follower. Be strong and not weak. Be one who builds up and not tears down. Be a life-giver and not a life-taker. Be a winner and not a loser. Be strong and determined to make a lasting contribution to society in this lifetime. Strive to have a profound impact on the lives of your children as well as others. Stop acting like a "tough guy" with no good sense. Obey your parents so that you can live a long, healthy, good life while on this earth.

People of All Ages

People of all ages are dying all around the world every day senselessly and needlessly just because they want to act like wild animals, be in a gang, or impress someone, or because they feel they just have to get their point across, or because they are just plain heartless and evil. People like this are not happy and hate to see anyone else happy. They don't want to succeed in life and don't want anyone else to succeed. They don't have this or that, and they don't want anyone else to have it. Someone hurt them or someone in their family, so they feel that they must also hurt someone. They feel the need to get even (and oftentimes they are seeking retribution against people they don't even know—innocent people!).

If you fit this description, then you are a person who doesn't want to work for a living. You would rather take what someone else has worked hard for. You steal and even kill for things that you have no right to, things that don't belong to you. You're too lazy to work and contribute to society like all other decent people. What must your parents and children think of you? The Bible states, "If a person will not work due to laziness, then neither shall he eat" (2 Thessalonians 3:10 KJV).

Get a *job*! Stop being a lazy, no-good, unproductive person. Stop being a leech!

Let me ask you these questions: Does your life matter? How do you feel when you steal from others? How do you feel when you take the life of an innocent human being? Do you like who you are? Do you know who you are? Have you looked deep down inside yourself? Do you have a conscience? Do the lives of others, including those of your so-called brothers and sisters, matter to you? My answer to this last question based on my own personal experience, and based on what I have heard and witnessed, would have to be *no*!

Too many of our African American people (young men especially) take the lives of their own people, thereby destroying their own selves. They kill and steal from the already poor black people who worked hard to get what little they have. You steal and kill, yet you don't want anyone to steal from you—nor do you want to die.

You all are nothing but lazy cowards looking for attention! Grow up and act like a human being. The only thing that you are proving and showing to your so-called friends or homeboys is that you can die instantly or else go to prison for most of your life or the rest of your life. Now who in their right mind wants that? Please do something constructive with the life that God gave you. You can do it! And you can start by repenting of your sins. Ask Jesus Christ for forgiveness of your sins. Ask Him to come into your life and give you a new heart, a new mind, and a life that's pleasing to Him. He will do it!

Gangs

The gangs I'm referring to here are organized groups of criminals—by their own admission and by choice. Young men and women, teenagers, and boys and girls who perhaps do not feel that they have the love and security of their parents and family, who have no respect for themselves or others, and who don't care about themselves or others are at risk of joining gangs. They have little or no self-esteem and little education. They may feel worthless, unloved, alone, scared, and bullied, so they seek others like themselves and hide in large groups to feel important, noticed, and safe.

Their purpose is to steal, kill, and destroy, which is just like Satan's purpose. By doing all of these devilish acts, they feel that they gain the respect and recognition of the group or their buddies or that they have now proven themselves to be loyal to their group. (How silly and ignorant is that?) Together they attack in numbers (even one individual) because they are cowards and do not have the bravery to stand up individually and fight one-on-one.

There are gangs of every race of people all around the world acting like savage beasts, as though they were raised in the woods by wild animals. What are you trying to prove, and to whom? Do you think that there is some glamour in it or that you're someone special because you're in a gang? Do you think that those who claim that they are now your family and have your back really are and really do? No, I don't think so. When you get involved with the law, then you will see how much these people care about you and have your back. They care only for themselves and what they can get for themselves. They also care about what illegal things they can make you do that hurt others so that they themselves won't get caught doing it. Simply put: you are a fool, and you're being used! Others see this, but you don't because your eyes have been blinded by Satan, and your understanding and conscience has been seared by lies and deceit.

There is nothing good or hip about being in a gang. It is a game that it organized by Satan to use, kill, steal from, and destroy people, especially young people. There is no hope in a gang or in any person in a gang. But there is hope in Jesus Christ. Ask God for help and strength, and come out from among them. He will receive and protect you. You don't have to fear human beings, because God will handle them. Stop allowing Satan to use you by allowing others to trick, use, and manipulate you. Repent right now, and ask Jesus Christ to forgive you of all your sins. Being in a gang doesn't make you powerful or special, but it does makes you look and sound ignorant, and it will cause you to live either a short life or else a long life in prison. However, it's your decision, your choice.

You really think you're bad and all that. Believe me, your day of reckoning and your day of judgment is coming soon if you do not repent and depart from evil. You will know, feel, and experience the wrath of God, and you will give an account to God for every life that He gave and that you took. You will reap all that you have sown and more. For every life that you have taken and every person you have tortured, you will constantly feel the pain, hurt, helplessness, sadness, and sorrow of those people forever. You will remember all that you did to them. And there will be no escape for you. You will be in constant torment, burning in a lake of unquenchable fire in hell for eternity along with your so-called buddies, the evil and wicked, Satan, and his demons. Tell me, who will you then call for help?

However, because God is merciful, because He loves you, because Jesus died on the cross at Calvary for your sins and rose on the third day for your justification, and because He is no respecter of persons, there is a way for you (yes, even you) to avoid eternal life in hellfire. But you must sincerely repent of your sins, your evil ways, and ask Jesus Christ for forgiveness— right now, before it's too late. This is your only way out. If you call on Jesus Christ right now for help, He will help you. He loves you and wants to give you eternal life. Embrace His love, and you will become a brand-new person; your life will never be the same. I guarantee it!

Don't you see? You are doing just what Satan and some other people want you to do, which is to destroy yourself. It is sad and bad enough that we must worry about young black men and women being mistreated or even killed by perverse-minded police officers, but it is even worse when they are being mistreated or killed by our own black men and women. You are really doing your enemies a favor by robbing and killing your own people. And you wonder why you are given no respect. Really?! You need to seek God now, while you may find Him, and call upon Him while He is near. Repent. Turn away from your sinful ways. Ask God to forgive you of your sins, come into your life, and make you a new creation in Him. Do it now!

All Lives Matter Regardless of Race

Our God is the Creator of all people, and He treats everyone (regardless of race) the same. Jesus Christ died on the cross for the sins of all people, and He rose from the dead on the third day for all lives. He favors no race or color. That doesn't matter to Him at all. We are all created in His image and His likeness. We all have the same body parts and odor. Our blood is the same color. There is no one good—no, not one—for we all have sinned and fallen short of His glory. We all need a Savior—Jesus Christ our Lord.

Yes, black lives do matter! So my question is, why are black people destroying black lives all around this world, and in black neighborhoods, by robbing, killing, selling drugs, raping and abusing our children and women, disrespecting the elderly, and even raping and killing them? What is wrong with you? And you want respect or feel that you deserve respect? Definitely not! I know what you do deserve and what you will get if you don't repent and change the way you're living. Ask Jesus to forgive you of your sins, and invite Him into your life. Many young black men are doing nothing with their lives but wasting it. If this applies to you, know that you are only destroying yourself and causing your race to be wiped from the face of this earth—way too soon.

Yes, the police are killing too many young black men, oftentimes for no good reason. If you are a police officer and your life is threatened by a young black man, I can understand why you might kill him, and I don't blame you for it. But if your life is not threatened, and if you support shooting someone in the back (while he is running away) because you thought he had a gun or that you saw a gun, then what you are doing is wrong. And why shoot to kill; why not shoot a suspect in the legs? That would stop them, and they would still be alive.

I believe that the majority of police officers reach for their guns and shoot out of fear and bigotry. And they have no conscience, no feeling or remorse for their actions. They never think about how they would feel if someone were to shoot and kill their young child, parent, spouse, siblings, or loved ones. (They don't realize or believe that they will reap what they sow and that what goes around comes around sooner or later. That's what the Word of God says, and it is true.)

This issue concerns me very much as I have two very young grandsons, a son-in-law (who is like a son to me), young nephews, and very young great-nephews. My son-in-law and nephews have never had problems with the law. All of them are hardworking, educated, intelligent, responsible, and respectable. They take excellent care of themselves and their families and endeavor to be the best people they can be. They take pride in who they are and in their race.

Black men and women: black lives do matter! So, please, stop hurting and killing one another! It is senseless and foolish. Be a better representative of yourself. Stop hurting others and committing crimes against people. If you do commit a crime, then you should be charged with it and serve ample time in prison (and this applies to any person or race). Young boys and men, when you are approached by a police officer, stop doing and saying the things that you know can and most likely will land you in jail or get you killed. By now, you know how the law and system works. So use your brains, not your mouth.

Dear people, all people of every race: let the process of healing and respecting one another start with *you*. Love and protect one another. Stop allowing Satan to use you against one another and doing exactly what he wants you to do. For he only wants to kill, steal from, and destroy you. Let us start building up one another instead of tearing each other down; let's start saving lives instead of taking lives. In God's eyes, all lives matter regardless of skin color. Let's unite peacefully with honor and respect for one another as a people. Let your actions speak for you. As God loves us, let us also love one another regardless of the color of anyone else's skin. God looks at our hearts, not our complexion or the color of our skin.

Many of you of every race and nationality have no shame, no morals, no conscience, low standards for yourself, no integrity, no faith in God, no fear of God, and no respect for yourself, for God, or for others. You are not trustworthy. You are a disgrace to society, your parents, and those who love you. You are like wild animals with no understanding and therefore cannot be tamed. And this is all because you choose the life you live.

Young people, choose to do something constructive and meaningful with your life here on earth so your family can be proud of you and you can be proud of yourself. Be industrious rather than lazy. Help others with their needs; be a giver and not a taker. God is not mocked; He knows and sees everything. And it is for certain that you will reap what you sow.

But know this: God sees every move you make, every step you take, and everything that you do (including to whom, where, and why), and He knows your every thought and every word even before you think it or say it. He will punish you for your evil and wicked works. You will wish that you had never been born and will wish that you had made better decisions and choices in life. You may think you are getting away with it, but your appointment to stand before Almighty God and Jesus Christ on Judgment Day is almost here.

And woe unto you if you do not sincerely repent now of your sins and ask Jesus to forgive you, come into your life, and be your Lord and Savior. Be the person that God created you to be. You have greatness inside of you, but it's up to you to develop it and allow it to materialize. God has a beautiful plan for your life, but He will not force it upon you; you have to want it and be willing to accept it. It's your free choice.

Let me address this to Caucasian police officers: it is a fact that there are more African American men and women (young and old) being killed by Caucasian police officers than any other race. (Also, you kill more than any other police officers of any other race or nationality.) *Stop* shooting and killing black men because of your fear, because you are prejudiced and just don't like black men or people of another race, or because of the way they look, walk, dress, talk, and so on.

Please know that in the eyes of God you are no better than anyone else (based on race or otherwise), for He made us all. You will stand before Almighty God one day and give an account of all the lives you have willfully and wrongfully taken. And you will be severely punished! God is not dead, and He never gave you authority to rule over or be overseers of African Americans or people of any other race. You are not superior even though you may think you are. We will all face God on Judgment Day, and He won't be looking at anyone's skin color, race, wealth, or profession; He'll be looking at your heart.

"I, the Lord, search the heart, I test [examine] the mind. Even to give every man according to his ways [conduct, actions], according to the fruit of his doings [what a person deserves based on his or her deeds]" (Jeremiah 17:10).

Women

Don't wait for someone else to pat you on the back or encourage you. Encourage yourself. You are a woman of great worth, faith, and integrity. You are a virtuous woman with high standards, morals, and values, and you protect your body, mind, and spirit. You love and respect yourself as well as others, and you deserve respect in return. You are a queen or a princess. You are beautiful, intelligent, educated, and successful. You are a leader who does what is right and not a follower of wrongdoing.

You are all that and then some. In Jesus Christ, you can do and achieve anything that you set your mind to do. You are unmovable and unstoppable. God, Creator of heaven and earth, made you wonderfully and fearfully. The Spirit of God who lives in you is greater and stronger than the devil and he who lives in the world. You are a winner and victorious. So look like it, stand like it, walk like it, dress like it, act like it, and talk like it. Let the redeemed of the Lord say so!

Men

Encourage yourself. You don't need anyone (either man or woman) to tell you what you already know. Give yourself a pat on the back and a high five. You are strong and educated. You are a provider for your family, a good father, a good husband, a gentleman, the protector of your family, a man of intelligence, a man of faith and integrity, and a man who has morals and values and is a lover of God rather than a lover of humankind. You are a good and honest man. You are a strong leader of righteousness and not a follower of unrighteousness. In Jesus Christ, you can do and achieve anything that you set your mind to do. You are unmovable and unstoppable. God, Creator of heaven and earth, made you. You are a winner and victorious. So dress like it, look like it, talk like it, and act like it. Be a follower of God and not of humankind.

To those of you who do not know Jesus Christ as your Lord and Savior, you need to ask Him to forgive you of your sins and repent. Turn away from your old way of living and turn to a new life and a new way of living. Say the short prayer in the following chapter and mean it with all of your heart. It's just that simple. Then, stay focused, stay in God's Word, study hard, and work diligently. Keep away from people who have no respect for God or for you, themselves, or others, people who do not want to achieve anything in life. They are just plain lazy with no goals or ambitions, and they allow Satan to rob them of the plans that God has preordained for their life and future. And now they wish the same fate for you.

Most often they only want to get you into trouble to prevent you from achieving your goals and realizing the wonderful plans and future that God has for you. They see God's greatness in you (even though you may not see it), and they see where you're headed, and because of their jealousy and envy, they want you to fail. Don't let Satan continue to blind, fool, and use you by listening to and following others who are doing bad things. Satan is the author of lies. He hates you and only wants to kill you, steal from you, and destroy you—physically, emotionally, and spiritually. And he wants to separate you from God. That is his only desire and assignment.

Finally, dear people, no matter who you are, please know and understand that you don't have to prove anything, and that you don't have to prove yourself, to anyone other than God. You have the power within you to say no to doing things you know are wrong (morally and otherwise) and against the law. Carefully and wisely choose the people you hang out with. Never be afraid to say no, and never allow anyone to push or force you into doing anything that you do not want to do. Never follow others just because you're afraid or concerned about how they might think or what they might say about you. How they feel doesn't matter, but how you feel, and the consequences of your actions, does and will matter to you.

You don't have to be a murderer, rapist, or thief, or a person who beats up and bullies people, or a member of a gang just to make yourself feel validated, like you're somebody special or someone to be feared. Be your own man or woman, and don't follow evil.

If you don't have Jesus Christ in your life, frankly, you are no one special. But if you do, then you are very special—and you don't need to shoot a gun, be in a gang, hurt others, murder people, or sell or use drugs, and you do not need to obey the voice of those whom Satan is using. If you truly want to be powerful, then repent of your sins and invite Jesus Christ into your life. Ask Him to baptize you with His Holy Spirit. Read the Bible. Get an education, get knowledge, get wisdom, and above all get understanding.

He can and will fill every void in your life. He can and will give you joy unspeakable and peace that surpasses all understanding. He will love you with an everlasting love and will never leave you or forsake you. He will protect you and lead and guide you on the right path, the way that you should go. Be careful of the company you keep, for your so-called friend is often your worst enemy.

Satan is the father of lies, and he wants to destroy your body and your soul. He kills, steals, deceives, and destroys. Think for yourself, respect yourself, respect God, respect others, have morals, and value life (your life and others' lives). Be the head and not the tail. Stop being intimidated and used by humankind and Satan. Stop being a complete idiot and a pawn in Satan's hand, someone he uses to do his dirty work and then toss to and fro. Be a real man or woman with character, bravery, integrity, intelligence, sophistication, and good common sense. Stand up! Say and do what you know is right.

Have dreams and pursue them. Have goals and seek after them; persevere and achieve them. Don't allow anyone who is being used by Satan to stop you from reaching for and obtaining all that God has for you (I don't care who it is he's using—and most of the time it's someone you trust and who is very close to you). Satan's goal and plan for you is that you spend eternity in hellfire with him, the wicked, and anyone who doesn't believe in Jesus Christ. Satan does not love you, but he knows that God the Father and Jesus Christ love you with Their lives.

Don't be foolish and let the devil (Satan) have his way with your life any longer. You have the strength and power within you (with God's help) to say no and to overcome him. Don't be afraid or be bulldozed and pressured by Satan. He's like a roaring lion seeking whomever he can destroy. But he has been defeated by Jesus Christ over two thousand years ago. Satan knows this, but he doesn't want you to know it—or believe it.

Prayer of Repentance and Salvation:

Will you please say this short prayer out loud to God and mean it with your heart?

Father God, I repent of my sins and ask for Your forgiveness. I believe that Your Son Jesus Christ died on the cross for my sins and that you raised Him from the grave on the third day. I confess this now with my mouth and believe it with all my heart. Thank You for coming into my life. Make me a new creation born again of Your Spirit. Let me no longer be conformed to this world, but transform me by renewing my spirit and mind with the things of God. Crucify the deceitful lusts of the flesh and the former conduct and actions of the old me. Thank You for saving my soul and making me whole. Now, endow me with Your Holy Spirit, and lead and guide me in the way that You would have me go. In Jesus's name I pray. Amen.

Hate Crimes and Prejudice

Since the dawn of time there has been some form of prejudice, with one race or group of people thinking that God has made them better than others (which is not true). They take advantage of people of color and of other races, and of the poor and less fortunate, although it is these latter people who invented, created, worked the fields of the former, raised their children, and helped make them rich. Our men and women—the people of this other race belittled them, stripped them of their dignity, abused them, raped them, misused them, dishonored them, mistreated them, sold their children into slavery, and even killed them for no reason other than hatred and fun.

Today, and unfortunately, some people of that race or in that group still think that they are better and richer than others. People are mistreating and killing people just because of skin color, gender, or sexual preference; where they live; where they came from; and/or their religion. There are even times when people judge and kill others based solely on how they look, talk, or dress. They don't give them a chance to say anything to defend themselves. They form their own opinions—they become judge and jury. If you are one of these people, then be very careful, because you will reap what you sow, and you will be judged by the same measure that you have judged others.

Then there are those who have been fooled into risking or taking their own lives to kill innocent people, believing that they will go to a place where there is peace, happiness, and a fabulous life, where they will have several virgin wives and all the rest. They really believe that they are literally doing God a favor by murdering people who are not of the same faith, belief, culture, or religion as they are, all because they hate another country. I feel so sorry for you all. Satan has lied and tricked you because he wants you to stay blind to the truth. His only desire is to keep you in darkness and destroy you. Satan wants you to spend eternity with him in the lake of unquenchable fire. And that is where you will be unless you repent of your sins, stop the hatred, stop killing people, and invite Jesus Christ into your heart and life.

The Bible states that there is only one God, one faith, and one baptism (Ephesians 4:5). He is not a God of hate but a God of love. God is not prejudiced. He loves everyone. He is no respecter of persons and will save all who call upon His name in faith and believe and accept His Son Jesus Christ. God is not a murderer; He gives life—eternal life—to those who believe in Him and who want and ask to be saved.

Don't be misguided and believe the lies you are being told by someone who is allowing Satan to use them to risk your life in hurting innocent people or taking innocent lives. Often that same person will not risk their own life for what they claim they believe in because they are afraid and do not really want to die. Why aren't they ready to go to this so-called place of peace and happiness where they can have so many wives and fringe benefits?

Maybe it is because they don't truly believe it themselves and they too were talked and pushed into these same false beliefs. So, they would rather have you risk your life because they count your life as nothing. And you are just weak and foolish enough to let them. You are shortening your life, which the one and only true and living God gave you, for humankind and Satan. Think about that! The blind leading the blind—and you all will fall into a ditch. All of you will stand before God one day and give an account and be punished for your evil ways. All of you will burn in unquenchable fire in hell forever.

Dear people, don't let anyone talk or push you into doing something that's wrong. No one can truly make you do anything that you don't want to do. No, not even if they put a gun to your head. Do not fear humankind or Satan, who can only destroy the body, but fear God, who has the power to destroy your body and soul in hellfire.

Please don't listen to anyone Satan uses, because you will pay for your crimes and the lives that you take for the rest of your eternal life in hellfire, along with the one who persuaded you to commit (and who has also committed) such horrible crimes. Hell is *not* a place of paradise, happiness, peace, or love as some people would have you believe. Instead it is a place that burns with unquenchable fire and brimstone. And all who go there will continuously feel and suffer indescribable pain and torment forever and ever.

You don't want to go to hell, as it was built for Satan and his fallen angels (demons), not for humankind. However, it is your choice because you were given a free will by God to choose whom you will serve, whether God or humankind, whether God or Satan. God's desire is that you choose Him. He loves you and wants to give you eternal life with Him in a place where there is indescribable joy, peace, and beauty. You will be in His presence forever just as He planned from the beginning. But still, the choice is ultimately yours.

In these last days, people are killing innocent people and pretending that they are *insane* because they know that they can get away with it without serving hard time. They say disturbing things and act certain ways to make everyone think that they have mental problems and are not taking their medication or that they should be on medication. Their attorneys will even stand with a client in this sort of lie, knowing full well that the individual committed the crime and that he or she is as sane as they are. Therefore, the attorney is just as guilty as the client and will be punished by God. People are literally getting away with murder.

You, sir, and you, madam, will stand in judgment before God, the Great Judge, and you will not be able to plea insanity for yourself. It will not work, and you will be without an excuse. Along with everything else that you have done, you will also be charged with the crimes that you committed to wrongfully hurt others. God will hold you accountable.

Attorneys: you who knew your clients were guilty of a crime yet lied for them and had them plead not guilty will, along with your clients, be judged by God according to your works and deeds. All will reap the seeds that they have sown, whether good or bad.

News Reporters

Stop being so quick to report certain information, and when you do report it, make sure that it is accurate. Don't just get a story; get a true story. Be more concerned about the truth and the safety of your country and its people than you are about being the first one to print a story or make a buck. You tell our country's enemies the how, when, and where without thinking or considering how they might use such information to attack and bring harm to the USA and its people. You tell them everything that they need to know to get the upper hand on us. Our enemies anxiously wait to hear from the media; they rely on the media to supply them with enough information so they can best plan their next attack. And you certainly don't fail or disappoint them. Remember, you are not exempt from harm if you live in the United States. So, *stop* feeding our enemies sensitive information that could cause harm, hurt, pain, sorrow, and death to the people of our country.

The United States of America

The USA supplies too much information to the news reporters, the media, and the people, thereby supplying this same information to its enemies, because they have eyes and ears everywhere. Certain pertinent information that comes from the White House as it relates to our homeland security and military plans should be keep *secret* and stay in the White House. We the people and the media don't have to know every decision that is made in the White House, or every strategic move that the government plans to make, or every step they take to secure this country and ensure the safety of its citizens. Why? Because the media will then spill this information and disseminate it worldwide, which means the enemies of the United States will know our vulnerabilities, our plans, and our every move, which in turn will help the enemy make their move. It is somewhat like a chess or checker game.

The USA will be more respected and successful in conquering its enemies by not always letting the left hand know what the right hand is going to do. Choose wise counselors. Learn how to be discreet, and carefully choose whom you discuss plans with. If the press or media are pressing you for answers, tell them something truthful, but you do not have to tell them everything. Be select in what you say. Remember, whatever you tell the media, you are telling the world, including our enemies. And I believe that the United States has many enemies. All who say and pretend they are friends of the USA are not!

I cannot stress this enough: the United States of America must be quiet and private about some things relating to military and homeland security plans. They must watch their moves. They must move with caution because their enemies are watching, listening, and waiting to hear something that will allow them to counteract the United States' plan or force us to move ahead with our plans. Unfortunately, oftentimes the USA plays right into the enemy's hand. How stupid they must think that some of us are. Stop revealing our *secrets* that should be kept *secret*. Stop making it so easy for our enemies to set traps to destroy our people and our homeland. Don't be deceived. You don't have any true friends, except maybe Israel.

As it stands right now, if our enemies desire to be informed of the USA's plans and intentions, all they have to do is turn on the television or radio or go look on social media. And oops—there it is! Think about what you are doing. Stop telling your enemies everything that you plan to do, including how, when, and where. Don't tell your enemy how you plan to apprehend them. Don't let your left hand know what your right hand is doing or plans to do. Keep your mouth shut on certain matters, and stop volunteering pertinent information.

I suggest that the leaders of the USA take heed of what I've said. Then you will keep our country and its citizens safer and out of harm's way. And our enemy will not have the chance to get an upper hand on us or know how to plan their next move. I believe that they look forward to us feeding them certain information, which in turn helps them strategize their next move or attack. And this applies to any person who wants to harm another human being, whether a US citizen or not. If you are not for us (the USA), then you are against us. Therefore, I consider you an enemy.

Television, Social Media, and Radio

These media will be the death of millions of US children and adults. You can see anything, hear anything, or find anything you want to know or *don't* want to know. You can learn how to do this or that, how to make something, how to get away with something, what to wear, what to say, etc. Whatever questions you have, you can find an answer on the internet. You can even learn how to build explosive devices, order weapons, make weapons, and lure small children and adults into Satan's trap, and you can see all sorts of disgusting, wicked, and outrageous things and pictures.

People can track you down and know your every move (some people are foolish enough to provide social media with such information and tell their life history), making Satan's job easier to keep track of you, attack you, and accomplish his deadly plan against you (and your family). Both television and social media put negative ideas in our children's heads, which can lead to their deaths or the death of others. This is all part of Satan's plan for their lives. He wants to kill, steal from, and destroy our kids—and you.

Most parents have little or no control over what their children hear and watch on television or social media, and many do not monitor what they watch. Also, if children don't have access at home, they will find a way to watch TV or use social media at a friend's house or the library. Then there are some parents who just do not care what their children watch, say, or do. Where is the supervision for these young innocent-minded children? You are responsible for your children, and you will be held responsible by God.

Certain programs (and there are many) should not be allowed to air on television. Our young children are impressionable and should not be subject to such trash. Our teenagers' hormones are active, and they're experiencing certain feelings in their bodies. They do not need to see all sorts of explicit sex scenes on television, which can put other thoughts in their heads (which could even lead them to commit sexual assault or rape). Flesh always want to be satisfied. Sometimes it doesn't care about the consequences, for example, who it hurts or what it must do to get what it wants.

I have a question for writers, producers, actors, and actresses: do you have young children, or perhaps little sisters, brothers, nieces, or nephews? And if so, would you let them watch some of the programs that you produce and/or perform in? Most scenes have sexual acts, bloody killings, and profanity (off the charts). Most of the things that children say and do is learned at home and from television and computer games. Do you have a conscience and morals? I think not. You care only about making money at any cost. And parents, where are you? What kind of life are you portraying for your children? What are you doing to prevent your children from watching such programs?

Turn off the television shows. They consist mostly of sex, violence, killings, racial hate, guns, drugs, and profanity, none of which should even be shown on television. Then there are countless games that are not suitable for young children or teenagers to play. Please stop purchasing those satanic bloody games for your children. That's not entertainment, but it is filling their heads with a lot of evil thoughts and their mouths with filthy words. Do you think that they're not going to act out what their eyes have seen and what their ears have heard? I've got news for you—they surely will. Also, parents, be careful what you watch on television and what you say and do around your children because most of the time they will copy you.

Weapons, Cowards, and Bullies

Where are the brave men and women? Everybody is a coward. They carry a weapon of some sort for fear of getting beat down by another. They are afraid of a fair fight. They must have a bunch of others just like themselves (scared bullies) with them just to beat one person. How shameful is that? What does that kind of action and display make you? And do you think this is honorable? Do you think you have gained the respect or fear of those around you? Do you think this makes you a big man or woman? Well, I, along with billions of others, think not! You're acting like an insane fool and a coward, one who lacks good judgment and common sense.

Only cowards and bullies use weapons (because they are scared and afraid of losing), and no decent person has respect for either a coward or a bully. Brave men and women will fight fair with their fists (hands), not with weapons, and they will fight one-on-one, not with help from so-called friends, because that's not a fair fight or a show of bravery at all; it is the fight of a coward and a bully. And you (and anyone who helped you) are the biggest coward and loser. Those who live by the sword shall also die by it. You will reap what you sow. So, believe it when I say that you're not getting away with anything. For God knows and sees everything.

Cowards and bullies use guns, knives, and such, and fight dirty, or else they get someone else to group with them who's also a coward or feels they must prove something to themselves or someone else and is stupid enough to do their dirty work for them for a price. Or they just hurt and kill for fun, allowing the devil to use them. You don't care if you get killed or go to jail. And Satan is just laughing at you, calling you a fool (and rightly so, because you are).

You are no better than the one who told you to do such horrible acts, and you all will burn forever in unquenchable brimstone and fire. (I don't encourage fighting, but if you must fight another man or woman, let it be an honest fight without deadly weapons. Stop being a coward. Fight clean, and show your homies the real you and what you're truly made of.)

One day soon, you and all evildoers will stand in judgment before God for your works and deeds. For everything that you have done, said, or even thought, good or bad, and for every person you have bullied, harmed, or murdered, you will have to give an account. And you will pay with your life for eternity—unless you sincerely repent now, before it's too late. Invite Jesus Christ into your heart and ask Him to forgive you of your sins. There is no other way of escape.

Please Stop. Lay Down Your Weapons

Stop the senseless beatings, shootings, and murders. Stop the drive-by shootings, which often kill our children and other innocent people. What do you think you are proving, and to whom? What did you accomplish other than hurting someone or taking the life of another human being (which you have no God-given right to do; you stole that life from God, so now you will pay with your own life), or getting yourself killed, or being sent to prison for most of your life or the rest of your life? That is not smart at all. That is just plain stupid. And you allowed your feelings or so-called friends to tell you what to do in a moment of rage (whatever the reason). Oftentimes, if these people have a little sense, they won't do themselves what they tell you to do because they don't want to get in trouble.

There is another, better way to handle situations. It doesn't have to be with a weapon, and it doesn't have to take someone's life. Killing someone doesn't make you a real man or woman, but it does makes you a cold-blooded murderer. And for certain, you will suffer the consequences with your eternal life.

You can be a better and smarter person. I am pleading with you to please stop robbing, cussing, hurting, fighting, stealing, and killing innocent people in cold blood. Stop beating people, including children of all ages and our defenseless elderly, and stop hurting lovable pets. Respect your parents and seniors. Very often the people you rob have little or no more than you have. And what really doesn't make sense is that after you rob people (young or old), you are so barbaric that you kill them. Why? Sooner or later you are going to get caught. And if you don't get caught by the law, trust me, you will get caught by God. What's more, you took something from a person that you had no right to take, something that they worked hard for, and you are so heartless and evil that you hurt or killed them. How barbaric and senseless is that? You took something from God that He gave that person (just as He gave you), which is *life*. You deserve to be punished here and now for your crimes. I, myself, have no pity for you.

Get some respect for yourself. Get off your lazy behind, get some ambition and pride for and in yourself, and find a job. Then you can have your own stuff. And what disgusts me even more, you're so evil that you rob and kill people who are blind. Why? They can't even see or identify you. What kind of person are you? You are no better than a wild savage animal. And if wild animals cannot be tamed to live in society among people, then they should be killed, or housed in a cage, or put someplace where they can't harm or kill anyone.

And stop using profanity, because it is very unbecoming for young people as well as adults. You can get your point across or converse in a civilized manner without acting uncivilized by cussing, talking loudly, using all sort of nasty words, and using God's name in vain. What does it prove or accomplish other than make you appear silly, unlearned, foolish, and primitive, or cause a fight and causing someone to get hurt or killed— and for what? It is such a waste of precious time.

Then your children grow up using the same language—or worse— that they've heard you and others around them using. When they cuss you and want to fight you, remember that you have only yourself to blame because they are only imitating and following you. They say and do what they heard you say and saw you do. How sad is that? Is that the legacy you desire to leave your children? Is that all you can offer them? Will your children say that the only thing they learned from you was meaningless filthy words and evil works? Will they have anything good and positive to say about you?

Doing all these wicked and evil things doesn't make you a superstar man or woman. It only shows you for what you are and proves who and what you truly are—and that is a deadbeat; a coward; a sadist; an inhuman, ignorant, evil person; a shell of a man or woman. And you are a child of Satan because you do what he tells you to do. You are not strong and brave; you are weak and scared. You have no morals, no values, no integrity, no respect for human life, and no respect for God, yourself, or others.

You have no dreams, no goals, no vision, no wisdom, no knowledge, no understanding, no good sense, no worth, and no hope. You want to blame everyone but yourself for your problems.

But get this news flash: your life is *your* responsibility. The choices you make are yours, not God's, not mine, and not anyone else's! And God will hold you, and only you, responsible for what you do with your life and the choices that you have made. For as sure as you live and as sure as you're going to die, you will stand before your Creator, Almighty God, one day soon and give an account of how you lived your life, including everything you have done on this earth, your contribution to society, how you have treated or mistreated others, and everything you have said or even thought. You will be judged and sentenced accordingly. Your eternal destiny (in heaven or hell) will be decided by God as you stand before Him to be judged.

Human Trafficking and Kidnapping

There are thousands of people (of all ages, but especially babies, young children, and teenagers) kidnapped and sold into slavery or sex slavery every year. It is a deplorable, inhumane, savage act, and something that a so-called human being should never do to another human being.

The people who are involved in human trafficking, abducting children and other young people to abuse them sexually, physically, emotionally, and mentally, selling them to others (or keeping them for themselves) as sex slaves, and forcing young boys to be in gangs and sell drugs, are no better than wild animals themselves. You are a poor excuse of a man or woman if you practice and participate in such horrible behavior. You will be judged by the almighty God, and you will have to pay with your eternal life for the wicked and evil things you have done.

You will reap what you sow. Right now, you may think that you are getting away with what you're doing, but I want you to know that God sees, hears, and knows everything. And one day soon, you will be judged and sentenced by Him. It will be unbearable and eternal, and you will wish that you had never caused harm to those people, God's children.

I beg you to stop what you are doing and free these people right now! Do this in the name of Jesus! These are God's people. They are not a commodity; they are human beings (which is more than I can say about you). No amount of money will save you from the wrath of the almighty God and His Son Jesus Christ. You will pay with your eternal life in the most horrifying place in total darkness, in indescribable pain and torment, in the lake that burns with brimstone and unquenchable fire forever, unless you repent right now. Stop what you know is so very wrong, and do what is right. Do it *now* while you still have time. God is watching you. Jesus Christ is coming soon!

Don't wait until tomorrow, because by then it could be too late for you. Don't worry about what humankind will do or say, for humans can only destroy the body. Instead worry about what God will do. He can and will destroy both body and soul in eternal hellfire, where there will be darkness, weeping, gnashing of teeth, and indescribable torment. Don't continue to allow the devil to use you to do evil. In the end, the life you save will be your very own.

Human trafficking must be stopped! It is not just a government issue or a government responsibility. It is everyone's. We all have a part or role to play. If you see or even suspect that your neighbor or someone else is human trafficking, holding someone against their will, then you should report it. It is your obligation as a citizen and as a moral human being. Also, you should want to do all that you can to help another and put an end to this inhumane thing called human trafficking. For the life you save may be that of a loved one or a friend, or that of someone else you know, or even your own. They just may be watching you too. Let us all fight this evil together.

So if you see something that doesn't look right, please say something and call your local police station. If you're traveling and see children looking afraid or anything else suspicious, write down the license plate number and a description of vehicle and the driver, if possible, and call 9-1-1 right away. Don't be afraid. You don't have to give any personal information about yourself. It's time for the people of God to destroy Satan's kingdom and human trafficking by fasting, praying, and helping one another. Raise awareness to end modern-day slavery. It will take more than a village (but that will help); it will take the prayers of the saints (people of God).

Criminals

Those of you who commit crimes should also be prepared to pay for the crime(s) you committed and serve the required time in jail or prison. Be prepared to suffer the consequences and be held accountable for your actions. No one forced you to commit the crime; it was your choice. So, you now must pay the consequences for that choice. Treat people the way you want to be treated, or be ready to face the time for doing the crime. And if you get away with it, it will only be for a short while. Remember, God knows where you are, and He sees and knows what you've done or are doing. And one day soon you will stand before Him on Judgment Day and receive your eternal sentence. Woe unto you if you have not sincerely repented and called upon the name of the Lord Jesus Christ for salvation. His grace is sufficient even for you.

Police Officers

First, let me say that I believe that there are many good police officers who are well respected and honest, who honor their position, and who abide by and uphold the law. They do the right thing. I certainly thank God for those individuals who remain true to their professional calling, true to themselves, and true to God.

However, there are also many police officers who are sworn to uphold the law but who are breaking the law. They are a disgrace to the badge that they wear and what it stands for. They use the law, their gun, and their position as a police officer for their own selfish reasons and advantage. They have sworn to uphold the law and to protect the people, yet they are killing the same people they have sworn to protect. Either they are trigger-happy, frightened cowards who don't know how to shoot a person who has no weapon in the leg or arm, without the intent to kill, or they have hatred in their hearts because of someone else's race or gender, or they simply don't care, or perhaps they panic with fear and, without thinking, pull the trigger, killing or seriously wounding innocent people. And sadly, these people have no conscience and are able to sleep well at night.

Regardless of people's skin color, be fair and treat people the way that you want to be treated or the way you would want someone else to treat your child, spouse, mother, father, sister, brother, or other loved one.

You, police officer, shoot because a person just doesn't look right to you, because they look suspicious to you, because you thought, or it looked like, they had a gun or knife (or other weapon of some kind) in their hand. Then you shoot a young child or teenager in the back (while running from you because they are afraid, knowing what you will do to them) in cold blood. Many men of color would rather face death than endure the injustice of this world's system. How sad.

This is such poor judgment on your part, police officer, and it is an outrage. You tell others not to break the law, yet you break that same law. You preach to others to obey the laws, yet you disobey them and then try to hide all your evil deeds. I'm not sure what your problem is (other than being just plan evil and wicked), but it is for certain that you do have one. Something is very seriously wrong with your heart and within the police department. And in all fairness to all people, something *must* be done now!

However, everyone must work together to rectify the problem and try to live in harmony and peace. One race is no better than another, and the color of a person's skin doesn't make the person. Instead, the heart and soul make the person. God doesn't see the color of a person's skin; He only sees the heart. God made all of us in His image. We all have the same color blood, and our bodies are made up of the same type of organs, vessels, cells, etc. The only difference is our outside covering, which is our skin and eye color and hair texture. And when Jesus Christ returns, our bodies will change and we will be just like Him. So none of this matters; our spirits look the same.

Most police officers feel that having a badge and gun makes them a (small) god and gives them the power and authority to mistreat people, break the law, and even kill innocent human beings without suffering any consequences and without any accountability. They feel that they can and will get away with it, and sad to say, most of the time they do. This is wrong, and God is not pleased. Do you think you are bad, that you have the power, and that you're getting away with doing your wicked and evil works? Let me assure you that you are not!

Almighty God knows and sees all things, and the day will come when everything that you have hidden, said, and done will be revealed. You will be judged by God. So get ready to stand before the one who has all power and give an account for all the wrong that you have done, for the harm to innocent people and the deaths of innocent people you have caused. For every life that you have taken unjustly, you will pay with your life—your eternal life in hellfire.

Humankind may allow you to get away with it here on earth, but God will not because He is righteous and just. He is no respecter of persons.

You will have to give an account of what you have done. And God will not take any excuses. You will be judged and sentenced strictly on the truth as to why you killed a person in cold blood and then lied about how it really happened. And you will pay with your eternal life for eternity in unquenchable hellfire.

The only way to avoid such a harsh punishment is to repent of your sins, turn from your evil ways, and ask God to forgive you of all your sins, come into your life, and make you a new creation in Jesus Christ. You should then seek those people who are still living whom you hurt or lied about, or their family members (if they are deceased), and ask them for forgiveness. Whether they forgive you or not, at least you asked. And if you can't find them, it is okay; you tried. God knows your heart. Now, He will protect you from your enemies, seen and unseen. He will replace your fear with courage. And He has promised never to leave you or forsake you in your time of need.

Personally, I feel that every police officer (as well as every judge) should have a psychological evaluation at least three times a year. This should be done randomly, without notice, and without fail. Police officers who are emotionally or mentally unstable should not be allowed to carry a gun, as it could be a danger to themselves and others. They too are ordinary human beings. They too have personal issues, problems, and hang-ups, just like the rest of us. Some of them may not have the ability to separate themselves from their personal problems or leave their personal problems at home. Instead, and sadly, they take their problems out on innocent people (simply because they can).

Please don't misunderstand me: I am a firm believer that if one commits a crime, then one should pay the penalty and do the time for it. Wrong is wrong. But police officers do not have the right to be the judge, jury, and executioner. I'm a firm believer that right is right, wrong is wrong, and everyone should be treated fairly. I don't care who you are, what color you are, how rich or poor you are, how you may feel, or what you may want to do.

My parents (despite the prejudice and hatred that we experienced and that surrounded us) taught my siblings and me to treat people the way we wanted to be treated. I got tired of them telling me that. I didn't always like treating people well, but most of the time I did it because I knew that God and my parents would be pleased with me.

Police officers have been given certain authority as it relates to the law, but this does not mean that they have the right to abuse and misuse such authority. It doesn't mean that they can shoot and kill anyone who looks shady, or asks them questions, or doesn't speak the way they want them to, or stands up for their civil rights or for those of another race or gender.

To all police officers, all judges, others in law enforcement, and all people: if you have hatred in your heart for any people for any reason—if your first thought is to cause bodily harm to others simply because their skin is of another color, or because they speak differently, or because they are from another country, or because you are prejudiced against any race— then you are very wrong. God is not pleased, and you will be judged by Him. And if you willingly withhold the truth about one of your colleagues when you know they mistreated someone, or set someone up and planted false information or evidence against them, or killed someone, then know that you are just as guilty as they are—and God will hold you responsible also. And if you allow fear to cloud good judgment, then being a police officer (regardless of your rank or title) is not the right job or profession for you.

Let me assure you, sir or madam, that you will reap what you sow and have sown. One day, you will stand before the almighty God, the one and only High Judge who is all-powerful and has all authority for your sentencing. You will be rewarded or punished according to your seed sown and your deeds, be they good or bad. Who will then be able to deliver you? I tell you, no one! For every person you have mistreated and lied about, for every precious life that you have taken unjustly, you must give an account. And you will pay a severe price forever—unless you sincerely repent of your sins and ask Jesus Christ for forgiveness. Ask Him to come into your life and create in you a clean heart and renew a right spirit within you right now. Ask Him to lead and guide your footsteps. Treat everyone with love, fairness, and respect. Treat them the way that you want to be treated, the way you would want your family treated.

Hear this: there is no excuse that you can give to God for when you shoot and kill another human being in cold blood who poses no harm or threat to you. You shoot to kill because of fear; you are afraid for your life just because it is a black man (regardless of his stature) or a person of another race or from another country.

> The eyes of the Lord are in every place, beholding the evil and the good. (Proverbs 15:3 KJV)

> Whoso sheddeth man's blood, by man shall his blood be shed: for in the image of God made he man. (Genesis 9:6 KJV)

> But why dost thou judge thy brother? or why dost thou set at nought thy brother? For we shall show all stand before the judgment seat of Christ. (Romans 14:10 KJV)

Judges

The law is lawlessness to and for certain people, and this is going to get worse. There are judges who will sell out to the devil for their own gratification even more than they do already. More than ever they will not do what is lawfully right because of fear, bribes, or prejudice or because they judge the person in front of them by the way the latter talks, looks, or dresses, by way of education, by the color of their skin, and by where they live or used to live.

Some judges are no better than the criminals they put in jail (which is where they themselves probably should be). They just hide in a black robe. Often, many of the people they find guilty are innocent. (However, let me be clear: I do believe that those who are guilty of the crime they committed should be held accountable and be punished. Right is right, and wrong is wrong.) Sadly, some of these men and women who hold some of the most honorable titles and highest positions break the same laws that they are sworn to uphold.

For many it is because of greed. They sell their honor, integrity, and dignity and even their souls—everything that they stand for and believe in—just for money (which will not last). For some it is because of their wealth or social status, or because of who they are, or because they are just plain prejudiced, biased against people of a certain race, color, religion, gender, nationality, or domicile. They are all wicked judges, and they will one day themselves stand before the almighty judge (Jesus Christ and God the Father) and be judged by Him. And believe me, He will judge righteously.

These corrupt judges will reap the seeds that they have sown. They will one day face the one and only High Judge who is truly just, holy, and righteous—Almighty God—to be judged and sentenced to eternal life in either heaven or hell (there is no in between.)

"Open your mouth for the speechless, in the cause of all who are appointed to die. Open your mouth, judge rightly, and plead the cause of the poor and needy" (Proverbs 31:8–9).

"He who justifies the wicked, and he who condemns the just, both of them alike are an abomination to the Lord. ... A wicked man accepts a bribe behind the back to pervert the ways of justice. ... But those who rebuke the wicked will have delight, and a good blessing will come upon them" (Proverbs 17:15, 23; 24:25).

In case you don't know, let me tell you more about the almighty God who created the world and everyone and all things in it. He is *omnipotent* (*all-powerful*): God has supreme power. He can do whatever He wants whenever He wants. But whatever He does is holy, righteous, and just. There is nothing that can be done that He cannot do. His power is infinite; there is no limit to it. He is also *omniscient* (*all-knowing*). God knows your past, present, and future. Nothing escapes or gets by Him. Nothing is known that can be known that God doesn't already know. Finally, He is *omnipresent* (*all-present*), meaning that He is everywhere at the same time. His divine presence encompasses the entire world or universe. There is no place in the heavens, on earth, or underneath the earth where you can run to hide from Him, because He is already there.

God doesn't take bribes. He hates all sinners but especially liars (people who speak not the truth knowingly and willingly), those with a proud look (who are arrogant or prideful or who look down on others, thinking more highly of themselves than they ought to), hands that shed innocent blood (cold-blooded murderers), hearts that devise wicked schemes and imaginations (plans, thoughts, and plots of evil to hurt others), feet that rush to do evil (people who run fast to do evil and wicked things), people who sow discord (by gossiping and spreading rumors that create tension), and false witnesses who speak lies (this type of lying could cause death or a jail sentence for an innocent person).

God believes in righteousness, truthfulness, and justice. He will not have any mercy for those who made up the law and have not kept it themselves, or who have not shown mercy to others, or who have been unfair and unjust to others. All will pay for all their wrongdoings and for mistreating all people from the least to the greatest, from the poorest to the richest, regardless of the color of their skin, their race, their gender, their religion, where they live, or some other trait or fact. You will reap what you sow. You will receive your sentence from the almighty judge one day soon, and it will be final. There will be no mistrials, no errors, and no appeals.

Listen, everyone! All branches of government, nations, judges, police officers, lawgivers, lawbreakers, criminals, wicked people, and evildoers, and all people who do not obey God and do not believe in Jesus Christ, hear the Word of the Lord God concerning the end of you who are evil and wicked. Almighty God sees and hears everything that you do. Your day of reckoning is coming. And you can bet your life—both physical and spiritual—on it! Please believe me, you're not getting away with anything.

Hear what the Word of God says concerning the evildoers and wicked and their destiny:

> Behold, I know your thoughts, and the devices which ye wrongfully imagine against me. (Job 21:27 KJV)

> Thus say the Lord: "Behold, I am fashioning a disaster and devising a plan against you. Return now everyone from his (their) own evil way, and make your ways and your doings good." (Jeremiah 18:11)

> For My eyes are on all their ways; they are not hidden from My face, nor is their iniquity hidden from My eyes. And I will repay double for their iniquity and their sin. (Jeremiah 16:17–18)

> There is no peace, saith the Lord, unto the wicked. (Isaiah 48:22 KJV)

> The wicked shall be turned into hell, and all the nations that forget God. (Psalm 9:17 KJV)

> Because the sentence against an evil work is not executed speedily, therefore the heart of the sons of men is fully set in them to do evil. Though a sinner does evil a hundred times, and his days are prolonged, yet I surely know that it will be well with those who fear God, who fear before Him. But it

will not be well with the wicked; nor will he prolong his days, which are as a shadow, because he does not fear before God. (Ecclesiastes 8:11–13)

For your hands are defiled with blood, and your fingers with iniquity; Your lips have spoken lies, your tongue has muttered perversity. No one calls for justice, nor does anyone plead for truth. They trust in empty words and speak lies; they conceive evil and bring forth iniquity. … Their works are works of iniquity, and the act of violence is in their hands. Their feet run to evil and make haste to shed innocent blood; their thoughts are thoughts of iniquity; wasting and destruction are in their paths. The way of peace they have not known, and there is no justice in their ways; they have made themselves crooked paths; whoever takes that way shall not know peace. (Isaiah 59:3–4, 6–8)

The wicked plotteth against the just, and gnasheth upon him with his teeth. The Lord shall laugh at him: for he seeth that his day is coming. (Psalm 37:12–13 KJV)

Thus says God to the wicked: "What right have you to declare My statues, or take My covenant in your mouth, seeing you hate instruction and cast My words behind you? When you saw a thief, you consented with him, and have been a partaker with adulterers. You give your mouth to evil, and your tongue frames deceit. You sit and speak against your brother; you slander your own mother's son. These things you have done, and I kept silent; you thought that I was altogether like you; but I rebuke you and set them in order before your eyes. Now consider this, you who forget God, lest I tear you in pieces, and there be none to deliver: Whoever offers praise glorifies Me; and to him who orders his conduct aright I will show the salvation of God." (Psalm 50:16–23)

The evildoers and the wicked, along with all unbelievers, Satan, and his followers—their eternal destination is hell.

The devil who deceived them was cast into the lake of fire and brimstone where the beast and the false prophet are. And they will be tormented day and night forever and ever. (Revelation 20:10)

But the cowardly, unbelieving, abominable, murderers, sexually immoral, sorcerers, idolaters, and all liars shall have their part in the lake which burns with fire and brimstone, which is the second death. (Revelation 21:8)

That the wicked is reserved to the day of destruction? They shall be brought forth to the day of wrath. (Job 21:30 KJV)

So, you see, your day is coming, and your punishment will be for eternity. Woe unto you. And let me remind you: you yourself chose where you would spend your eternal life.

Therefore, I say to the righteous:

Fret not thyself because of evildoers, neither be thou envious against the workers of iniquity. For they shall soon be cut down like the grass, and wither as the green herb. ... For evildoers shall be cut off: but those that wait upon the Lord, they shall inherit the earth. For yet a little while, and the wicked shall not be: yea, thou shalt diligently consider his place, and it shall not be. (Psalm 37:1–2, 9–10 KJV)

Dear people, you won't get away with all the wrong, evil, and wickedness that you have done unless you repent and are saved right now. Because of God's mercy and grace, He will give you another chance. You must ask Jesus to forgive you of your sins, accept Him as Lord and Savior, believe and have faith in Him and His work at Calvary, and do good and what you know is right. Stop listening to and following the devil (and those whom he uses), who is only leading you to total and eternal destruction. Won't you please start listening to and following God our Father, and Jesus Christ our Savior, who will lead you into unspeakable joy, peace, and eternal life?

God says: "The heart is deceitful above all things, and desperately wicked; who can know it? I, the Lord, search the heart, I test the mind, even to give every man according to his ways, according to the fruit of his doings" (Jeremiah 17:9–10).

This is the nature of humankind, of a human being's heart. This is why Jesus said that we must be spiritually born again. We must be reborn with His Spirit. We must believe, repent, and ask Jesus to forgive us of our sins and cleanse us from all unrighteousness. We must invite Him into our hearts. When you do this, He will give you a new heart, and you will become a new creation in Jesus Christ our Lord. Your old perverted way of thinking will change; you will have a new way of thinking and living. You will be transformed by the renewing of your mind with the Word of God. You will be reborn by His Holy Spirit and will now belong to the family of God. This is why Jesus Christ came to die on the cross for our sins and why God raised Him from the grave on the third day: for our justification. We can once again be in right standing with God our Creator and Father. We can fellowship with Him and have the opportunity to live forever in His presence.

The devil (Satan, who deceived and tricked you), along with his demons, false prophets, and all who do not believe in the gospel of Jesus Christ, will be cast into the lake of fire and brimstone. And they will be tormented day and night constantly, forever and ever. There will be no end to this indescribable, unthinkable, unbearable, excruciating pain and suffering. It will be too late to call to God or Jesus for help, for They will neither hear nor help you.

No, it is not too late for you, but you must have a sincere heart. Confess that you are a sinner, ask God to forgive you, turn from your evil and wicked ways, believe in Jesus Christ, and invite and accept Him into your heart and life. Ask Him to cleanse you from all unrighteousness.

God the Father is righteous. He is just. He loves you and doesn't want you or anyone else to perish. His desire is that we will live for eternity with Him and share in His glory. He extends mercy and grace to everyone and does not have any favorites. He is a God of truth, honor, and integrity, and He can't be bought. He is the same yesterday, today, and forever. He sees the end from the beginning.

One day soon, you will stand in His courtroom, before His throne, and be judged for every person you have judged unjustly and sentenced; for all the people you have killed in cold blood; for every man, woman, boy, and girl you have misused, abused (physically, emotionally, verbally, mentally, and/or spiritually), molested, raped, beaten, kidnapped, sold, robbed, and/or murdered; and for all the evil and horrible inhumane things that you have said and done. And you will be severely punished.

For all the people you arrested and sent to prison unfairly, you will be held accountable. You will have to give an account for every single person. You will be judged with the same measure that you have used to measure and judge others, and you will be rewarded accordingly. You will be treated the same way you treated others (good or bad). You will reap what you have sown. And you will not be able to give an excuse or lie your way out this time. You will be judged and sentenced according to your works.

Remember, God is sovereign. He is the Almighty One who has supreme power. He has the power to take your breath this very second. And following your death, He can put your spirit in heaven (or paradise, the place He has prepared for us) or in hell (a place of indescribable torment prepared for Satan, his demons, the wicked, and all those who reject Jesus Christ). All liars will have their place in the lake of fire that burns forever. The righteous judge and lawgiver is coming! Ready are not, believe it or not, prepared or not, Jesus is coming again!

Listen dear people, God our Father has a wonderful plan for your life and a wonderful future for you, not the wicked plan that you may have now, which will only lead you to eternal destruction. Satan comes to steal from, kill, and destroy you. Be assured that Satan, and all of your so-called friends, doesn't truly care about you or what happens to you or your family. But Jesus Christ truly does care. He came so that you might live your life to the fullest here on earth and so that you could spend your eternal life with Him. He truly loves you (but hates sin). If you will repent of your sins and give your life to Him, He will never leave you or forsake you. You can give Him all your cares because He loves you. He's got you covered.

God demonstrated His love for us by sending His only begotten Son Jesus Christ, and Jesus demonstrated His love for us by dying on the cross for our sins, thereby paying our sin debt. We have been redeemed! God the Father raised Jesus from the grave on the third day for our justification and with all power, as He holds the keys to life and death. We have been forgiven and restored to God, and He has accepted us back into a right relationship with Him. All praise and glory be unto His Son Jesus Christ!

He loves and cares so very much for you, for your family, and for all people. His grace and mercy endures forever. Please put away your hatred, prejudices, and weapons. Stop selling drugs to our children. Stop threatening young men and women and forcing them to sell drugs. Stop beating women, children, and men and forcing them to sell their bodies. Stop all the robbing and killing of innocent people. Throw away your guns, knives, and other deadly weapons. For those who live by the sword shall (eventually) die by the sword. Because as sure as you are alive right now, your payback day is coming! God our Father and Jesus Christ His Son hear and see everything you are doing. So, you are *not* getting away with anything.

One day soon, you will be judged and sentenced by God according to your deeds. He will repay fury to His adversaries and recompense to His enemies. All the wicked, evildoers, and unbelievers will be cast into hell, in the lake that burns with fire and brimstone forever, with Satan. All who love and have faith in God and His Son Jesus Christ and who do what is right will live forever with Him in that indescribably beautiful and awesome place that Jesus has prepared for us.

Let us love and respect one another, pray for one another, and protect each other, including our children, our parents, our grandparents, and seniors (elderly people). Stop trying to be who you were not made to be, and give your heart and life to Jesus Christ right now. Become the person that He created you to be in the beginning.

You have the power within you to change your life, your way of thinking, your attitude, and your situation right now. God has put inside of us a gift that can be used to help others and to glorify Him. Search yourself to find out what that gift is. Stir it up, and use it. There is a better way. You don't have to spend your eternal life in torment in a place that burns with fire and brimstone. Invite Jesus Christ into your life right now and ask Him to forgive you of all your sins.

You will have a brand-new outlook on life. Your old life and way of doing things will no longer have dominion over you. You will no longer have the desire to hurt others or to impress others, trying to prove that you are someone other than who you truly are, who God created you to be, and who you are in Him. Read your Bible and pray for God's guidance. God will transform your life, making you a new creation in Him. Your life will never be the same again, and you will have eternal life with Him and our heavenly family when your life is over here on this earth.

Don't listen to Satan (Lucifer, the devil) any longer! Once you have asked Jesus to forgive you of your sins and invite Him into your life, neither Satan nor humankind will have dominion over you or your life. You now belong to God the Father and to Jesus Christ His Son, our Lord and Savior. You are now free! And whom the Son sets free is free indeed (John 8:36). Hallelujah! Jesus loves you, and He wants to save your soul. He came so that you could have a full and abundant life here on earth and eternal life with Him in the place that He has prepared for all who love, accept, obey, and have faith in Him.

Remember: the decisions you make will have consequences. What you decide to do today will determine where you will spend your tomorrows, your eternity. Please choose carefully and prayerfully. Make sure it is a decision that you can eternally live with. Once you cross over to the other side (i.e., once you die in this life), it will be impossible for you to change your mind or your final eternal destination.

Prayer

Please say this short prayer with me, and mean it with all your heart:

> Dear God, I repent and ask You to forgive all my sins. Come into my life and cleanse me from all unrighteousness. I confess with my mouth and believe in my heart that Jesus Christ is the Son of God. I believe that He died on the cross for my sins and that You raised Him from the grave on the third day for my justification. I accept Jesus Christ as my Lord and Savior. Thank You for salvation! In Jesus's name, I pray. Amen.

My Prayer for You

Father God, thank you for hearing the prayers of my brothers and sisters who have opened the door of their hearts to You. You said in Your Word that You will forgive them of their sins and that you will remember their sins no more (Hebrews 8:12). According to Your Word they are saved if they confessed with their mouth the Lord Jesus and believe in their hearts that You have raised Him from the dead. "For with the heart one believes unto righteous, and with the mouth confession is made unto salvation" (Romans 10:10). You also said that whosoever calls upon the name of the Lord shall be saved (Romans 10:13). Father, we are calling upon You right now in the name of Jesus. So, along with You and the angels in heaven, I rejoice with my brothers and sisters for their salvation. You save to the uttermost, and whom Your Son Jesus Christ sets free is free indeed.

And Father, I pray that You will fill my brothers and sisters with Your Holy Spirit to enable them to do the work You have called them to do and to live a holy life while here on this earth. I pray that their minds will be transformed as they renew them with Your Word. As they pray, fast, and study Your Word, they will draw closer to You, as You will to them. I pray that You will reveal Yourself to them. Let them feel Your awesome love, presence, and power in their lives. When they are weak, show yourself strong in and through them. Thank You for Your love, Your mercy, and Your amazing grace that You have bestowed upon us all. I love You. I pray in the name that is above every name here on earth and in heaven. In the name of Jesus! Amen.

Dear friends, God is no respecter of persons. It doesn't matter what race or nationality you are; what skin color, hair texture, or eye color you have; how you talk; what your profession is; how much money you earn; or where you live. None of these things make any difference; they mean nothing to Him. God the Father and Jesus Christ His Son, our Savior, love everybody. Jesus is Lord over all of us and is rich to all who will call upon Him for salvation (Romans 10:12–13). When Jesus died on the cross at Calvary over two thousand years ago and God raised Him from the grave three days afterward for our justification, it wasn't just for a select group of people; it was for the sins of the whole world, which includes every person who has been born and ever will be born.

Therefore, my dear friends, whoever you are, if you hear the voice of God today (through a person, a song, a dream, the television, or whatever), do not be stubborn and close your ears and your heart. Listen and obey Him. Call upon Him right now, because tomorrow, or even the next moment, may be too late. Salvation is a free gift given to all by God who will accept, believe, and place their faith in the finished work of Jesus Christ our Lord. We can do or say nothing to earn it. It is only by the grace of God—His free gift to us. For it is because of and by this *grace* that we are saved through faith; it doesn't have anything to do with who we are or what good works we ourselves have done or will ever do, as salvation cannot be earned (see Ephesians 2:8–9).

God has great plans for us and a sure destiny. His thoughts for us are good: "For I know the thoughts that I think toward you, saith the Lord, thoughts of peace, and not of evil, to give you an expected end" (Jeremiah 29:11 KJV).

You see how much He loves us and cares. God wants to give you and me a happy future and hope for eternal life in His kingdom.

He is waiting to hear from you; He's longing to do great and miraculous things just for you. Yes, you! No matter who you are, no matter what you have done or what dark cloud hovers over you, just call upon Jesus Christ and ask Him to forgive you of your sins. Invite Him into your heart, repent of your sins, and live according to His Word. Remember that our God's grace is sufficient for whatever you need, and His mercy endures forever. Just trust Him and live a righteous life. Love, respect, and help one another. Be the best person that you can be, and value all lives. Try to live in unity with all people as much as possible. Try not to see the color of people's skin; instead take note of their character, integrity, and kindness and the way they treat you.

"Beloved, let us love one another: for love is of God; and every one that loveth is born of God, and knoweth God. He that loveth not knoweth not God; for God is love. In this was manifested the love of God toward us, because that God has sent His only begotten Son into the world, that we might live through Him" (1 John 4:7–9 KJV).

If we cannot love one another here on earth in this life, then we do not qualify and cannot live in heaven, God's kingdom, the New Jerusalem, with God, Jesus Christ, and our heavenly family. Jesus Christ is coming again, just as He promised that He would. Job (14:14) asked the question, if a person dies, will he or she live again? Jesus answers that question in John 14:1–3: "Let not your heart be troubled: ye believe in God, believe also in Me. In My Father's house are many mansions: if it were not so, I would have told you. I go to prepare a place for you. And if I go and prepare a place for you, I will come again, and receive you unto Myself; that where I am, there ye may be also."

This is Jesus's promise. I believe it. And this is my hope and the hope of every believer in Jesus Christ. We await His return to take us to our new eternal residence. I pray that you will believe it too. However, one day all will have the opportunity to find out the truth for themselves. I hope that it will not be too late for you.

"Blessed be the God and Father of our Lord Jesus Christ, who according to His abundant mercy has begotten us again to a living hope through the resurrection of Jesus Christ from the dead, to an inheritance incorruptible and undefiled and that does not fade away, reserved in heaven for you [us], who are kept by the power of God through faith for salvation ready to be revealed in the last time" (1 Peter 1:3–5).

"Now hope does not disappoint, because the love of God has been poured out in our hearts by the Holy Spirit who was given to us" (Romans 5:5).

The Rapture and the Millennial Kingdom

There are those who believe that before the return of Jesus Christ, there will be an event or encounter referred to as the Rapture (which refers to a snatching away, a being caught up).

Many believe that the Rapture is when Jesus Christ will suddenly, silently, and secretly come (His feet will not touch the ground) for His saints, true born-again believers in Him who are alive. Countless Christians in Jesus Christ will disappear from the face of the earth and will rise up to meet Him in the air, where mortal bodies will be transformed in a moment, in the twinkling of an eye, from mortality to immortality and be given glorified bodies. And He will take His children home to live with Him forever.

There are different denominational, theological, and personal views concerning the Rapture as to when it will take place—before the seven years of tribulation (so the people of God won't have to suffer through it), in the middle of the tribulation period, or at the end of the tribulation period—or if it will take place at all.

Those people who believe that the church will be raptured before the seven years of tribulation (at which time the Antichrist will be revealed and will bring devastation upon the earth and the people such as never before since creation. War, hunger, hatred, and dictatorship will cause the death of many believers, as well as unbelievers) begin are generally recognized as "pretribulationists." They believe also that they will accompany Jesus, along with all the angels and believers, on His Second Coming to earth.

Some people believe that the church will go through the middle period, the first three and a half years of the seven years of tribulation, and then the Rapture will take place. Those who believe this are known as "midtribulationists."

There are those who are called "posttribulationists," and they believe that the church will go through the whole seven years of the tribulation. They believe that the church will be raptured only at the Second Coming of Jesus Christ.

"Because thou hast kept the word of my patience, I also will keep thee from the hour of temptation, which shall come upon all the world, to try them that dwell upon the earth" (Revelation 3:10 KJV).

The millennial period, also known as the millennial kingdom, follows after the tribulation period. This is when Jesus Christ will reign here on earth for one thousand years. Again, there are various views and opinions concerning the purpose of the thousand-year reign, or if it will happen at all. Some believe that during this period, all the believers who made it into the millennial kingdom will have a time of rest before Satan is released from the bottomless pit to test the saints of God a final time to determine their love, faith, trust, and belief in Jesus Christ and God the Father.

If you truly have a personal intimate relationship with Jesus Christ, and if He has been rooted and grounded in your heart, then passing such a test won't be that difficult. However, those who do reject Jesus Christ's rule or do not comply with His will and fail the test will, at the end of the thousand years, be destroyed in everlasting fire.

Remember that your religion or how long you've been a member of a church has nothing to do with it. You must be born again. You must ask Jesus Christ to forgive you of your sins, repent, believe, have faith, and accept Jesus as your Lord and Savior. Those who endure until the very end shall be saved and will spend eternity in the kingdom of God.

Note that 1,000 years equals about 52,143 weeks. But remember what the apostle Peter stated in 2 Peter 3:8: "But, beloved, be not ignorant of this one thing, that one day is with the Lord as a thousand years, and a thousand years as one day" (KJV).

Psalm 90:4 reads, "For a thousand years in thy sight are but as yesterday when it is past, and as a watch in the night" (KJV). So don't wait until tomorrow—not even the next second. Call upon the name of Jesus Christ our Lord for salvation right now, while He is near.

Be prepared at all times. Be watchful and be prayerful because we do not know when these things will happen or when Jesus is coming. But I am certain that according to His Word, and according to what I feel within my spirit, Jesus Christ will return, and the white throne judgment of God will occur. I pray that we will all be prepared for whatever occurs on that day.

At the end of the millennial period, before we saints and believers in Christ can reign in glory with our resurrected and glorified bodies on the new earth in the New Jerusalem, we must stand before God, the High Judge, and be judged. This next great event is the white throne judgment, when everybody must appear before the judgment throne of God to be judged and rewarded based on all they have done and said (good or bad).

Then *all* will be assigned to their eternal home, whether it be in God's kingdom or in hell (with Satan that old devil, fallen angels, demons, the wicked, the evil, and all unbelievers) in a lake of that will forever burn with unquenchable fire and brimstone, in torture, darkness, and total separation from God. Some believe that there will be two judgments, that the Christians (believers in Christ) will be judged at the judgment seat by Jesus Christ, the Lamb of God, and the unbelievers will be judged by God the Father at the white throne judgment, where all will be judged and rewarded or punished according to their deeds (good or bad) and every word they have spoken.

"Therefore the ungodly shall not stand in the judgment, nor sinners in the congregation of the righteous. For the Lord knoweth the way of the righteous: but the way of the ungodly shall perish" (Psalm 1:5–6).

There are scriptures that you can read at your leisure regarding the tribulation period of seven years, the return of Jesus Christ for His church (His bride), the millennial period, and the white throne judgment. I can't tell you when all these things or events will take place, nor will I argue or debate about it, because I have no time for such. I must prepare for when all these things do take place or happen.

I want to be found worthy to go back and spend eternity with my God, Lord, and Savior and the rest of my heavenly family when Jesus arrives. It is in God's own time as to when He will come back for me (body or spirit) and take me home. It doesn't matter to me when, or in what order events take place, just as long as He comes for me as promised. So, I don't really have to try to figure it out, and neither do you. Just be robed and prepared when He calls you to your eternal home.

Pray and ask God to give you knowledge, wisdom, and understanding as you read His Word (the Holy Bible) and as you read this book with expectation. If you're sincere, He will hear you and grant your request.

A few scriptures that most people refer to as proof of the Rapture (while others refer to these same scriptures in reference to Jesus Christ's return) are as follows:

> I tell you at night there will be two men in one bed: the one will be taken and the other will be left. Two women will be grinding together: the one will be taken and the other left. Two men in the field: the one will be taken and the other left. (Luke 17:34–36)

> For the Lord Himself shall descend from heaven with a shout, with the voice of an archangel, and the trump of God: and the dead in Christ shall rise first: Then we which are alive and remain shall be caught up together with them in the clouds, to meet the Lord in the air: and so shall we ever be with the Lord. (1 Thessalonians 4:16–17 KJV)

> Behold, I shew you a mystery; we shall not all sleep, but we shall all be changed, In a moment, in the twinkling of an eye, at the last trump: for the trumpet will sound, and the dead will be raised incorruptible, and we shall be changed. For this corruptible must put on incorruption, and this mortal must put on immortality. (1 Corinthians 15:51–53 KJV)

> Scriptures for the millennial kingdom and the white throne judgment are as follows:

> Then I saw an angel coming down from heaven, having the keys to the bottomless pit and a great chain in his hand. He laid hold on the dragon, that serpent of old, who is the Devil and Satan, and bound him for a thousand years; and he cast him into the bottomless pit, and shut him up, and set a seal on him, so that he should deceive the nations no more till the thousand years were finished. But after these things he must be released for a little while. (Revelation 20:1–3 KJV)

And I saw thrones, and they sat upon them, and judgment was given unto them; and I saw the souls of them that were beheaded for the witness of Jesus, and for the word of God, and had not worshipped the beast, neither his image, neither had received his mark upon their foreheads, or in their hands; and they lived and reigned with Christ a thousand years. But the rest of the dead lived not again until the thousand years were finished. This is the first resurrection. Blessed and holy is he that hath part in the first resurrection; on such the second death hath no power, but they shall be priests of God and of Christ, and shall reign with him a thousand years. (Revelation 20:4–6 KJV)

When the Son of Man comes in His glory, and all the holy angels with Him, then He will sit on the throne of His glory. All nations will be gathered before Him, and He will separate them one from another, as a shepherd divides his sheep from the goats. And He will set the sheep on His right hand, but the goats on His left. Then the King will say to those on His right hand, "Come, you blessed of My Father, inherit the kingdom prepared for you from the foundation of the world." … Then He will say to those on His left hand, "Depart from Me, you cursed, into everlasting fire prepared for the devil and his angels." … And these will go away into everlasting punishment, but the righteous into eternal life. (Matthew 25:31–34, 41, 46)

And I saw a great white throne and Him who sat on it, from whose face the earth and heaven fled away. And there was found no place for them. And I saw the dead, small and great, standing before God, and books were opened. And another book was opened, which is the Book of Life. And the dead were judged according to their works, by the things which were written in the books. The sea gave up the dead who were in it, and Death and Hades delivered up the dead who were in them. And they were judged, each one according to his works. Then Death and Hades were cast into the lake of fire. This is the second death. And anyone not found written in the Book of Life was cast into the lake of fire. (Revelation 20:11–15)

When Jesus Christ returns with the angels and the saints, for the rest of His saints, His children, His Church, and His Bride to judge everyone according to their deeds; and to separate the righteous from the unrighteous; it will not be in secret. Everyone will see Him ascending from heaven; and His feet will touch the Mount of Olives in Jerusalem. Jesus, His angels, and saints will fight Satan, his army of demons, and wicked enemies at a place that is called Armageddon in the Hebrew. (Revelation 16:16 KJV)

There Satan will forever be defeated along with all of God's and Israel's enemies.

Jesus will set up His kingdom here on a purified earth, where He will reign and rule the nations with a rod of iron. And He will give eternal life to all those who believed, trusted, and accepted Him and put their faith Him.

We will spend eternity with Him in that indescribably beautiful place that He has prepared for us. The unrighteous will be cast in the lake of unquenchable fire and brimstone that burns forever, along with Satan, demons, the beast, false prophets, and all unbelievers (those who did not believe and accept Jesus Christ). They will spend their eternity in unbearable torment, darkness, and total separation from God and Jesus.

On that day the trumpet of God will sound, and everyone, even the dead, will hear it. The dead will rise from the grave, and every eye will see Him coming in the clouds. He will not come in secret or as a baby this time, but as King of Kings and Lord of Lords, in awesome and great power. His kingdom will be established on a new earth, and He will rule forevermore. We will for eternity be in His presence. Hallelujah! Glory to God!

It is not meant, nor is it necessary, for us to know all of God's plan, as some things are still a mystery—and I'm okay with that. I am satisfied with, elated about, and honored by what He has chosen to share and reveal to me and to us. I am happy to know that I will spend my eternal life with Him wherever He is. Listen, you just be prepared for when these events happen, for when He comes.

And the seventh angel sounded: and there were great voices in heaven, saying, The kingdoms of this world are become the kingdoms of our Lord, and of his Christ; and he shall reign for ever and ever. (Revelation 11:15 KJV)

And they shall see his face; and his name shall be in their foreheads. (Revelation 22:4 KJV)

He shall rule them with a rod of iron; they shall be dashed to pieces like a potter's vessels. (Revelation 2:27)

Behold! The Second Coming of Jesus Christ Is Near: He Wants Us to Be Prepared for His Arrival

Behold, the day! Behold, it has come!
—Ezekiel 7:10

Prepare to meet your God!
—Amos 4:12

But of that day and hour no one knows, not even the angels
in heaven, nor the Son, but only the Father. Take heed,
watch and pray for you do not know when the time is.
—Mark 13:32–33

It is like a man going to a far country, who left his house
and gave authority to his servants, and to each his work, and
commanded the doorkeeper to watch. Watch therefore, for you
do not know when the master of the house is coming—in the
evening, at midnight, at the crowing of the rooster, or in the
morning—lest, coming suddenly, he find you sleeping.
—Mark 13:34–36

Let not your heart be troubled; you believe in God, believe also
in Me [Jesus]. In My Father's house are many mansions; if it were
not so, I would have told you. I go to prepare a place for you.

And if I go and prepare a place for you, I will come again and
receive you to Myself; that where I am. There you may be also.
—John 14:1–3

For he hath prepared for them a city.
—Hebrews 11:16 (KJV)

Before the Lord: for he cometh, for he cometh to judge the earth: he
shall judge the world with righteousness, and the people with his truth.
—Psalm 96:13 (KJV) (See also Psalm 98:13 KJV)

And as is appointed for men to die once, but after this the judgment, so
Christ was offered once to bear the sins of many. To those who eagerly
wait for Him he will appear a second time, apart from sin, for salvation.
—Hebrews 9:27–28

And to wait for His Son from heaven, whom He raised from the
dead, even Jesus who delivers us from the wrath to come.
—1 Thessalonians 1:10

When Christ who is our life appears, then you
also will appear with Him in glory.
—Colossians 3:4

For I know that my redeemer liveth, and that he
shall stand at the latter day upon the earth.
—Job 19:25 (KJV)

For the Son of Man shall come in the glory of his Father with his
angels; and then he shall reward every man according to his works.
—Matthew 16:27 (KJV)

Verily I say unto you, There be some standing here, which shall not
taste death, till they see the Son of Man coming in his kingdom.
—Matthew 16:28 (KJV)

I am blowing the trumpet and sounding the alarm: Jesus is coming! Are you prepared to meet Him? Are you prepared to go back with Him to that place He has prepared for you? Are you ready to stand before Almighty God to be judged? For only a fool knows that someone is coming or that something big is going to happen and yet makes no preparation for it.

God tells us, warns us, and pleads with us to be ready for this inevitable event. People have talked about it, read about it, written about it, joked about it, and sung about it. The Word of God is extremely clear about the Second Coming of Jesus Christ. And whether one believes it or not, it doesn't really matter, because Jesus is still coming. And He wants us to be ready and prepared for His arrival.

We all need to ask ourselves these questions: "Am I fully prepared for His coming? Is there anything in my life that I'm doing that may not be pleasing to Him and that is not in line with His Word? Is there anything that I am doing that will hinder me or keep me from going back with Him when He comes?" Or you may ask the question, "How do I prepare for Jesus's return?"

Well, I'm glad you asked. All of these questions and more are answered in my book, and it is an easy read because it's scriptural. My dear friends, you must be prepared spiritually, emotionally, and mentally. You must be born again by the Spirit of God. You must not be conformed to the world, doing things the way the world does. You must be transformed by renewing your mind with the Word of God, the things of God, and by doing things His way. If you claim to be a Christian, you must repent, change, and forsake your old way of thinking and living.

You must live a righteous life before God. My brothers and sisters, you cannot continue to deliberately, constantly, and knowingly live in sin. You must stop, tell Jesus that you are sorry, and ask Him to forgive you of your sins, *if indeed you want to be prepared for His coming.*

Will you please say this short prayer with me with your whole heart? This prayer is for those who have not received Jesus Christ into their lives, as well as for those who have but who, for some reason, know that they need to do it again (they and God know why):

> Lord Jesus, I am so sorry for all of my sins. I ask that You forgive me; create in me a new and clean heart; cleanse me

from all unrighteousness; baptize me with Your Holy Spirit to help me live a holy and fruitful life; and prepare me for Your coming. I believe that You are the Son of God, that You died on the cross for my sins and those of the world, that God raised You from the grave on the third day, and that You are now seated at the right hand of God the Father in heaven. I invite You into my heart and into my life as my Lord and Savior. I fully surrender to You. Change and rearrange my life so that I can be more like You. Give me a heart of love and compassion for people. Help me to prepare for Your coming so that I will be ready upon Your arrival. I want to be found worthy to go back with You. Thank You for saving my soul and making me whole. O Lord, thank You for the gift of salvation and eternal life. In Your name, I pray. Amen.

Take inventory of your life and compare your list with His list (the Bible). Make sure that you're prepared when Jesus returns. Or if you should depart this life here on earth before He returns, be prepared to meet Him on the other side (of this life). It is for certain that whether you live or die, you will stand before Him for judgment.

Make sure that you are living a life that is pleasing to God, obeying His Word, and doing the work that He told you to do. Jesus Christ is coming back! Start preparing so that you will be ready when He appears. Let us get our hearts, minds, and souls right with God. Let us clean and get our houses in order. Let us live a life of holiness before God. More than anything in this world, I pray that we will all be prepared for that glorious day when Jesus returns to earth.

I am basically speaking to two groups of people. I'm sure that you can find yourself in one of these groups:

The Believers

The believers are Christians who believe in the doctrine of Jesus Christ. They believe in the Trinity (Father, Son, and Holy Spirit). They believe that God the Father loves us so much that He was willing to give up His only beloved Son Jesus Christ to come into the world and suffer unbearable pain, shame, and temporary separation from Him as Jesus gave His life on the cross, shedding His precious blood for the sins of the world. Why?

Because He loves us, He desires that we all be saved, and He wishes to give us the chance to have eternal life with Him.

Believers are also called the saints, the holy ones, and the children of God. They have been sanctified and set apart for God. These are the people who have acknowledged and confessed their sins to Jesus Christ, asked Him to forgive them of their sins, invited Him into their hearts and lives, and accepted Him as their Lord and personal Savior. They confessed with their mouths and believe in their hearts that Jesus Christ is Lord and Savior, that He died on the cross for their sins, and that God raised Him from the grave on the third day for their justification. They have been born again by the Spirit of God and washed in the blood of Jesus, and the Holy Spirit now dwells (abides, lives) inside them. They are each now a new creation in Jesus Christ and a member of the family of God. They have repented, changed their minds and old ways of living, and turned away from their old sinful lives and the choices they made.

They now choose and endeavor to live a holy life and to know God's way—a new way of living life according to His Word (the Bible). For God is holy and requires us to live holy lives also (1 Peter 1:15–16). Their desire is to please Him (and not humankind) and to be obedient to His Word, will, and ways. Their hope (and my hope) is to ultimately spend eternity with God the Father, our Creator, and Jesus Christ His Son, our Lord, Savior, and King, in the place that Jesus has prepared for us. (See John 14:3.)

Believers also believe that Jesus is now in heaven, seated at the right hand of God the Father. They have faith in Him, believe in Him, and trust His Word. They believe in the Second Coming of Jesus Christ. He is coming again to this earth to take His children home to live with Him forever and to righteously judge and reward all people (the dead and the living) based on all that they have said and done. For God sent Jesus to save you and me and everyone who so chooses to believe and have faith in Him and receive His grace and mercy.

Please read the entire chapter of 1 Corinthians 15 for more on the resurrection of Jesus Christ, believers in Jesus Christ, and the resurrected body. There is a natural body and there is a spiritual body. First, we have a natural body because of our physical birth. When by faith we accept Jesus Christ as Lord and Savior, this qualifies us to receive a spiritual body. The Spirit of God indwells us, and we become born again. And one *must be* born again, for flesh and blood cannot inherit or live in God's kingdom. (Read John 3:3–8; 1 Corinthians 15:50.)

Do not compromise the Word of God for anyone or anything. Be sure that your life is in order. Love one another; pray for, forgive, have compassion for, and be kind to one another. Share the gospel of Jesus Christ and His love with others, and win souls for God's kingdom. Love God the Father and Jesus Christ His Son, our Lord and Savior, with all your mind, heart, and soul, and obey His Word. Put no one above Him; make Him your first priority. Do not quench the Holy Spirit; allow Him to lead and guide you into all truths. Watch, pray, and stay in the Word of God. Prepare now so that you will be ready to meet Jesus Christ, our Lord, King, and Savior, when He comes.

The Unbelievers

These are the people who do not believe that Jesus Christ is God's Son. They have not asked Jesus Christ for forgiveness of their sins, and they have not accepted Him as their Lord and personal Savior. They do not believe in God or in His Son Jesus Christ. "The fool has said in his heart, There is no God" (Psalm 14:1 KJV). Maybe they believe in God but do not believe that Jesus Christ is God's Son. They don't believe that Jesus died on the cross for their sins, that God raised Him from the dead on the third day for our justification, and that He is alive, seated in heaven with God the Father. They do not believe in the resurrection power of God or in the coming of Jesus.

Perhaps they believe in a higher power, not knowing who or what it is. Maybe they just don't believe in anything or anyone that they cannot see, hear, feel, or touch. Or perhaps they think that they still have time to repent, to give their life to Jesus Christ another day or at some other time. But some other time, even the next second, is not promised to us and therefore may be too late.

Get your life and your house in order while you still have *this time— this moment*. Invite Jesus Christ into your heart right now, and ask Him to forgive you of your sins, be your Lord and Savior, and fill you with the Holy Spirit to help you walk the path of righteousness.

Whether you believe in God the Father or Jesus Christ His Son, our Lord and Savior, and whether you believe His Word (the Bible), doesn't matter. Nor does your disbelief change anything, because God's Word is true. Heaven and earth will pass away, but His Word stands forever. Repent and save yourself for the kingdom of God is at hand! God loves you and wants you to spend eternity with Him in that beautiful place He has prepared for us. But you must be prepared when He comes, and you must be born again spiritually. For whether we live or die, we will one day meet Him face-to-face and see Him as He really is. We will be judged according to whether or not we believe in Him and by our works, and we will be rewarded accordingly. It will be determined by God where you (your spirit) will spend eternal life.

So if you hear His voice in your heart today, do not harden your heart or allow someone else to say something negative to change your mind. (For that is only a trick of Satan the devil. He wants you to spend eternity with him in torment amid hellfire and brimstone. That is his plan for you.) For what does it profit a man or woman to gain the entire world and yet lose his or her soul? What would you give in exchange for your soul?

Try God and Jesus Christ His Son. You have nothing to lose and everything to gain, which means eternal life. Talk to Him with your whole heart and tell Him what you're feeling. Yes, He already knows, but He wants to converse with you one-on-one. He wants a personal relationship with you so that He can reveal Himself to you even more. God's plan for you is life. He seeks to give you abundant and eternal life. He wants you to live in His presence in the New Jerusalem with its indescribable beauty and unspeakable joy, full of His glory.

Dear friends, our eyes have not seen and our ears have not heard of the beauty, joy, and magnificent things that God has prepared and has waiting for those who love Him. He doesn't want anyone, regardless of who you are or what you have done (so long as you ask Jesus Christ to forgive you of your sins and repent), to be lost. He has given everyone a chance to choose eternal life. Believe and trust in God the Father and in His Son Jesus Christ. Be ready and prepared when Jesus comes. He is coming back just as He has said in His Word. God loves us very much and wants us to be prepared when Jesus comes.

Right now, I'm reminded of the ten virgins in the Bible in Matthew 25:10–12. The story goes as follows:

Five of these virgins were wise in that their lamps were filled with oil and they had also brought extra oil with them. They were ready and well prepared as they waited patiently for the bridegroom to come. However, the other five virgins were called foolish because, as they waited for the bridegroom, they ran out of oil and had not brought extra oil with them. They thought that they were ready and had prepared for this day, but they were not fully prepared or equipped for the bridegroom's coming. They asked the five wise virgins to share their oil, but the wise virgins refused because they feared they would run out, that they would fall short and therefore not be ready and prepared to meet the bridegroom whenever he arrived.

They were fully equipped and prepared for this event, and they weren't going to allow anyone to perhaps cause them to miss this long-awaited moment and opportunity. This was their hope; they had been preparing and were watchful. They had prepared for this day when the Bridegroom would come and take them back with Him and live forever. After all, the five foolish virgins had the same opportunity that the wise virgins had had to prepare for the Bridegroom's (Jesus Christ's) return. But they were slack, unequipped, unwilling, unorganized, and lazy. They remained in their comfort zone, unalert, with no true expectancy. And, might I add, they were not very smart.

So, while the five foolish virgins left to go get oil for their lamps, the bridegroom came. The five wise virgins and those who were prepared went into the wedding to see the bridegroom, and the door was shut. The five foolish virgins returned and asked the Lord to open the door for them, but the bridegroom replied that he did not know them. They had not taken this event (which is symbolic of Christ's return) seriously; they had not wholeheartedly prepared and therefore weren't ready for this glorious moment. Sadly, they were left behind.

"While the bridegroom tarried, they all slumbered and slept. And at midnight there was a cry made, Behold, the bridegroom cometh; go ye out to meet him" (Matthew 25:5–6 KJV).

"And while they went to buy, the bridegroom came; and they that were ready went in with him to the marriage: and the door was shut. Afterward came also the other virgins, saying, Lord, Lord, open to us. But he answered and said, Verily I say unto you, I know you not" (Matthew 25:10–12 KJV).

I pray that you and I will be part of that group of people who will be wise and who will be prepared to meet Jesus Christ, our Bridegroom, and go back with Him when He comes. Don't be in the foolish group; don't take any chances. Keep your lamp filled with oil, and make sure you lack nothing. Repent, and ask Jesus Christ to come into your life right now. Ask Him to forgive you of your sins and be your Lord and Savior. He loves you and wants you to be prepared to go back with Him when He returns. Jesus Christ is coming!

Will you please say this short prayer with me?

Lord Jesus, I believe that You are the Son of God. I need You right now. Reveal Yourself to me. I want to believe. Help me with my unbelief. Forgive me of my sins and come into my life. I believe that You are the Son of God, that You died on the cross for my sins, and that God raised You from the grave on the third day for my justification. Open my eyes and ears spiritually so that I can see and hear You clearly. Save my soul and make me whole. I surrender myself to You; have Your way in my life. In Your name I pray. Amen.

If you sincerely, with your whole heart, meant what you just said, then you are saved! Congratulations. Welcome to the family of God. To God be the glory! Jesus Christ is coming and will arrive upon this earth very soon. He wants us to be prepared for His return.

Now, please hear the words of the Lord our God, and prepare your heart for His return:

I am Alpha and the Omega, the beginning and the end, the first and the last. (Revelation 22:13 KJV)

Sing and rejoice, O daughter of Zion: for, lo, I come, and I will dwell in the midst of thee, saith the Lord. (Zechariah 2:10 KJV)

Many nations shall be joined to the Lord in that day, and shall be my people: and I will dwell in the midst of thee, and thou shalt know that the Lord of hosts hath sent me unto thee. (Zechariah 2:11 KJV)

Be silent, O all flesh, before the Lord: for he is raised up out of his holy habitation! (Zechariah 2:13 KJV)

The great day of the Lord is near; it is near, and hasteth quickly, even the voice of the day of the Lord: the mighty man shall cry there bitterly. That day is a day of wrath, a day of trouble and distress, a day of wasteness desolation, a day of darkness and gloominess, a day of clouds and thick darkness. A day of trumpet and alarm against the fenced cities, and against the high towers. (Zephaniah 1:14–16 KJV)

"I will stretch out My hand against ... those who have turned back from following the Lord, and have not sought the Lord, nor inquired of Him." Be silent in the presence of the Lord God; for the day of the Lord is at hand. (Zephaniah 1:4, 6–7)

Behold, the Lord comes with ten thousands of His saints, to execute judgment on all, to convict all who are ungodly among them of all their ungodly deeds which they have committed in an ungodly way, and of all the harsh things which ungodly sinners have spoken against Him. (Jude 1:14–15)

"Now, therefore," says the Lord, "turn to Me with all your heart, With fasting, with weeping, and with mourning. So, rend your heart and not your garments; return to the Lord your God, For He is gracious and merciful, slow to anger and of great kindness; and He relents from during harm." (Joel 2:12–13)

And in those days men shall seek death, and shall not find it; and shall desire to die, and death shall flee from them. (Revelation 9:6 KJV)

And I will bring distress upon men, that they shall walk like blind men, because they have sinned against the Lord: and their blood shall be poured out as dust, and their flesh as the dung. (Zephaniah 1:17 KJV)

Neither their silver nor their gold shall be able to deliver them in the day of the Lord's wrath; but the whole land shall be devoured by the fire of His jealousy: for he shall make even a speedy riddance of all them that dwell in the land. (Zephaniah 1:18 KJV)

"I will utterly consume everything from the face of the land," says the Lord; "I will consume man and beast; … birds, fish of the sea, and the stumbling blocks along with the wicked. I will cut off man from the face of the land," says the Lord. (Zephaniah 1:2, 3)

Blessed are those who do His commandments that they may have the right to the tree of life; and may enter through the gates into the city—the New Jerusalem. But outside are dogs and sorcerers and sexually immoral and murderers and idolaters, and whoever loves and practices a lie. (Revelation 22:14–15)

But the fearful, and unbelieving, and abominable, and murderers, and whoremongers, and sorcerers, and idolaters, and all liars, shall have their part in the lake which burneth with fire and brimstone: which is the second death. (Revelation 21:8 KJV)

Do you not know that the unrighteous will not inherit the kingdom of God? Do not be deceived. Neither fornicators, nor idolaters, nor adulterers, nor homosexuals, nor sodomites, nor thieves, nor covetous, nor drunkards, nor revilers, nor extortioners will inherit the kingdom of God. (1 Corinthians 6:9–10)

But I do not want you to be ignorant, brethren, concerning those who have fallen asleep, lest you sorrow as others who have no hope. For if we believe that Jesus died and rose again, even so God will bring with Him those who sleep in Jesus. For this we say to you by the word of the Lord, that we who are alive and remain until the coming of the Lord will by no means precede those who are asleep. For the Lord Himself will descend from heaven with a shout, with the voice of an archangel, and with the trumpet of God. And the dead in Christ will rise first. Then we who are alive and remain shall be caught up together with them in the clouds to meet the Lord in the air. And thus, we shall always be with the Lord. (1 Thessalonians 4:13–17)

And he did evil, because he prepared not his heart to seek the Lord. (2 Chronicles 12:14 KJV)

To the end he may establish your hearts unblameable in holiness before God, even our Father, at the coming of our Lord Jesus Christ with all his saints. (1 Thessalonians 3:13 KJV)

For God hath not appointed us to wrath, but to obtain salvation by [through] our Lord Jesus Christ, Who died for us, that, whether we wake or sleep, we should live together with him. (1 Thessalonians 5:9–10 KJV)

And the Lord my God shall come, and all the saints with thee. (Zechariah 14:5 KJV)

Oh, what a beautiful day and what an awesome sight it will be for those who love and have obeyed God, for those who have long hoped and waited for this moment.

And they shall call them, the holy people, the redeemed of the Lord. (Isaiah 62:12 KJV)

Nevertheless we, according to his promise, look for a new heavens and a new earth, wherein dwelleth righteousness. Wherefore, beloved, seeing that ye look for such things, be diligent that ye may be found of him in peace, without spot and blameless. And account that the longsuffering of our Lord is salvation. (2 Peter 3:13–15 KJV)

He who overcomes shall be clothed in white garments; and I will not blot out his name from the Book of Life; but I will confess his name before My Father and before His angels. He who has an ear, let him hear what the Spirit says. (Revelation 3:5–6)

When the Son of Man comes in His glory, and all the holy angels with Him, then He will sit on the throne of His glory. All the nations will be gathered before Him, and He will separate them one from another, as a shepherd divides his sheep from the goats. And He will set the sheep on His right hand, but the goats on the left. Then the King will say to those on His right hand, "Come you blessed of My Father, inherit the kingdom prepared for you from the foundation of the world." (Matthew 25:31–34)

More than anything in this world, I want to be in this group of people at the right hand of God when He makes the separation. I want to hear My Father say: "Well done, Sarah. Come and spend eternity with Me in My kingdom."

Please don't find yourself in that group of people He sends to His left hand, because you will spend your eternal life in torment and total separation from God our Father and Jesus our Savior.

Then shall He say also unto them on the left hand, "Depart from Me, you cursed, into the everlasting fire prepared for the devil and his angels: "For I was hungry, and you gave me no food; I was thirsty, and you gave Me no drink; I was a stranger and you did not take Me in, naked and you did not clothe Me, sick and in prison and you did not visit Me.'" (Matthew 25:41–43)

Assuredly, I say to you, inasmuch as you did not do it to one of the least of these, you did not do it to Me. ... And these will go away into everlasting punishment, but the righteous into eternal life. (Matthew 25:45, 46)

My dear friends, seek God the Father and Jesus Christ His Son, our Lord and Savior, with all your heart. Don't try to understand everything concerning the things of God; stop trying to figure Him out. Just believe, have faith in Him, and trust Him. Seek His forgiveness, and invite Him into your heart. Ask Him to be Lord and Savior in your life. Seek righteousness and His will. Talk to Him from your whole heart, for He will hear and answer you. I promise, you will not be disappointed.

And now, little children, abide in him; that, when he shall appear, we may have confidence, and not be ashamed before him at his coming. (1 John 2:28 KJV)

And to give you who are troubled rest with us when the Lord Jesus is revealed from heaven with His mighty angels, in flaming fire taking vengeance on those who do not know God, and on those who do not obey the gospel of our Lord Jesus Christ. These shall be punished with everlasting destruction from the presence of the Lord and from the glory of His power, when He comes, in that Day, to be glorified in His saints and to be admired among all those who believe, because our testimony among you was believed. (2 Thessalonians 1:7–10)

Behold, I come as a thief. Blessed is he that watcheth, and keepeth his garments, lest he walk naked, and they see his shame. (Revelation 16:15 KJV)

And, behold, I come quickly; and my reward is with me, to give to every man according to his work shall be. (Revelation 22:12 KJV)

I am Alpha and Omega, the beginning and the end, the first and the last. (Revelation 22:13 KJV)

I, Jesus, have sent My angel to testify to you these things in the churches. I am the Root and the Offspring of David, the Bright and Morning Star. (Revelation 22:16)

Behold, the Lord God will come with a strong hand, and his arm shall rule for him; behold, his reward is with him, and his work before him. He shall feed his flock like a shepherd; he shall gather the lambs with his arm, and carry them in his bosom, and shall gently lead those who are with young. (Isaiah 40:10–11 KJV)

Now I saw heaven opened, and behold, a white horse. And He who sat on him was called Faithful and True, and in righteousness He judges and makes war. His eyes were like a flame of fire, and on His head were many crowns. He had a name written that no one knew except Himself. He was clothed with a robe dipped in blood, and His name is called The Word of God. And the armies in heaven, clothed in fine linen, white and clean, followed Him on white horses. Now out of His mouth goes a sharp sword, that with it He should strike the nations. And He Himself will rule them with a rod of iron. He Himself treads the winepress of the fierceness and wrath of Almighty God. And He has on His robe and on His thigh a name written: King of Kings and Lord of Lords. (Revelation 19:11–16)

"I am Alpha and the Omega, the Beginning and the End," says the Lord, which is, and which was, and which is to come, the Almighty. (Revelation 1:8)

I am He who lives, and was dead, and behold, I am alive forevermore. Amen. And I have the keys of Hades and of Death. (Revelation 1:18)

Surely, I come quickly. Amen. Even so, come, Lord Jesus. (Revelation 22:20)

Woe unto those who have not prepared for Jesus's coming; have not sought Him; have not obeyed the voice of Almighty God; have stopped or turned back from following God; have not received correction; have not believed and trusted in Him; have not drawn near to Him; and have neither believed in nor received Jesus Christ, God's Son, as Lord and Savior.

Woe unto those who have not asked God to forgive them of their sins and invited Jesus into their lives, who have not believed that He died on the cross for our sins and that God raised Him from the grave on the third day for our justification (with all power in His hands and the keys of life and death). For He is the Savior of the world. He is the way, the truth, and the life. He is King of Kings and Lord of Lords. He is the Alpha and the Omega, the Beginning and the End. He is that which was, that which is, and that which is to come. Glory to God!

Jesus promised us that He would go and prepare a place for us (our eternal home), that He would come back one day for us, and that we will live with Him forever (John 14:1–4). He is a God who cannot lie and is true to His Word. We should comfort and encourage one another as often as we can, knowing that our Lord and Savior is coming again.

I pray that you and I will be prepared when Jesus Christ comes and that we will be found worthy to go back with Him. I pray that He will be pleased with us and take us to live with Him forever in the New Jerusalem here on the new purified earth or in that place He has prepared for us.

You can read Revelation chapters 21 and 22 for more information concerning a new heaven and earth, where we will spend eternity with Jesus Christ our Lord and Savior, God our Father, our loved ones, the angels, and all the believers and saints of God. You will be in awe with unspeakable joy and happiness as you read about the immaculate beauty and wonder of this place. It is seemingly too much for the human mind to grasp. Truly, eyes have not seen a place such as our new eternal home, our New Jerusalem.

Please go to a church that teaches and preaches the gospel of Jesus Christ according to the Word of God (Bible) without compromise. I'm sure that the pastor and ministerial staff will be happy to help you and answer any questions that you may have. Study the Bible for yourself and attend Bible school or Bible study. Pray and talk to God anytime you want, as He is available 24/7, 366 days a year. He never sleeps or slumbers and never gets tired of us calling Him and conversing with Him.

Remember, my friends, that God loves you so much that He gave His Son Jesus Christ to die for our sins. He was our sacrifice; He was our ransom, He took our place on the cross and paid the price with His precious blood for our redemption. We have been reconciled to God and can have a personal relationship with Him. We can go boldly to the throne of grace to God our Father in prayer and let Him know how we feel about all things. Jesus Christ is now seated in heaven at the right hand of God as our High Priest, Advocate, Mediator, and Intercessor.

For those of you who have not invited Jesus Christ into your heart and life: Ask Jesus to forgive you of your sins. Tell Him that you believe that He is the Son of God, that He died on the cross for your sins and those of the world, that He rose from the grave on the third day, and that He is now seated at the right hand of God the Father in heaven. Invite Him into your heart as Lord and Savior. Tell Him that you want to be well prepared for His soon return for His children.

May the mercy and grace of God our Father and our Lord Jesus Christ be with us all.

Be Watchful, Be Sober, and Be Prayerful. Be Prepared for Jesus Christ's Return

Watch therefore, for ye know neither the day nor
the hour wherein the Son of Man cometh.
—Matthew 25:13 (KJV)

But let us, who are of the day, be sober, putting on the breastplate
of faith and love; and as a helmet, the hope of salvation.
—1 Thessalonians 5:8 (KJV)

And that servant, which knew his lord's will, prepared not himself,
neither did according to his will, shall be beaten with many strikes.
—Luke 12:47 (KJV)

Be ye therefore ready also: for the Son of Man
cometh at an hour when ye think not.
—Luke 12:40 (KJV)

Take ye heed, watch and pray: for ye know not when the time is.
—Mark 13:33 (KJV)

Be watchful, be sober, be prayerful, be brave, be strong, and stand in the faith. Let no one deceive you. Prepare, so that you will be ready for the Second Coming of Jesus Christ. Do not be shaken by the cares of this world. Continue to have faith. Trust, rely on, and believe every word and promise of God. If you haven't already done so, repent of your sins, ask God to forgive you, and invite Jesus Christ into your life as Lord and

Savior. For He is the way, the truth, and the life, and no one can come or get to God the Father unless one first comes through Jesus His Son. We must stay alert and be prepared at all times, having the *expectation* of His arrival at any given moment.

> Therefore let us not sleep, as do others; but let us watch and be sober. (1 Thessalonians 5:6 KJV)

> Be sober, be vigilant; because your adversary the devil as a roaring lion, walketh about seeking whom he may devour. (1 Peter 5:8 KJV)

> But watch thou in all things, endure afflictions. (2 Timothy 4:5 KJV)

> Watch and pray, that ye enter not into temptation: the spirit indeed is willing, but the flesh is weak. (Matthew 26:41 KJV)

> Let your waist be girded and your lamp burning; and you yourselves be like men who wait for their master, when he will return from the wedding, that when comes and knocks they may open to him immediately. Blessed are those servants whom the master, when he comes, will find watching. And if he should come in the second watch, or come in the third watch, and find them so, blessed are those servants. (Luke 12:35–38)

> Blessed is that servant, whom his master will find so doing when he comes. Truly, I say to you that he will make him ruler over all that he has. But if that servant says in his heart, "My master is delaying his coming," and begins to beat the male and female servants, and to eat and drink and be drunk, the master of that servant will come on a day when he is not looking for him, and at an hour when he is not aware, and will cut him in two and appoint him his portion with the unbelievers. (Luke 12:43–46)

> For you yourselves know perfectly that the day of the Lord so comes as a thief in the night. For when they say, "Peace and safety!" then sudden destruction comes upon them, as labor

pains upon a pregnant woman. And they shall not escape. (1 Thessalonians 5:2–3)

Be watchful, and strengthen the things which remain, that are ready to die, for I have not found your works perfect before God. Remember therefore how you have received and heard; hold fast and repent. Therefore if you will not watch, I will come upon you as a thief, and you will not know what hour I will come upon you. (Revelation 3:2–3)

Watch therefore and pray always that you may be counted worthy to escape all these things that will come to pass, and to stand before the Son of Man. (Luke 21:36)

Watch therefore, for you do not know when the master of the house is coming—in the evening, at mid night, at the crowing of the rooster, or in the morning—lest, coming suddenly he finds you sleeping. And what I say to you, I say to all: Watch! (Mark 13:35–37)

Signs of Jesus Christ's Return: The Last Days

Dear friends, I believe, based on the Word of God, that we are now living in the last days. Human beings will continue to destroy themselves, but God will rescue and deliver His children from the hand of the wicked and will destroy the evil and wicked people forever. For the righteous and the unrighteous cannot, and will not, live together in the kingdom of God.

We are indeed living in the most perilous, dangerous, and devastating times that the world has ever faced. God warned us that these times would come. He told us that people will be lovers of themselves, lovers of money, and boasters. He warned us that people would have proud hearts and be blasphemers. He said that children would be disobedient to parents and that people would be unthankful, unholy, unloving, unforgiving, slanderous, without self-control, headstrong, haughty, and brutal. He said that people would be despisers of good, traitors, and lovers of pleasure rather than lovers of God, and that they would have a form of godliness but deny its power. God warns us to turn away from and not associate with such people (2 Timothy 3:1–5).

The Word of God tells us that evil people and impostors will grow worse and worse, deceiving and being deceived (2 Timothy 3:13). Sadly, this is so true. Some people act worse than wild animals. Some people tell so many lies, and tell them so well, that oftentimes even they themselves believe what they say. Their conscience has been seared as with a hot iron, and they just don't care.

Now the Spirit expressly says that in latter times some will depart from the faith, giving heed to deceiving spirits and doctrines of demons (1 Timothy 4:1). This too is already happening.

There are numerous signs of Jesus's return that are mentioned in the Bible that have already passed or are happening right now. Others will happen in the future. And there are many scriptures pertaining to these signs—too many for me to write about with explanations in this book. However, some suggested reading is the book of Revelation. Start with chapters 1–3, and read Jesus's letters to the seven churches. You may find yourself in one of these churches. If you do, please hear what the Spirit of God is saying to you. Jesus Christ knows and sees all. He gave Himself for the church, and He is coming back for a church (His bride) without spot or wrinkle to present to God the Father.

"Behold, the days come, saith the Lord God, that I will send a famine in the land, not a famine of bread, nor a thirst for water, but of hearing the words of the Lord: And they shall wander from sea to sea, and from north even to the east, and they shall run to and fro to seek the word of the Lord, and shall not find it" (Amos 8:11–12 KJV).

Read the Word of God (the Holy Bible) daily. Meditate on it, memorize it, and hide its words in your heart. In this way, no one can ever take it from you, you will always be full, and you'll never suffer famine.

As the disciples sat on the Mount of Olives (Matthew 24), they asked Jesus privately to tell them when certain things would happen and what the sign of His coming and the end of the age would be. And Jesus answered them as follows:

> Take heed that no man deceive you. For many will come in my name, saying, I am Christ; and shall deceive many. And ye shall hear of wars and rumors of wars; see that ye be not troubled; for all these things must come to pass, but the end is not yet. For nation shall rise against nation, and kingdom against kingdom; and there will be famines, and pestilences, and earthquakes, in divers places. All these are the beginning of sorrows. (Matthew 24:4–8 KJV)

> Then they shall deliver you up to be afflicted, and shall kill you: and ye shall be hated of all nations for my name's sake. And then shall many be offended, and shall betray one another, and shall hate one another. And many false prophets shall rise and shall deceive many. And because iniquity shall abound, the

love of many shall wax cold. But he that shall endure to the end, the same shall be saved. And this gospel of the kingdom shall be preached in all the world for a witness unto all nations; and then the end shall come. (Matthew 24:9–14 KJV)

Therefore, when you see the "abomination of desolation," spoken of by Daniel the prophet [see Daniel 9:27; 11:31; 12:11], standing in the holy place (whoever reads, let him understand), then let those who are in Judea flee to the mountains. Let him who is in the field not go back to get his clothes. But woe to those who are pregnant and to those who are nursing babies in those days! And pray that your flight may not be in the winter or on the Sabbath. (Matthew 24:15–20)

For then there will be great tribulations, such as has not been since the beginning of the world until this time, no, nor ever shall be. And unless those days were shortened, no flesh would be saved; but for the elect's sake those days will be shortened. (Matthew 24:21–22)

Then if anyone says to you, "Look, here is the Christ!" or "There!" do not believe it. For false christs and false prophets will rise and show great signs and wonders to deceive, if possible, even the elect. See, I have told you beforehand. (Matthew 24:23–25)

For as the lightning comes from the east and flashes to the west, so also will the coming of the Son of Man be. (Matthew 24:27)

Immediately after the tribulation of those days the sun will be darkened, and the moon will not give its light; the stars will fall from heaven, and the powers of the heaven will be shaken. Then the sign of the Son of Man will appear in heaven, and then all the tribes of the earth will mourn, and they will see the Son of Man coming on the clouds of heaven with power and great glory. (Matthew 24:29–30)

And he shall send his angels with a great sound of a trumpet; and they shall gather together his elect from the four winds, from one end of heaven to the other. (Matthew 24:31 KJV)

Now learn a parable from the fig tree; when his branch is yet tender, and putteth forth leaves, ye know that summer is nigh: ... So likewise ye, when ye shall see all these things, know that it is near, even at the doors. (Matthew 24:32, 33 KJV)

But of that day and hour knoweth no man, no, not the angels of heaven, but my Father only. But as the days of Noah were, so shall also the coming of the Son of Man be. For as in the days that were before the flood they were eating and drinking, marrying and giving in marriage, until the day that Noah entered into the ark, and knew not until the flood came, and took them all away; so shall also the coming of the Son of Man be. (Matthew 24:36–39 KJV) (Read Genesis 6–8 regarding the Flood)

Jesus goes on to say the following in other chapters concerning the end times and the great tribulation:

And I will show wonders in the heavens and in the earth: Blood and fire and pillars of smoke. The sun shall be turned into darkness, and the moon into blood, before the coming of that great and awesome day of the Lord. (Joel 2:30–31)

The earth quakes before them, the heavens tremble; the sun and moon grow dark, and the stars diminish their brightness. (Joel 2:10)

And there will be signs in the sun, in the moon, and in the stars; and on the earth distress of nations, with perplexity, the sea and the waves roaring; men's heart failing them from fear and the expectation of those things which are coming on the earth, for the powers of the heavens will be shaken. (Luke 21:25–26)

Now brother will deliver up brother to death, and a father his child; and children will rise up against parents and cause them to be put to death. (Matthew 10:21)

You will be betrayed even by parents and brothers, relatives and friends; and they will put some of you to death. And you will be hated by all for My name's sake. (Luke 21:16–17)

So you also, when you see these things happening, know that the kingdom of God is near. (Luke 21:31)

Listen to what God says in Zechariah 14:12 concerning those who will fight Israel in the future: "And this shall be the plague with which the Lord will strike all the people who fought Jerusalem: Their flesh shall dissolve while they stand on their feet, their eyes shall dissolve in their sockets, and their tongues shall dissolve in their mouths. It shall come to pass in that day, that a great panic from the Lord will be among them. Everyone will seize the hand of his neighbor and raise his hand against his neighbor's hand."

What does this sound like to you?

This prophecy was spoken by the prophet Joel and came to pass on the Day of Pentecost:

And it shall come to pass afterward, that I will pour out my Spirit on all flesh; and your sons and your daughters shall prophesy, your old men shall dream dreams, your young men shall see visions: And, also upon my servants, and upon the handmaids in those days will I pour out my Spirit; and they shall prophesy. And I will show wonders in the heavens and in the earth: Blood and fire and pillars of smoke. The sun shall be turned into darkness, and the moon into blood, before the coming of the great and awesome day of the Lord. And it shall come to pass that whoever calls on the name of the Lord Shall be saved. (Joel 2:28–32 KJV) (See also Acts 2:1–22 KJV)

And when these things begin to come to pass, then look up, and lift up your heads; for your redemption draweth nigh. (Luke 21:28 KJV)

For the Lord Himself will descend from heaven with a shout, with the voice of an archangel, and with the trumpet of God. And the dead in Christ will rise first. Then we who are alive and remain shall be caught up together with them in the clouds to meet the Lord in the air. And thus, we shall always be with the Lord. Therefore comfort one another with these words. (1 Thessalonians 4:16–17)

Read about the series of punishments, plagues, and judgments that will come upon the earth just before Jesus's return. You will read about a scroll sealed with seven *seals* (Revelation 5–8) and about the seven *trumpets*, the *last plagues*, and the *bowls* of the wrath of God pours out upon the earth (many believe this happens during the tribulation period) (Revelation 8–16).

Revelation 11:3–13 speaks about the two witnesses (also referred to as the two olive trees and the two lampstands standing before the God of the earth) (Revelation 11:4; Zechariah 3:14). There has been much speculation as to who they all are, but no one really knows. It is believed by some that these two witnesses will appear just before Christ returns. They will prophesy for 1,260 days (3.5 years) sometime during the seven-year tribulation period. God will give them great power to perform miracles, and they will destroy their enemies with fire they blow from their mouths.

They will have power to call a famine and drought, turn water to blood, and strike the earth with various plagues. (*Note:* These are some of the same miracles performed by Elijah and Moses. See 2 Kings 1:9–15; 1 Kings 17:1–7; Luke 4:25; Exodus 7:20. Also read Exodus 7–11 for more on the ten plagues God performed through Moses [water becoming blood, and then the frogs, lice, flies, pestilence, hail and thunderstorms, locusts, darkness, and death of the firstborn of Egypt].)

After the two witnesses have completed their assignment and finished their testimony, the beast that will be released from the bottomless pit will make war against them and kill them. Many people will rejoice over their deaths because they had tormented them (probably with their final message of repentance and the wrath of God, among other things). No one will bury them, and their bodies will lie in the streets for three and a half days, after which time our God will raise them up from the dead, and a voice from heaven will say to them, "Come up here."

The people will hear the voice and see the two witnesses ascend to heaven in a cloud. In the same hour there will be a great earthquake, and a tenth of the city population will fall, with seven thousand killed. The rest of the people, afraid, will gave glory to God. (I believe this indicates that people can and will be saved during this period if they wholeheartedly repent, ask Jesus to forgive their sins, and believe and accept Him as their Lord and Savior. These people will give glory to God.)

In Revelation chapter 13, a beast rises out of the sea having seven heads and ten horns, and upon his horns ten crowns, and on his heads a blasphemous name. Verse two describes the beast as looking like a leopard, with feet are like those of a bear and a mouth like that of a lion. The dragon gives the beast his power, his throne, and great authority. After seeing one of the heads, which seems to have been mortally wounded, on the beast and seeing that the fatal wound is healed, the whole world will follow the beast and marvel at it. Many people will worship the dragon and the beast and will believe that there is no one else who is like or can be compared to the beast or who can make war (and win) against him. Many Jews and nonbelievers will believe that this is the messiah that is to come, but it is not, because Jesus Christ is the true Messiah (He came the first time over two thousand years ago, and He's coming a second time very soon, I believe in the twenty-first century).

Power will be given to the dragon and beast to continue for forty-two months. They will be given a mouth to talk against God and Jesus Christ and to blaspheme Christ's name, His church, and those who dwell in heaven. God will allow Satan to give power and authority to them to make war and persecute God's people—the believers in Jesus Christ. The beast and the dragon will overcome the saints (believers) and all kindreds, tongues, and nations.

Pay close attention to verse 8, which reads: "All who dwell on the earth will worship him [the beast], whose names have not been written in the Book of Life of the Lamb slain from the foundation of the world." Following is verse 9: "If anyone has an ear to hear, let him hear." It is very important that you read all of Revelation chapter 13 regarding another beast coming up out of the earth who has two horns like a lamb and speaks like a dragon. He too has power as the first beast and makes the people worship the first beast. This beast will perform great signs and miracles and will deceive many people. He will cause all people, small, great, rich, poor, free, or slave, to receive a mark (666, which is the mark of the beast) either on their foreheads or right hands. And those who do not have the mark (666), or the name of the beast, will not be able to buy or sell anything. The number of the beast, 666, is the number of a man. And this man is believed to be the Antichrist.

Whatever you do, or whatever happens, *do not take the mark (666) or the name of the beast.* If you do, you will burn in total darkness and torment in the lake of fire and brimstone forever and ever. Some believe that when the seventh trumpet sounds, Jesus Christ will return, while others do not (Revelation 11:15). The kingdoms of this world will become God the Father and His Son Jesus Christ. And He will reign as King of Kings and Lord of Lords forever and ever. His final plan and purpose for His creation, His special people (the holy and righteous), will have now been completed. The righteous will forever be in His presence. Where He is, there we will be also as Jesus promised.

Don't forget to read Revelation 14:8 and chapters 17–18, about the judgment of the woman, the great harlot—"And on her forehead a name was written: Mystery, Babylon the Great, the Mother of Harlots and of the Abominations of the Earth" (17:5)—and the fall of Babylon the Great. There is much to be said, and there have been various opinions regarding the meaning of the foregoing verse (as to what or who is Babylon, the woman, and the beast).

Revelation 19:7–8 speaks about the marriage of the Lamb (Jesus Christ), Jesus's return with the saints of God. Revelation 19:11, 14 reads as follows: "Now I saw heaven opened, and behold, a white horse. And He who sat on him was Faithful and True, and in righteousness He judges and makes war. … And the armies in heaven, clothed in fine linen, white and clean, followed Him on white horses."

And there is discussion of war between God and Satan. "And I saw the beast, the kings of the earth, and their armies, gathered together to make war against Him who sat on the horse and against His army. Then the beast was captured, and with him the false prophet who worked signs in his presence, by which he deceived those who received the mark of the beast and those who worshiped his image. These two were cast alive into the lake of fire burning with brimstone. And the rest were killed with the sword which proceeded from the mouth of Him who sat on the horse. And all the birds were filled with their flesh" (Revelation 19:19–21).

There is lots more to read in Revelation about what's going to happen before Christ's return during the tribulation, the great white throne judgment (chapter 20), and what will happen just before Christ and His children reign on earth in the New Jerusalem (chapters 21–22).

You can also read more about end-time prophecy in Daniel (chapters

7–9) as he tells us the main fact about his dreams and visions and some interpretations of the four great beasts, the ten horns, the Ancient of Days (God), and one like the Son of man (Jesus Christ).

In chapter 8, Daniel's vision is about the ram with two horns and a male goat that has a noticeable horn between his eyes. The angel Gabriel interprets the dream for Daniel. And in chapter 9 of Daniel, verses 24–27, he talks about the prophecy of the seventy weeks. In short, it is believed that the Antichrist will make a peace covenant with Israel for seven years. (I believe this is done only to gain the Jews' trust for whatever scheme he has in mind.) The Jews will reject him when he sits himself in the place of worship (God's holy place) and proclaim that he is God. The Jews will not tolerate this because it is an abomination unto God. Read Daniel chapter 11.

> And forces shall be mustered by him, and they shall defile the sanctuary fortress; then they shall take away the daily sacrifices, and place there the abomination of desolation. (Daniel 11:31)

> And the king shall do according to his will; and he shall exalt himself, and magnify himself above every god, and shall speak marvellous things against the God of gods, and shall prosper till the indignation be accomplished: for that that is determined shall be done. (Daniel 11:36 KJV)

> And from the time that the daily sacrifice shall be taken away, and the abomination that maketh desolate set up, there shall of desolation is set up, there shall be a thousand two hundred and ninety days. (Daniel 12:11 KJV)

> When ye therefore shall see the abomination of desolation, spoken of by Daniel the prophet, stand in the holy place (whoso readeth, let him understand). (Matthew 24:15 KJV)

So, within three and one-half years, the Antichrist will break the covenant he made with the Jewish people and show his true self. He will be the cause of much fighting between Christians, Jews, all peoples, and all nations, as well as the cause of much death.

Ezekiel 38–39 also speaks about end-time prophecy involving much about a World War III and the battle of Armageddon. It speaks about an invasion of Israel by all of its enemies as a result of the latter's hatred and greed. Some of those enemies are thought to be Magog (present-day Russia), Persia (present-day Iran), Put (present-day Libya), Togarmah (present-day Turkey and Armenia), Gomer (present-day Germany, which is believed to include the southern parts of the former USSR), and Cush (present-day Ethiopia). In addition to the foregoing, I believe that North Korea and China will have a major role to play in this scene also, if only with the USA. But people of the United States of America, don't you be fooled. Those countries that claim to be friends of the USA could very well be our enemies. We have some (if not all) of the same enemies as Israel. But Israel is not worried, because the God of Israel will protect and fight for Israel and will destroy all nations who come against Israel.

Hear what the Word of God says concerning Israel:

The nations also will know that I, the Lord, sanctify Israel, when My sanctuary is in their midst forevermore. (Ezekiel 37:28)

"And it will come to pass at the same time, when Gog comes against the land of Israel," says the Lord God, "that My fury will show in My face. For in My jealousy and in the fire of My wrath I have spoken; surely in that day there shall be a great earthquake in the land of Israel. ... I will call for a sword against Gog throughout all My mountains," say the Lord God. "Every man's sword will be against his brother." (Ezekiel 38:18–19, 21)

And I will bring him to judgment with pestilence and bloodshed; I will rain down on him, on his troops, and on many peoples who are with him, flooding rain, great hailstones, fire, and brimstone. Thus, I will magnify Myself and sanctify Myself, and I will be known in the eyes of many nations. Then they shall know that I am the Lord. (Ezekiel 38:22–23)

"So, I will make My holy name known in the midst of My people Israel, and I will not let them profane My holy name anymore. The nations shall know that I am the Lord, the

Holy One in Israel. Surely it is coming, and it shall be done," says the Lord God. "This is the day of which I have spoken." (Ezekiel 39:7–8)

But when you see Jerusalem surround by armies, then know that its desolation is near. (Luke 21:20)

I believe that day is very near. However, God will protect Israel and will destroy all of its enemies. God will fight Israel's battle.

In addition to reading your Bible, get a good study guide on Revelation and Daniel, or search the Web for information about these books. Study Revelation 1–22 and Daniel 37–38. It is truly revealing and amazing reading. It can be very scary for some people, especially if they are not familiar with God's Word. However, I find it fascinating to see things that were written in the Bible thousands of years ago unfolding today, happening right before my eyes. I am very excited and striving to be prepared for Jesus's return to earth. I ask that you, if you haven't already, please get your house in order because whether you believe it or not, and whether you are prepared or not, Jesus Christ is coming soon.

If you find yourself in the valley of decision, why don't you call upon Him right now, invite Him into your life, and accept Him as your Lord and Savior? He will save you from all the devastation and destruction that is coming upon this earth. Jesus loves you; He died and rose again to save you from the wrath to come and to give you the gift (the most perfect gift that can be given to anyone) of eternal life and unspeakable joy, glory, and peace living with Him.

You can read Matthew 24:3–51; Mark 13:4–37; Luke 21:7–36, 17:20–36; and the book of Revelation for more on end-time signs of Jesus's return and what will happen before His return and during the great tribulation. I encourage you to read these verses so that you may be ready, be fully prepared, and better understand what is happening now in these last days. You will know what *will and must* take place upon this earth. You will understand why current events are happening and unfolding as they are. However, I tell you a truth: the worst is yet to come. Stay with God so that God will stay in and with you.

Christians Will Not Be Totally Unaware of That Day

But concerning the times and the seasons, brethren, you have
no need that I should write to you. For you yourselves know
perfectly that the day of the Lord so comes as a thief in the night.
But you, brethren, are not in darkness, so that this Day should
not overtake you as a thief. You are all sons of light and sons
of the day. We are not of the night, nor of darkness. Therefore,
let us not sleep, as others do, but let us watch and be sober.
—1 Thessalonians 5:1, 2, 4–6

But take heed to yourselves, lest your hearts be weighed down
with carousing, drunkenness, and cares of life, and that Day
come on you unexpectedly. For it will come as a snare on all
who dwell on the face of the earth. Watch therefore and pray
always that you may be counted worthy to escape all these things
that will come to pass, and to stand before the Son of Man.
—Luke 21:34–36

Born-again Christians will not be totally unaware or left in the dark
concerning Jesus's return so long as we stay in the Word of God; stay in
fellowship with God; be obedient to Him; watch, pray, and be sober; treat
everyone with kindness and respect; do what is good, not what is evil;
be patient with ourselves and with others; demonstrate the love of God
through us; and rejoice in the joy of the Lord and His promises.

In everything, every situation or problem, give thanks to the Lord our
God and worship Him. For God is still worthy, and it is His will for us in

Jesus Christ that we worship Him. For God is faithful; He will do what He says. He can't fail, and He can't lie. We are to love, encourage, have compassion for, and be supportive of each other; build up one another; and exhort one another daily or as often as possible—and so much more today as we *see* the signs showing us that the time of Jesus's return is approaching quickly.

As Christians, we are children of the day and of the light; therefore, we are to stay alert and sober and be suited with the breastplate of faith and love and the helmet of hope and salvation (1 Thessalonians 5:8). God will not let that great day of His return come upon us, His children, without warning.

Although we do not know the exact day or the hour (only God the Father knows), we do know that God's Word is true: Jesus is coming! And He wants to make us aware and wants us to be prepared for His return. Stay in His Word and do what He has told you to do. Because ready or not, prepared or not, and whether you believe it or not, Jesus Christ is coming!

And now, my family of God, avoid sin. And if you do sin, quickly ask Jesus to forgive you, for He is our Advocate, and if we confess our sins, He is faithful and just to forgive us. Stay with God and abide in Him, and He will abide in you. Do all that He has told you to do. Live a righteous life, live a peaceful life with others (with as much peace as is within you), and be obedient to God so that you will have confidence in knowing that you will be counted worthy and not be ashamed when He appears at His Second Coming here on earth.

"And let us consider one another in order to stir up love and good works, not forsaking the assembling of ourselves together, as is the manner of some, but exhorting one another, and so much the more as you see the Day approaching" (Hebrews 10:24–25).

My brothers and sisters, may the God of peace Himself sanctify you wholly and set you apart for His glory and His precious jewels. I pray that your whole spirit, soul, and body be prepared and seen as blameless at the coming of our Lord and Savior Jesus Christ. Watch, pray, and stay in the Word of God.

Destruction Is Near: Who Will Be Saved?

Destruction upon destruction is cried.
—Jeremiah 4:20

For My people are foolish, they have not known Me.
—Jeremiah 4:22

Your ways and doings have procured these things for you. This is your
wickedness, because it is bitter, because it reaches to your heart.
—Jeremiah 4:18

And I will execute vengeance in anger and fury on
the nations that have not heard [obeyed].
—Micah 5:15

The wicked and the unrighteous will be punished, but the righteous will
be saved. Our God is holy and righteous. Our God is a God of justice, and
His judgment is just. On that day when Jesus Christ returns from heaven
with His mighty angels, He will reward us with His rest from the wicked
and unrighteous. He will punish those who have troubled us for so long
in flaming fire, taking vengeance on those who do not know Him, on
those who do not obey (or have not obeyed), and on those who have heard
the gospel of Jesus Christ our Lord and Savior but chose not to accept or
believe God's Word.

These people will be punished with everlasting destruction and
banishment from the presence of the Lord, and from the glory of His
power, when He comes on that great and awesome day to be glorified by

His saints and to be admired by all those who believe and trust in Him (2 Thessalonians 1:9–10).

Jesus Christ offers everyone—whosoever will believe, have faith, and come to Him—a better way and gives all a chance to choose eternal life and live in His presence forever. But some will reject the way, the truth, and the life, the one who shed His precious blood and gave His life for our sins on the cross at Calvary over two thousand years ago.

If we reject eternal life, which He has provided for us through His blood, it is no one's fault but our own. We have only ourselves to blame. And remember that you rejected Jesus Christ; He did not reject you. He came to save you, to give you eternal life, because He loves you and desires a people who will worship Him in spirit and in truth, a people who will praise and glorify Him and reign with Him forever. Our God is awesome, good, merciful, and full of grace.

The God of heaven, earth, and everything in it is calling you. Listen! Can't you hear Him? He desires to save you and all people. He doesn't want anyone to perish.

> Come my people, enter thou into thy chambers, and shut thy doors about thee: hide thyself as it were for a little moment, until the indignation be overpast. For, behold, the Lord cometh out of his place to punish the inhabitants of the earth for their iniquity: the earth also shall disclose her blood, and shall no more cover her slain. (Isaiah 26:20–21 KJV)

> The Lord is good, a stronghold in the day of trouble; and he knoweth them that trust in him. And darkness will pursue his enemies. (Nahum 1:7–8 KJV)

> God is jealous, and the Lord revengeth; the Lord revengeth, and is furious: the Lord will take vengeance on his adversaries, and he reserveth wrath for his enemies. The Lord is slow to anger, and great in power; and will not at all acquit the wicked. (Nahum 1:2–3 KJV)

> But the Lord is the true God; he is the living God, and an everlasting King: at his wrath the earth shall tremble, and the

nations shall not be able to abide his indignation. (Jeremiah 10:10 KJV)

Hear, O earth! Behold, I will certainly bring calamity on this people—the fruit of their thoughts, because they have not heeded My words nor My law but rejected it. (Jeremiah 6:19)

But this is what I commanded them, saying, "Obey My voice, and I will be your God, and you shall be My people. And walk in all the ways that I have commanded you, that it may be well with you." Yet they did not obey or incline their ear, but followed the counsels and the dictates [stubbornness, imagination] of their evil hearts, and went backward and not forward. (Jeremiah 7:23–24)

Thus, says the Lord: "Will one fall and not rise? Why has this people slidden back? … They hold fast to deceit, they refuse to return. I listened and heard, but they do not speak aright. No man repented of his wickedness, Saying, 'What have I done?' Everyone turned to his own course, as the horse rushes into the battle.'" (Jeremiah 8:4, 5–6)

"Do they provoke Me to anger?" says the Lord. "Do they not provoke themselves to the shame of their own faces?" Therefore, thus says the Lord God: "Behold, My anger and My fury will be poured out on this place—on man and on beast, on the trees of the field and on the fruit of the ground. And it will burn and not be quenched." (Jeremiah 7:19–20)

For you have trusted in your wickedness; you have said, "No one sees me," Your wisdom and your knowledge have warped you [led you astray]; and you have said in your heart, "I am, and there is no one else besides me." Therefore, evil shall come upon you; and you shall not know from where it arises. And trouble shall fall upon you; you will not be able to put it off. And desolation shall come upon you suddenly, which you shall not know. (Isaiah 47:10–11)

Thou art wearied in the multitude of thy counsels: Let now the astrologers, the stargazers, the monthly prognosticators, stand up, and save thee from these things that shall come upon thee. Behold, they shall be as stubble, the fire shall burn them; they shall not deliver themselves from the power of the flame: There shall not be a coal to warm at, nor a fire to sit before it. (Isaiah 47:13–14 KJV)

But the day of the Lord will come as a thief in the night, in which the heavens will pass away with a great noise, and the elements will melt with fervent heat; both the earth and the works that are in it will be burned up. Therefore, since all these things will be dissolved, what manner of persons ought you to be in holy conduct and godliness, looking for and hastening the coming of the day of God, because of which the heavens will be dissolved, being on fire, and the elements will melt with fervent heat? (2 Peter 3:10–12)

Wow! Can you imagine that the elements, everything on planet Earth, will be destroyed—melted and burned up? Repent right now, ask God to forgive you of your sins, and invite Jesus Christ into your heart. Live a righteous life (in your body and through your conduct), not a life of evil and wickedness. Read God's Holy Word (the Bible), and learn more about Him. Talk to Him, and He will talk to you through His Word (among other ways that He chooses). Live a life that God will be pleased with. The wages of sin is death, but the gift of God through Jesus Christ is eternal life.

People Will Believe When They See Jesus Christ Coming on Clouds from Heaven, but It Will Be Too Late

When Jesus Christ returns, everyone will see Him coming on the clouds from heaven, and then they will believe, but it will be too late to repent or change their mind or way of living. It will be too late to cry out to Him and ask for forgiveness of their sins. It will be too late to read His holy Word. It will be too late to say, "I love You. I believe in You. Save me." Please believe the Word of God right now, and please believe me: Jesus is coming very soon, any day now!

Repent today, ask Him to forgive you of your sins, and accept Him as Lord and Savior right now. Do not put it off for tomorrow, or for some other time, because time, not even the next moment or second, is promised to no one. Do it *now* while you have this *time*, this *chance*. Do it before Jesus comes.

He gave Himself, took our sins upon Himself as He died on the cross, and rose from the grave on the third day so that we (through Him) might be delivered from this present evil world and be reconciled to God according to His will. Jesus loves us so very much, and He wants us to be saved. He wants us to be prepared to go back and live with Him forever.

Today, right this very moment, if you hear His voice within your spirit speaking to you, please do not harden your heart. Listen and obey Him. Say, "Here I am, Lord. What do You want me to do" (Hebrews 4:7)? For when Jesus Christ appears in the clouds, it will be too late for anyone to ask Him to save them, too late to say you're sorry for the things that you have done and said.

"For the time is at hand. He who is unjust, let him be unjust still; he who is filthy, let him be filthy still; he who is righteous, let him be righteous still; he who is holy, let him be holy still" (Revelation 22:10–11).

"The fool hath said in his heart, There is no God. They are corrupt, they have done abominable works, there is none that doeth good" (Psalm 14:1 KJV).

Everyone has sinned. If you say that you have not, then you are a liar. What's worse, you're calling God a liar. And God Almighty cannot lie because He can't—He is Truth.

I pray that you are prepared and that He will find us all busy working for His kingdom when He arrives. Dear friends, Jesus Christ our Lord, Savior, and King is coming soon!

Hell Is a Real and Eternal Place of Indescribable Torment, a Lake that Burns Eternally with Unquenchable Fire

> Ye serpents, ye generation of vipers, how can
> you escape the damnation of hell?
> —Matthew 23:33 (KJV)

Hell is real and is far beyond the grave. The evil and wicked will not be able to escape its damnation. Hell is in the lowest part of the earth (Ephesians 4:9; Matthew 12:40). Hell is also called the "pit" (or the "bottomless pit") and the "abyss" (Isaiah 14:9, 15; Ezekiel 32:18, 21–25; Revelation 9:2).

Hell is a place of total darkness and torment, and it burns with a furnace and lake of fire and brimstone that cannot be quenched. It is a place where there is wailing, weeping, and gnashing of teeth; where worms and maggots do not die; and where there is no rest or peace. It is a place of constant indescribable torture and pain. It is a place of total and eternal separation from God.

Hell was originally designed and prepared for Satan (Lucifer, the devil), and his fallen angels (demons, evil spirits) after they made war with God in heaven and tried to take over. They were cast out of heaven, and their final eternal residence is hell. (Read Isaiah 14 and Ezekiel 28.) But hell has now been enlarged (renovated if you will) to accommodate the wicked, evildoers, the unrighteous, and all those who have not believed in Jesus Christ and have rejected Him as God's Son and Lord and Savior of the world. If you do not believe or just aren't sure that there is a place called hell, just keep reading. I pray that you will hear and believe the Word of God.

There was a certain beggar named Lazarus, and a rich man. Both men died. The beggar was carried by the angels to Abraham's bosom. And being in torments in Hades, he [the rich man] lifted up his eyes and saw Abraham afar off, and Lazarus in his bosom. Then he [the rich man] cried and said, "Father Abraham, have mercy on me, and send Lazarus that he may dip the tip of his finger in water and cool my tongue; for I am tormented in this flame." But Abraham said, "Son, remember in your lifetime you received your good things, and likewise Lazarus evil things; but now he is comforted, and you are tormented. And besides all this, between us and you there is a great gulf fixed, so that those who want to pass from here to you cannot; nor can those from there pass to us." Then he [the rich man] said, "I beg you therefore, father, that you would send him to my father's house, for I have five brothers, that he may testify to them, lest they also come to this place of torment." Abraham said to him, "They have Moses and the prophets; let them hear them." And he [the rich man] said, "No, father Abraham; but if ones goes to them from the dead, they will repent." But he [Abraham] said to him, "If they do not hear Moses and the prophets [also the preachers, teachers, evangelists, and ministers and the gospel of Jesus Christ], neither will they be persuaded though one rise from the dead." (Luke 16:19–31)

You don't want to spend eternity in hell, this place of torment. Don't be like the rich man who didn't believe anything until it was too late. He couldn't even warn those whom he loved so dearly to get their lives right with God; to repent, believe, have faith, and accept Jesus Christ as their Lord and Savior; to be loving, compassionate, respectful, kind, and generous to all people regardless of race, color, or creed; and to aid those who were in need while here on this earth so that they could avoid going to such a horrible place of eternal damnation.

Notice that the rich man was *conscious* of who he was and where he was, just as he was conscious of the one he mistreated or ignored. He couldn't help himself, nor could he help his family who were still living on earth. And he had feelings. All five of his senses were operational (he could see, hear, feel, taste, and smell). He knew that it was too late for him;

his destination was final and eternal. He also knew that he did not want his loved ones to come to this place of continuous and eternal pain and torture when they died. Please don't think that when you die in this life it's all over. *No*, it's just the beginning of an eternity, which has no end.

> And everyone not found written in the Book of Life was cast into the lake of fire. (Revelation 20:15)

> Cast into outer darkness; … there will be weeping and gnashing of teeth. (Matthew 8:12, 22:13)

> Cast into hell, into the fire that shall never be quenched—where their worm does not die, and the fire is not quenched. (Mark 9:43–44)

> So it will be at the end of the age. The angels will come forth, separate the wicked from the just, and cast them into the furnace of fire. There will be wailing and gnashing of teeth. (Matthew 13:49–50)

Hell is a real place, my friends. Please *do not bet or risk* your eternal life thinking that it's not, because you will surely lose. Please don't gamble with your eternal life. Nothing on this earth is worth spending eternity in such a place as hell.

> I provide a few scriptures, below, giving reference to hell (Hades, the pit, the bottomless pit, the abyss, Sheol):

> For You will not leave My soul in Hades, nor will You allow Your Holy One to see corruption. (Acts 2:27)

> And I say also unto thee. That thou art Peter, and on this rock I will build my church; and the gates of Hell shall not prevail against it. (Matthew 16:18 KJV)

> For thus says the Lord God: … "Then I will bring you down with those who descend into the Pit, to the people of old, and I will make you dwell in the lowest part of the earth, in places desolate from antiquity [ancient times], with those who go

down to the Pit, so that you may never be inhabited; and I shall establish glory in the land of the living. I will make you a terror, and you shall be no more; though you are sought for, you will never be found again," says the Lord God. (Ezekiel 26:20–21)

Then shall he say also unto them on the left hand, Depart from me, ye cursed, into everlasting fire, prepared for the devil and his angels. (Matthew 25:41 KJV)

And cast ye the unprofitable servant into the outer darkness: there shall be weeping and gnashing of teeth. (Matthew 25:30 KJV)

For they have all been delivered to death, to the depths of the earth, among the children of men who go down to the Pit. (Ezekiel 31:14)

Thus says the Lord God: "In the day when it went down to hell, I caused mourning. ... When I cast it down to hell together with those who descend into the Pit. ... They also went down to hell with it, with those slain by the sword; and those who were its strong arm dwelt in its shadows among the nations." (Ezekiel 32:15–17)

But I will show you whom you should fear: Fear Him who, after He has killed, has power to cast you into hell; yes, I say to you, fear Him! (Luke 12:5)

But he knoweth not the dead are there; and that her guests are in the depths of hell. (Proverbs 9:18 KJV)

Upon the wicked He will rain coals; fire and brimstone and a burning wind shall be the portion of their cup. (Psalm 11:6)

So it will be at the end of the age. The angels will come forth, separate the wicked from among the just, and cast them into the furnace of fire. There will be wailing and gnashing of teeth. (Matthew 13:49–50)

The strong among the mighty shall speak to him out of the mist of hell. ... They have gone down. (Ezekiel 32:21)

To go to hell, into the fire that shall never be quenched—where their worm does not die, and the fire is not quenched. (Mark 9:43–44; see also 9:45–48)

Let death seize upon them, and let them go down quick into hell: for wickedness is in their dwellings, and among them. (Psalm 55:15 KJV)

Hell from beneath is excited about you, to meet you at your coming; it stirs up the dead for you. ... Your pomp is brought down to Sheol. ... The maggot is spread under you, and worms cover you. (Isaiah 14:9, 11)

Yet thou shall be brought down to hell, to the sides of the Pit. (Isaiah 14:15 KJV)

The sea gave up the dead who were in it, and Death and Hades delivered up the dead who were in them. And they were judged, each one according to his works. Then Death and Hades were cast into the lake of fire. (Revelation 20:13–14)

Therefore hell (Sheol) hath enlarged herself, and opened her mouth without beyond measure. ... And he who is jubilant, shall descend into it. (Isaiah 5:14)

For Sheol cannot thank You, Death cannot praise You; those who go down to the pit cannot hope for Your truth. (Isaiah 38:18)

Therefore, my friends, stay sober and keep a very careful watch (be vigilant), because the devil is your adversary, and he is walking about as a roaring lion, seeking whom he can destroy. And believe me, he wants to kill you. But we must resist him and totally submit our lives to Jesus and depend on Him.

Read what David wrote (I really love this): "As for me, I will call upon the God, and He will save me. Evening and morning and at noon I will pray, and cry aloud, and He shall hear my voice" (Psalm 55:16–17).

Isn't that wonderful? You do not have to go to hell. No matter what you have done, the grace and mercy of God is available to you. Why don't you call upon God right now with your whole heart and ask Him to forgive you of your sins and save you? If today you hear His voice (in your heart; through dreams, visions, or the Bible; in the words of this book; or from another servant of God), please don't be stubborn. Do not let anyone talk you out of it, and do not put off repenting for some other time, because then it may be too late. Seek the Lord *right now* while He may be found, while He is speaking to you, and call upon Him while you are alive, while He is near, and while you are in a right place for Him to hear you.

I feel within my spirit that we should take this moment to pray. If you sincerely want to be saved from spending your eternal life in torment and darkness in hellfire, and if you'd rather spend eternity with God our Father and Jesus Christ our Savior in that paradise of a place He has prepared for His children, then please say this short prayer with me and mean it with all your heart:

> Lord Jesus, I'm sorry for my sins and ask for Your forgiveness. I invite You into my heart. I confess with my mouth and believe in my heart that You are the Son of God and that You shed Your precious blood and died on the cross for my sins. I believe that God raised You from the grave on the third day. I believe that You are coming back again soon, and I want to be ready and prepared for Your coming so I can go back and spend my eternal life with You in the place You have prepared for Your children. I surrender all to You; use me for Your glory. Baptize me with Your Holy Spirit to empower me to live an honorable life pleasing to You. Allow me to be a witness for You and to do the work You have called me to do. In Your name I pray, amen.

Dear friends, my heart is filled with joy knowing that you are now part of the family of God. The angels and everyone in heaven is also rejoicing. For your name is now written in the Lamb's book of life. Now Satan no longer has a reserved place for you in hell. Your reservation has just been canceled. Hallelujah! Glory to God!

May I Pray for You?

Father God, I feel an urgency within my spirit to pray for my brothers and sisters right now. According to Your Word, they have confessed with their mouths that Jesus Christ is Lord, Savior, and Your Son, and they have believed in their hearts that You, Father God, raised Him from the dead—and they are saved. For with the heart one believes unto righteousness, and with the mouth confession is made unto salvation. You said that whoever calls on Your name will be saved. These, your people, have heard and believe Your Word and therefore have called upon You.

Based on their faith and belief, and their confession with their mouths with their whole hearts, I thank You for their salvation. Let no weapon formed against them prosper. I ask that You condemn every tongue that should rise against them falsely. For this is now part of their heritage as Your children. Protect them and their family from Satan and his evil ones. I ask that You supply their needs according to Your riches in glory by Christ Jesus and that You give them their hearts' desires according to Your will.

Encourage them, embrace them in Your loving arms, heal their bodies and the bodies of their family members of all sickness and disease, mend the brokenhearted, and renew and transform their minds by and in Your Word. Baptize them with Your Holy Spirit to enable and empower them to do the work You have called them to do, to witness to others of Your love, grace, and mercy, and to live a holy life in this life here on earth.

Father, I pray that when their hearts feel empty, You will fill them with Your love and power. I pray that when they feel alone or afraid, they will put their trust in You. Strengthen them spiritually, physically, mentally, and emotionally with Your strength and joy that surpasses all understanding. You promised us that You would never leave us or forsake us.

Show them dreams and visions, Father, to draw them nearer to You and to assist them in building up their faith. Show Yourself strong in their lives as You prove Yourself to them. Thank You for Your favor, mercy, and grace bestowed upon them. I know that Your thoughts of them and Your plans for them are good. Fulfill Your plans and purpose in their lives. Not their will, but let Your will be done. Thank You, Father, for saving their souls, making them whole, and preparing them for the Second Coming of Your Son Jesus Christ.

In the name of Jesus—the name above all names—I pray. Amen.

Satan (a.k.a. Lucifer, the Devil, Adversary, Dragon, Serpent of Old, Accuser of the Brethren) Is Real

And He [Jesus] said to them, "I saw Satan
fall like lightning from heaven."
—Luke 10:18

For those of you who do not believe in the existence of Satan, I have listed a few scriptures to verify that he does indeed exist. He was an anointed angel in heaven with a high position. He was the seal of perfection, full of wisdom and power, and was said to be the most beautiful of all God's creation. But that wasn't enough for him. He was not satisfied; he desired and sought after the position of the Most High God. He wanted to be like God. He wanted to be worshipped. He wanted the glory, the praise, and the honor that is due and given to God the Father.

Satan allowed his beauty, pride, jealousy, position, and power to get the best of him, and as a result he became the perverted evil being that he is today. So, Satan, along with some other evil angels following him, started a coup. There was a war in heaven, and Satan and his followers (fallen angels, also known as demons, evil spirits, and unclean spirits— *they too are real*) were thrown out of heaven down into the lower part of planet Earth. Satan's name was changed from Lucifer to Satan after his fall. Always remember that God will not share His glory with anyone. So, take heed how you stand (with what you say and do, and how you allow others to praise you, be very careful), or you just might fall *hard*.

And another sign appeared in heaven: behold, a great, fiery red dragon having seven heads and ten horns, and seven diadems on his head. His tail drew a third of the stars of heaven and threw them to the earth. And the dragon stood before the woman who was ready to give birth, to devour her Child [Jesus] as soon as it [He] was born. ... And war broke out in heaven: Michael and his angels fought with the dragon; and the dragon and his angels fought, but they did not prevail, nor was there place found for them in heaven. So, the great dragon was cast out, that serpent of old, called the Devil and Satan, who deceives the whole world; he was cast to the earth, and his angels were cast out with him. (Revelation 12:3–4, 7–9)

Then he [Rehoboam, son of Solomon] appointed for himself priests for the high places, for the demons, and the calf idols which he had made. (2 Chronicles 11:15)

For the accuser of our brethren, who accused them before our God day and night, has been cast down. (Revelation 12:10)

Therefore rejoice, O heavens, and you who dwell in them! Woe to the inhabitants of the earth and the sea! For the devil has come down to you, having great wrath, because he knows that he has a short time. (Revelation 12:12)

And the dragon was enraged with the woman, and he went to make war with the rest of her offspring, who keep the commandments of God and have the testimony of Jesus Christ. (Revelation 12:17)

Satan and his demons are still enraged with God and continue to make war with His children because of their own eviction and expulsion from heaven. Satan detests with a passion not only God and Jesus Christ but also anyone who calls on the name of Jesus for salvation. Satan's only desire is to get even with God by destroying His children (those who give their hearts to Him and have accepted Jesus as their Savior and Lord) physically and spiritually.

His malicious demon spirits constantly try to deceive and make war against the people of God. They want to kill, steal from, and destroy you before you come into the knowledge of truth; before you believe and put your faith and trust in Jesus Christ; before you believe that Jesus died on the cross for your sins (and the world); and before you believe that God raised Him from the grave on the third day for your justification with all power in His hands as holder of the keys of life and death.

You see, Satan knows how much God loves us and how much He wants to give us eternal life and have us live in His presence. But Satan doesn't want this to happen and will do all within his power, through scheming, lying, deception, and any other means, to prevent it. He doesn't want us to spend our eternal life with God, Jesus, and our heavenly family in a place of beauty, a place of unexplainable and unspeakable joy, peace, and happiness, forever loving, exalting, worshipping, honoring, and praising Him. For he knows that is why God created us. That is what God wants (for He inhabits the praises of His people), and that is also what Satan used to do when he lived in heaven.

Satan tries to imitate God to fool the people. But remember: he is the father of lies, a thief, a killer, a destroyer, a deceiver, and an accuser of the brethren. His goal is to keep us from believing, receiving, and having faith in God the Father and Jesus Christ our Redeemer. He doesn't want us to believe and accept Jesus Christ as the Son of God, Savior, and Lord, because the moment that we do, we will then belong to God and will be sealed with His Spirit. Satan can't let this happen because he would have lost the war again—and this time forever!

His desire is keep us spiritually blind to the truth, love, forgiveness, mercy, kindness, faithfulness, and grace of God. He wants to keep us in bondage. But we have been set free through the blood of our Lord and Savior Jesus Christ, and there's nothing Satan can do about it so long as we stay connected to Jesus.

Please understand that Satan does not love you. He hates God, Jesus, you, and me and desires only to destroy our spirits and separate us from God so that he can take as many as he can to spend their eternal lives with him (and his demons) in a place called hell that was originally prepared for just them, in a lake that burns forever with unquenchable fire and brimstone. He is a deceiver and a liar, and he spends much of his time trying to make you think that he doesn't exist. He wants to get in your mind and control you.

Satan will stop at nothing until he has convinced you to curse God, until he has convinced you to stop loving Him, believing Him, and trusting Him, and until you finally walk away from Him. He will even tell you to take your own life. Why? Because once you do that, you give Satan and his demons a green light to enter into your heart and your life. You abandon your gift from God, which is to spend your eternal life with Him, your loved ones, your friends, and the whole family of God.

Listen, Jesus Christ came into this world to destroy the works of Satan. And He has done just that. Therefore, we have the victory! Thanks be unto Him.

"He who sins is of the devil, for the devil has sinned from the beginning. For this purpose, the Son of God [Jesus Christ] was manifested, that He might destroy the works of the devil" (1 John 3:8).

The Jews were in a discussion claiming that Abraham is their father. Jesus said to them: "You are of your father the devil [Satan], and the desires of your father you want to do. He was a murderer from the beginning, and does not stand in the truth, because there is no truth in him. When he speaks a lie, he speaks from his own resources, for he is a liar and the father of it" (John 8:44).

> Satan was thrown out of heaven by God. Thus says the Lord God to Lucifer/Satan:
>
> You were the seal of perfection, full of wisdom and perfect in beauty. You were in Eden, the garden of God; every precious stone was your covering: The sardius, topaz, and diamond, beryl, onyx, and jasper, sapphire, turquoise, and emerald with gold. The workmanship of your timbrels and pipes was prepared for you on the day you were created. You were the anointed cherub who covers; I established you; you were on the holy mountain of God; you walked back and forth in the midst of fiery stones. You were perfect in your ways from the day you were created, til iniquity was found in you. (Ezekiel 28:12–15)
>
> By the abundance of your trading you became filled with violence within, and you sinned; therefore, I cast you as a profane thing out of the mountain of God; and I destroyed you, O covering cherub, from the midst of the fiery stones. Your heart was lifted

up because of your beauty; you corrupted your wisdom for the sake of your splendor; I cast you to the ground, I laid you before kings, that they might gaze at you. (Ezekiel 28:16–17)

How you are fallen from heaven, O Lucifer, son of the morning! How you are cut down to the ground. You who weakened the nations! For you have said in your heart: "I will ascend into heaven, I will exalt my throne above the stars of God; I will also sit on the mount of the congregation on the farthest sides of the north; I will ascend above the heights of the clouds, I will be like the Most High." Yet you shall be brought down to Sheol [or hell], to the lowest depths of the Pit. Those who see you will gaze at you, and consider you, saying: "Is this the man who made the earth tremble, who shook kingdoms, who made the world as a wilderness and destroyed its cities, who did not open the house of his prisoners?" (Isaiah 14:12–17)

Hell [or Sheol] from beneath is excited about you, to meet you at your coming; it stirs up the dead for you, all the chief ones of the earth; it has raised up from their thrones all the kings of the nations. They all shall speak and say to you: "Have you also become as weak as we? Have you become like us? Your pomp is bought down to Sheol [or hell], and the sound of your stringed instruments; the maggot under you, and the worms over you." (Isaiah 14:9–11)

So, Satan is finished, and he knows that. But he won't stop until you are in the same place for eternity that he will be in and you are finished too. Please don't let that happen!

During the millennial period, Satan will be loosed from the bottomless pit for the final time (before the white throne judgment) to make havoc and deceive God's people.

"He [an angel from heaven with the key to the bottomless pit] laid hold of the dragon, that serpent of old, who is the Devil and Satan, and bound him for one thousand years; and he cast him into the bottomless pit and shut him up, and set a seal on him, so that he should deceive the nations no more until the thousand years were finished. But after these things he must be released for a little while" (Revelation 20:2–3).

"Now when the thousand years have expired, Satan will be released from his prison and will go out to deceive the nations which are in the four corners of the earth, Gog and Magog, to gather them together to battle, whose number is as the sand of the sea" (Revelation 20:7–8).

Satan (the devil, Lucifer) is also known as the tempter and deceiver (Matthew 4:3; 1 Thessalonians 3:5; Genesis 3:1, 4–5, 13; Revelation 20:10); the father of lies (John 8:44); the king and angel of the bottomless pit (the abyss, hell) whose name in the Hebrew is Abaddon (which means destruction) but who in Greek has the name Apollyon (which means destroyer) (Revelation 9:11); Beelzebub, ruler of demons (Matthew 12:24); the ruler of the darkness of this age (world) (Ephesians 6:12); the evil one (John 17:15; Matthew 6:13); the wicked one (Ephesians 6:16); the god of this world (age) (2 Corinthians 4:4); a murderer, thief, and destroyer (John 10:10; 2 Thessalonians 2:3; Job 15:21); the prince of the power of the air; and the spirit who now works in the children of the disobedient (Ephesians 2:2).

My friends, Satan knows his fate and where he's going, where he and his demons, the beast, false prophets, and all who do not believe and have faith in Jesus Christ will spend eternity. Do you know where you will spend your eternal life? Would you please believe and accept Jesus Christ, the Son of God, as your Savior and Lord right now?

Satan is not your friend. He is your worst enemy. He wants to make your life miserable here on earth and try to trick you into spending your eternal life with him in the lake of unquenchable fire and brimstone. He doesn't want you to be happy here on earth or to spend eternity with God because he knows how much God loves you. He knows that Jesus Christ died and rose for you, and he knows God's plan for your life. Satan is the enemy of God, of Jesus Christ, and of all who give their hearts to and believe in Jesus and want to follow Him. Satan is always at war in one way or another with God's people. But I bring you good news! Soon that will be over. Let us endure until the end. For he or she who does endures to the end will be saved and will inherit eternal life.

"The devil, who deceived them, was cast into the lake of fire and brimstone where the beast and the false prophet are. And they will be tormented day and night forever and ever" (Revelation 20:10).

Now I ask you: do you really want to spend eternity with Satan?

It appears that Satan still maintains access or has permission to appear before God even after his fall from heaven. He is always accusing and opposing the people, especially those who believe and have faith in God the Father and Jesus Christ His Son, our Lord and Redeemer.

"And the Lord said to Satan, 'From where do you come?' So, Satan answered and said, 'From going to and fro on the earth, and walking back and forth on it'" (Job 1:7). Also read Job 1:6, 8–12; 2:1–7 for conversations between God and Satan regarding Job.

Read what the prophet Zechariah wrote in Zechariah 3:1–2: "Then he showed me [Joshua, the high priest] standing before the angel of the Lord, and Satan [the adversary] standing at his right hand to oppose him. And the Lord said to Satan, 'The Lord rebuke you, Satan!'"

Now the serpent was more cunning than any beast of the field which the Lord God had made. And he said to the woman, "Has God indeed said, 'You shall not eat of every tree of the garden'?" (Genesis 3:1).

Satan had a conversation with Eve, trying to tempt her and influence her by arousing her lust, her desire to satisfy the flesh, and her desire to have the power of wisdom and knowledge, some of the very same things that men and women seek after today and that some will sell their souls for.

When God asked the woman why she had done this thing, she replied, "The serpent deceived me, and I ate" (Genesis 3:13). Satan is known as the greatest deceiver of the world. He's devious, cunning, and the father of lies. (Read Revelation 12:9).

"And Satan stood up against Israel, and provoked David to number [take a census of] Israel" (1 Chronicles 21:1 KJV). "They sacrificed to devils [demons]" (Deuteronomy 32:17 KJV).

Then Jesus said to him, "Away with you Satan! For it is written, 'You shall worship the Lord your God, and Him only you shall serve'" (Matthew 4:10). "You believe that there is one God. You do well. Even the demons believe—and tremble" (James 2:19)!

Satan is not your buddy or friend. Don't give him any opportunity in your life, and prevent him from reaching your family. Do not open the door if you hear him knocking; don't even crack it open. Rebuke him in the name of Jesus. Resist him. Do not entertain his thoughts. Submit and commit to God, and keep your heart and mind stayed on Him. He will protect you and keep you in perfect, amazing peace.

"Be sober [self-controlled], be vigilant [watchful]; because your adversary the devil walks about like a roaring lion, seeking whom he may devour" (1 Peter 5:8).

Jesus spoke to Paul on the road to Damascus, at which time Paul was converted. God appointed him as a minister and witness (to the things he had seen and things that would be shown to him) to the Gentiles. His ministry was revealed, and his name was changed from Saul to Paul. As Paul stood before King Agrippa, he recounted that encounter and what Jesus said to him: "To open their eyes, in order to turn them from the darkness to light, and from the power of Satan to God, that they may receive forgiveness of sins and an inheritance among those who are sanctified by faith in Me [Jesus]" (Acts 26:18).

So many people are taken captive by Satan. They don't want to hear the truth. In love, and meekness we must pray for them and tell them what the Word of God says. Even if they oppose we must still pray and ask God to grant them forgiveness and repentance; and lead them into the knowledge and truth of His word.

In humility correcting those who are in opposition, if God perhaps will grant the repentance, so that they may know the truth, and that they may come to their senses and escape the snare of the devil, having been taken captive by him to do his will. (2 Timothy 2:25–26)

For they are spirits of demons, performing signs, which go out to the kings of the earth and of the whole world, to gather them to the battle of that great day of God Almighty. (Revelation 16:14) (For cross-reference regarding this battle, read 2 Thessalonians 2:9; Revelation 17:14, 19:19, 20:8.)

The coming of the lawless one is according to the working of Satan, with all power, signs, and lying wonders, and with all unrighteous deception among those who perish, because they did not receive the love of the truth, that they might be saved. (2 Thessalonians 2:9–10)

Lest Satan should get an advantage of us; for we are not ignorant of his devices. (2 Corinthians 2:11 KJV)

> And the scribes who came down from Jerusalem said of Jesus, "He has Beelzebub," and, "By the ruler of the demons He casts out demons." So, He [Jesus] … said to them … "How can Satan cast out Satan?" (Mark 3:22–23)

> And the Lord said, "Simon [Peter], Simon! Indeed, Satan has asked for you, that he may sift you as wheat." (Luke 22:31)

That old devil is still after God's children. He's still after you! Remember, we have the victory in and through Jesus Christ our Lord and Redeemer.

People of God, in order for us to withstand living in these wicked and evil days and to defeat and outwit the devil, we must remain strong in our Lord and in His almighty power, and we must wear at all times the proper armor and use the weapons that are guaranteed to defeat him. We must realize that our fight is not against flesh and blood but is a *spiritual* battle against principalities, powers, rulers of the darkness of this age (world), and hosts of wickedness in heavenly places (Ephesians 6:12–13). This fight, our opposition and struggle, is against unseen spiritual demonic forces of darkness (Satan, his army of demons, and followers of evil).

Therefore, let us "Put on the whole armor of God, so that [we] may be able to stand against the wiles [schemes, tricks] of the devil" (Ephesians 6:11).

Ephesians 6:12–18 tells us how to stand and describes the type of armor we should put on and the benefits of wearing such armor. It tells us that we should always pray, be watchful, and persevere with supplication to the Spirit for all the saints of God.

Dear friends, Satan is real. Of course he doesn't want us to know this so that God can be blamed for anything that goes wrong in our lives and on earth. There are satanists, demonic spirits, witches, sorcerers, mediums, and those who practice spells, charms, and evil. And these people will agree with me, as will God's servants (especially those who cast out demons or evil spirits). However, if you still choose not to believe, I'm sorry, as there's nothing more I can say or do. One day soon, you will find out for certain; this I guarantee. I pray that it will not be too late. I pray for your deliverance and salvation in Jesus's name. Amen.

What Will Happen to Satan, His Demons (Fallen Angels), His Followers, the Beast, the False Prophet, and All Who Rejected Jesus Christ as Lord and Savior?

The Bible is very clear as to what will happen to Satan, his demons, his followers, the beast, the false prophet, the evil and the wicked, and unbelievers (those who have rejected Jesus Christ as Lord and Savior). Satan knows full well that he will spend eternity in torment and darkness in the lake that burns with fire and brimstone that can't be quenched. There is nothing he can do to change it.

He knows that he is doomed, and he wants you to be doomed forever with him. He knows that he no longer has a choice, as he made his decision when he started the war in heaven against God. But he also knows that you do have a choice. Why not choose today whom you will serve and spend your eternal life with? You do not have to spend eternity with Satan, demons, the wicked, and those who chose not to believe, obey, or accept Jesus as Lord and Savior in that awful place of eternal darkness in fire, torture, and suffering. Remember, you still have a choice.

> The way of life winds upward for the wise, that he may turn away from hell below. (Proverbs 15:24)

> Then the beast was captured, and with him the false prophet who worked signs in his presence, by which he deceived those who received the mark of the beast and those who worshipped

his image. These two were cast alive into the lake of fire burning with brimstone. (Revelation 19:20)

For God did not spare the angels who sinned, but cast them down to hell, and delivered them into chains of darkness, to be reserved for judgment. (2 Peter 2:4)

The wicked shall be turned into hell, and all the nations that forget God. (Psalm 9:17)

But the cowardly, unbelieving, abominable, murderers, sexually immoral, sorcerers, idolaters, and all liars shall have their part in the lake which burns with fire and brimstone, which is the second death. (Revelation 21:8)

And these will go away into everlasting punishment, but the righteous into eternal life. (Matthew 25:46)

Then shall he say also unto them on the left hand, Depart from me, ye cursed, into everlasting fire, prepared for the devil and his angels. (Matthew 25:41 KJV)

And shall cast them [the wicked] into a furnace of fire: there shall be wailing and gnashing of teeth. (Matthew 13:42 KJV)

Upon the wicked he shall rain snares, fire and brimstone, and a horrible tempest: shall be the portion of their cup. (Psalm 11:6 KJV)

In flaming fire taking vengeance on those who do not know God, and on those who do not obey the gospel of our Lord Jesus Christ. These shall be punished with everlasting destruction from the presence of the Lord and from the glory of His power. (2 Thessalonians 1:8–9)

The destruction of transgressors and of sinners shall be together, and those who forsake the Lord shall be consumed. ... Both will burn together, and no one shall quench them. (Isaiah 1:28, 31)

For the wages of sin is death; but the gift of God is eternal life through Jesus Christ our Lord. (Romans 6:23 KJV)

Pray that your name is written in the Book of Life. Because anyone's name that is not found written in the Book of Life will be cast into the lake of fire. (Revelation 20:15 KJV)

The Great White Throne Judgment: God's Righteous Judgment

But let judgment run down as waters, and
righteousness as a mighty stream.
—Amos 5:24

And there is no creature hidden from His sight, but all things are
naked and open to the eyes of Him to whom we must give account.
—Hebrews 4:13

All will be judged according to their works, deeds, and words and the lives they have lived. No excuses will be accepted, and no exceptions will be made. Remember, it was your choice.

Our God is a holy, merciful, and loving God. He is also righteous, fair, and just to all people. He wants us to live a holy life so that we can qualify to live with Him forever. What will you do when Jesus Christ comes for you? What are you going to do when you stand before God on Judgment Day? God's judgment upon sin is coming. He will judge everyone on the face of this earth who has not believed by faith in the gospel of Jesus Christ and accepted Him as their Lord and Savior. All will be judged according to their words and works.

Your race, social status, profession, money, car(s), and house(s); who you are; where you live; and your fame will not matter. The greatest and the least, the richest and the poorest—all will be judged fairly and sent to the place where they will spend their eternal lives. There will be final consequences for not serving Jesus Christ, God's Son, and for rejecting Him, just as there will be rewards for accepting Him as Lord and Savior and serving Him only. Don't let sin have dominion over you and be your ruin, causing you to miss heaven and the chance to spend your eternal life in the presence of God, Jesus Christ His Son, your loved ones, and the family of God.

> For since the creation of the world His invisible attributes are clearly seen, being understood by the things that are made, even His eternal power and Godhead, so that they are without excuse, because, although they knew God, they did not honor or glorify Him as God, nor were thankful, but became futile in their thoughts, and their foolish hearts were darkened. Professing to be wise, they became fools, and changed the glory of the incorruptible God into an image made like corruptible man—and birds and four-footed animals and creeping things. (Romans 1:20–23)

> Therefore, God also gave them up to uncleanness, in the lusts of their hearts, to dishonor their bodies among themselves, who exchanged the truth of God for the lie, and worshipped and served the creature rather than the Creator, who is blessed forever. Amen. (Romans 1:24–25)

> For this reason, God gave them up to vile passions. For even their women exchanged the natural use for what is against nature. Likewise, also the men leaving the natural use of the woman, burned in their lust for one another, men with men committing what is shameful, and receiving in themselves the penalty of error which was due. (Romans 1:26–27)

> And even as they did not like to retain God in their knowledge, God gave them over to a debased mind, to do those things which are not fitting; being filled with all unrighteousness, sexual immorality, wickedness, covetousness, maliciousness; full of envy, murder, strife, deceit, evil-mindedness, they are whisperers, backbiters, haters of God, violent, proud, boasters, inventors of evil things, disobedient to parents, undiscerning, untrustworthy, unloving, unforgiving, unmerciful; who, knowing the righteous judgment of God, that those who practice such things are deserving of death, not only do the

same but also approve of those who practice them. (Romans 1:28–32)

Therefore you are inexcusable, O man, whoever you are. … But we know that the judgment of God is according to truth against those who practice such things. And do you think this, O man, you who judge those practicing such things, and doing the same, that you will escape the judgment of God? Or do you despise the riches of His goodness, forbearance, and longsuffering, not knowing that the goodness of God leads you to repentance? (Romans 2:1–4)

But in accordance with your hardness and your impenitent heart you are treasuring up for yourself wrath in the day of wrath and revelation of the righteous judgment of God, who "will render to each one according to his deeds": eternal life to those who by patient continuance in doing good seek for glory, honor, and immortality; but those who are self-seeking and do not obey the truth, but obey unrighteousness—indignation and wrath, tribulation and anguish, on every soul of man who does evil. … For there is no partiality with God. Everyone will be judged fairly. (Romans 2:5–9, 11) (For God is a God of righteousness and justice.)

Yet the … people say, "The way of the Lord is not fair." But it is their way which is not fair! When the righteous turns from his righteousness and commits iniquity, he shall die because of it. But when the wicked turns from his wickedness and does what is lawful and right, he shall live because of it. Yet you say, "The way of the Lord is not fair." O house of Israel, I will judge every one of you according to his own ways. (Ezekiel 33:17–20)

The hand of the Lord shall be known to His servants, And His indignation to His enemies. For behold, the Lord will come with fire and with His chariots, like a whirlwind, to render His anger with fury, And His rebuke with flames of fire. For by fire and by His Sword. The Lord will judge all flesh; and the slain of the Lord shall be many. (Isaiah 66:14–16)

And they shall go forth and look upon the corpses of the men who have transgressed against Me. For their worm does not die, and their fire is not quenched. (Isaiah 66:24)

In that day, the deaf shall hear the words of the book, and the eyes of the blind shall see out of obscurity and out of darkness. The humble also shall increase their joy in the Lord, and the poor among men shall rejoice In the Holy One of Israel. For the terrible one is brought to nothing, the scornful one is consumed, and all who watch for iniquity are cut off. (Isaiah 29:18–20)

For what if some did not believe? Will their unbelief make the faithfulness of God without effect? Certainly not! Indeed, let God be true but every man a liar. As it is written: "That You may be justified in Your words and may overcome when You are judged." (Romans 3:3–4)

For we must all appear before the judgment seat of Christ, that each one may receive the things done in his body, according to what he has done, whether good or bad. (2 Corinthians 5:10)

Then I saw another angel flying in the midst of heaven, having the everlasting gospel to preach to those who dwell on the earth—to every nation, tribe, tongue, and people—saying with a loud voice, "Fear God and give glory to Him, for the hour of His judgment has come; and worship Him who made heaven and earth, the sea and springs of water." (Revelation 14:6–7)

Thus says the Lord God: … "An end! The end has come upon the four corners of the land. Now the end has come upon you, and I will send My anger against you; I will judge you according to your ways, and I will repay you for all your abominations. My eye will not spare you, nor will I have pity; but I will repay your ways, and your abominations will be in your midst; then you shall know that I am the Lord!" (Ezekiel 7:2–4)

Behold, the Lord comes with ten thousands of His saints, to execute judgment on all, to convict all who are ungodly among them of all their ungodly deeds which they have committed in an ungodly way, and of all the harsh things which ungodly sinners have spoken against Him. (Jude 14–15)

"And I will come near you for judgment; I will be a swift witness against sorcerers, against adulterers, against perjurers, against those who exploit wage earners and widows and orphans, and against those who turn away an alien—because they do not fear Me," says the Lord of hosts. (Malachi 3:5)

You have said, "It is useless to serve God." (Malachi 3:14)

"Therefore I will judge you, … everyone according to his ways," says the Lord God. "Repent, and turn from all your transgressions, so that iniquity will not be your ruin. Cast away from you all the transgressions which you have committed; and get yourselves a new heart and a new spirit. For why should you die …? For I have no pleasure in the death of one who dies," says the Lord God. "Therefore turn and live!" (Ezekiel 18:30–32)

But I will punish you according to the fruit of your doings. (Jeremiah 21:14)

For the wrath of God is revealed from heaven against all ungodliness and unrighteousness of men, who suppress the truth in unrighteousness, because what may be known of God is manifest in them, for God has shown it to them. (Romans 1:19–20)

The Lord tests the righteous, but the wicked and the one who loves violence His soul hates. … For the Lord is righteous, He loves righteousness; His countenance beholds the upright. (Psalm 11:5, 7)

And at that time your people shall be delivered, everyone who is found written in the book. And many of those who sleep in the dust of the earth shall wake, Some to everlasting life, some to shame and everlasting contempt. (Daniel 12:1–2)

Let us pray with all our hearts and souls that our names are written in the book of life.

Then I saw a great white throne and Him who sat on it, from whose face the earth and the heaven fled away. And there was found no place for them. And I saw the dead, small and great, standing before God, and books were opened. And another book was opened, which is the Book of Life. And the dead were judged according to their works, by the things which were written in the books. The sea gave up the dead who were in it, and Death and Hades delivered up the dead who were in them. And they were judged, each one according to his works. Then Death and Hades were cast into the lake of fire. This is the second death. And anyone not found written in the Book of Life was cast into the lake of fire. (Revelation 20:11–15)

The devil, who deceived them, was cast into the lake of fire and brimstone where the beast and the false prophets are. And they will be tormented day and night forever and ever. (Revelation 20:10)

Dear friends, it is for certain that one day we must all appear before the judgment seat of Christ to give an account of our deeds and how we lived; for everything that we have thought, said, and done; for whom or what we believe in; and for what we have done and haven't done (and that which we should have done) for Jesus Christ. There is just no way of escaping it, and there will be no excuse that anyone can give to get out of it when standing before Almighty God on Judgment Day.

If you do not believe that Jesus Christ died on the cross for your sins and that God raised Him from the grave on the third day, and if you do not repent and ask Jesus to forgive you of your sins and be your Lord and Savior, then (according to the Word of God) you will spend eternity in a place called hell, suffering indescribable pain and torment in the lake that burns with unquenchable fire and brimstone forever and forever.

"Therefore as the tares are gathered and burned in the fire, so it will be at the end of this age. The Son of Man will send out His angels, and they will gather out of His kingdom all things that offend, and those who practice lawlessness, and will cast them into the furnace of fire. There will be wailing and gnashing of teeth. Then the righteous will shine forth as the sun in the kingdom of their Father. He who has ears to hear, let him hear" (Matthew 13:40–43)!

God's Kingdom: Who Will Enter and Who Will Not

Make sure your name written in the Lamb's book of life.

Our God is a holy God. God's kingdom is His holy place, and only the holy and righteous (those who live according to His Word and speak the truth in their hearts, who love Jesus Christ and have accepted Him by faith as Lord and Savior, and who do no evil and cause no harm to others) shall enter and dwell with Him for eternity.

God has already told us in His Word with clarity those who *will* and will *not* enter the kingdom of heaven. It is true that God is merciful, faithful, just, and full of grace. It is true that God loves us, but He cannot and will not tolerate us living continuously in sin. It is true that Jesus Christ loves us, forgives us, and has paid the price for our sin with His life and blood by way of the cross and that as a result of this, God has given us the gift of eternal life.

It is true that when we fall short, when we sin, Jesus is our Advocate and High Priest and makes an appeal to the Father on our behalf. It is true that He is faithful and just to forgive us of our sins and cleanse us from all of our iniquities, for we have been reconciled to God through Jesus Christ. But it is also true that if we deliberately continue in sin, there will be serious consequences. You will eventually pay for every choice that you have made and will make, and if you sin, you will receive your wages for your sins. And the wages for sin is death (Romans 6:23).

My friends, unless we are sincere in our hearts, living a right lifestyle, our religious rituals and behavior are worth nothing. You may be able to fool some of the people some of the time, but you can't fool God any of the time.

"For if we sin willfully after we have received the knowledge of the truth, there no longer remains a sacrifice for sins, but a certain fearful expectation of judgment, and fiery indignation which will devour the adversaries" (Hebrews 10:26–27).

In a dream, I once heard a voice say to me, "Sin doesn't come without consequences." For whatever you do in life (good or bad), it will always generate consequences. Therefore, if you don't believe in God the Father, or in His Son Jesus Christ, there will be serious consequences. If you don't believe that Jesus died on the cross for your sins and that God raised Him from the grave on the third day for your justification, there will be serious consequences. If you don't repent of your sins, ask God for forgiveness, and invite Jesus Christ into your life, there will be serious consequences. If you neglect God's wonderful grace, there will be serious consequences.

If you claim that you're a Christian and you have only a form of godliness, deny the power of God, mislead the people of God, are disobedient to God and His Word, have your own personal agenda, and do your will and not God's will, then there will be very serious consequences. If you serve or worship any god other than Almighty Jehovah God, who is the one and only true God, then there will be very serious consequences.

You can't blame God for the wrong choices that you make in life. You made those choices of your own free will. You know right from wrong, yet you chose to do wrong. Whether good or bad, whatever decision you make in life will always have consequences. God looks deep into the heart and searches it. He looks at your motives to discover why you chose to do what you did or say what you said.

Don't let the consequences of sin keep you from you from entering into the kingdom of God. Don't spend your eternity with Satan in torment in a lake that burns forever with unquenchable fire and brimstone.

In order to enter into God's kingdom, to enter the gates to the city of New Jerusalem, one must believe in the gospel of Jesus Christ and be born again by the Spirit of God. One must have faith in Christ. One must be washed in the blood of Jesus and thereby be sanctified, holy, and righteous. One must obey God and do His will. Strive to enter into God's kingdom with all your might.

Those who have believed in the gospel of Jesus Christ, have asked Him to forgive them of their sins, have trusted and have faith in Jesus, and have accepted Him as their Lord and Savior will enter into God's kingdom.

"He who walks uprightly, and works righteousness, and speaks the truth in his heart; he who does not backbite with his tongue, nor does evil to his neighbor, nor does he take up a reproach against his friend; in who eyes a vile person is despised; but honors those who fear the Lord; he who swears to his own hurt; keeps his word; and does not change regardless of the circumstances or consequences; and he who does not take a bribe against the innocent" (Psalm 15:2–5). People like this will enter into God's kingdom.

"He who has clean hands and a pure heart, who has not lifted up his soul to an idol, nor sworn deceitfully, He shall receive blessing from the Lord, and righteousness from the God of his salvation" (Psalm 24:4–5). People like this will enter into God's kingdom.

Those who worship, honor, and praise God; those who abide in Him and are obedient; and those do His will, will enter into the kingdom of God. Those whose names are written in the Lamb's book of life will enter the kingdom of God.

Now, let us take a look at who will *not* enter into God's kingdom:

Jesus answered, "Most assuredly, I say to you, unless one is born of water and the Spirit, he cannot enter the kingdom of God. That which is flesh is flesh, and that which is born of the Spirit [of God] is spirit." (John 3:5–6)

Many won't enter in because of their unbelief. (Hebrews 3:19)

But there shall by no means enter it anything that defiles, or causes an abomination or a lie, but only those who are written in the Lamb's Book of Life. (Revelation 21:27)

But the cowardly, unbelieving, abominable, murderers, sexually immoral, sorcerers, idolaters, and all liars shall have their part in the lake which burns with fire and brimstone, which is the second death. (Revelation 21:8)

Do you not know that the unrighteous will not inherit the kingdom of God? Do not be deceived. Neither fornicators, nor idolaters, nor adulterers, nor homosexuals, nor sodomites, nor thieves, nor covetous, nor drunkards, nor revilers, nor extortioners will inherit the kingdom of God. (1 Corinthians 6:9–10)

But outside [the kingdom] are dogs and sorcerers and sexually immoral and murderers and idolaters, and whoever loves and practices a lie. (Revelation 22:15)

Having given themselves over to sexual immorality and gone after strange flesh, are set forth as an example, suffering the vengeance of eternal fire. (Jude 1:7)

Flee sexual immorality. Every sin that a man does is outside the body, but he who commits sexual immorality sins against his [or her] own body. (1 Corinthians 6:18)

For I say to you, that unless your righteousness exceeds the righteousness of the scribes and Pharisees, you will by no means enter the kingdom of heaven. (Matthew 5:20)

Not everyone who says to Me, "Lord, Lord," shall enter the kingdom of heaven, but he who does the will of My Father in heaven. (Matthew 7:21)

He who believes in the Son has everlasting life; and he who does not believe the Son shall not see life, but the wrath of God abides on him. (John 3:36)

Many will say to Me in that day, "Lord, Lord, have we not prophesied in Your name, cast out demons in Your name, and done many wonders in Your name?" And then I will declare to them, "I never knew you; depart from Me, you who practice lawlessness!" (Matthew 7:22–23)

Anyone who has rejected Moses' law dies without mercy on the testimony of two or three witnesses. Of how much worse punishment, do you suppose, will he be thought worthy who has trampled the Son of God underfoot, counted the blood of the covenant by which he was sanctified a common thing, and insulted the Spirit of grace? (Hebrews 10:28–29)

For we know Him who said, "Vengeance is Mine, I will repay," says the Lord. And again, "The Lord will judge His people." (Hebrews 10:30)

For, "It is a fearful thing to fall into the hands of the living God." (Hebrews 10:31)

Please do not reject or abandon Jesus Christ, the Son of God, our Lord and Savior. Do not allow Satan to trick or deceive you into spending your eternal life in the lake that burns forever with fire and brimstone (the place called hell or Hades), where you will be tormented continuously, day and night, and you will forever be separated from God and your saved loved ones. Don't listen to Satan; he is a liar, and he hates us. He especially hates God and Jesus Christ.

There is absolutely nothing that you or I have done that God our Father and Jesus Christ His Son, our Lord, Savior, and King, won't forgive us for (except blasphemy against the Holy Spirit). All you have to do is talk to Him, admit that you are a sinner, ask Him to forgive you of your sins, and invite Him into your life. Jesus loves you and wants everyone to come to repentance and be saved, and God is married to the backslider. Dear friends, please don't wait until it is too late. Call upon the name of Jesus now!

It doesn't matter what you have done (Jesus has already paid the price for everyone with His precious blood), and it doesn't matter who you are— your race, the color of your skin, or whether you are rich or poor—God is Lord over all and offers salvation to *all* who call upon Him in faith with a sincere heart. He is rich in love, mercy, and grace and is always ready to save (Romans 10:12).

God our Father and Jesus Christ His Son, our Lord and Savior, love us so very much and want everyone to come unto repentance and be saved. God has a good plan and purpose for our lives. He desires to write your name in the book of life. That is why He gave and sent His only beloved Son Jesus Christ to earth to die on the cross for our sins and raised Him from the grave on the third day for our justification, so that we could be in right standing with Him, fellowship once again with Him (as in the beginning of time before Adam and Eve disobeyed Him in the Garden of Eden), and be given eternal life.

False Prophets, Priests, Pastors, Preachers, Teachers, et al., Will Be Judged and Rewarded or Punished according to Their Deeds

Behold, a whirlwind of the Lord has gone forth in fury—a violent whirlwind! It will fall violently on the head of the wicked. The anger of the Lord will not turn back Until He has executed and performed the thoughts of His heart. In the latter days you will understand it perfectly.
—Jeremiah 23:19–20

(I believe that we're now living in the latter days, or last days.)

And so we have the prophetic word confirmed, which you do well to heed as a light that shines in a dark place, until the day dawns and the morning star rises in your hearts; knowing this first, that no prophecy of Scripture is of any private interpretation, for prophecy never came by the will of man, but holy men of God spoke as they were moved by the Holy Spirit.
—2 Peter 1:19–21

Thus says the Lord concerning the prophets who make My people stray; who chant "Peace" while they chew with their teeth, but who prepare war against him who puts nothing into their mouths: Therefore you shall have night without vision, and you shall have darkness without divination; the sun shall go down on the prophets; and the day shall be dark for them. So the seers shall be ashamed, and the diviners abashed; indeed they shall all cover their lips; for there is no answer from God.

—Micah 3:5–7

False leadership in the church and around the world today is unbelievable and is on the rise like never before. There are countless men and women who call themselves (or who have the title of) prophet, pastor, bishop, apostle, teacher, preacher, priest, pope, evangelist, minister, deacon, deaconess, prophetess, or missionary and who claim that they are called, are ordained, and are being used by God—but they are not.

These are men and women who should have been giving all the people spiritual and moral advice and guidance chose to sell out their true calling and gifts from God to Satan in exchange for money, fame, a name, and material things that will all fade away someday. In all fairness, some of them may have started out in the ministry with good intentions, but they've allowed Satan and the love of mammon to creep into their hearts. Then there are those who deliberately set out to devise tricks and get-rich-quick schemes. They see only dollar signs.

There are even fortune-tellers, sorcerers, and so-called white witches who claim that they do good work for God to help people, but they do not. They are no different from the black witches that Satan uses.

These people all have a form of godliness and speak elegant and enticing words, and some may even pretend to perform a miracle every now and then. They will tell you what you want to hear based on your vulnerability but not what you need to hear according to God's Word. And they may even get some basic things right about your life (which is the same as most people). Understand that they can only give you false hope and lies.

They are greedy for money, fame, and material things, and many do not care who they hurt to obtain what they want. But God has something waiting for them if they don't repent, because He knows, sees, and hears everything, and Judgment Day is coming.

People of today will allow anyone to teach or preach to them. They will listen to and follow other people knowing full well what the Word of God says. Even knowing this, they choose to follow these men and women (who are hungry for fortune and fame, not winning souls for Jesus

Christ. Their lives haven't changed; they are still drug users, homosexuals, lesbians, adulterers, fornicators, liars, and evil wicked men and women) instead of God, His Word, and eternal life.

Men and women who claim that they are servants and messengers of God yet who commit adultery, fornication, and abominable acts are *still* liars, drug users, abusers, thieves, sex offenders, killers, prejudiced people, and haters who are only concerned about money, materialistic things, and themselves. They have not truly repented. Many are bold and do not deny their sexuality. Men are marrying men, women are marrying women, and transgender people are marrying, thinking that this is right in the sight of God. Others just don't care about God, and they do whatever they so desire to satisfy their flesh.

Do you really think that you will get away with your wickedness? Do you really think that God doesn't see you and know your heart? Or perhaps you think that at some point (but not right now, not today) you will repent from your evil ways.

Hear the Word of God, so now you can't say (when you stand before God one day) that you did not know.

> So, God created man in His own image; in the image of God He created him; male and female He created them. ... He blessed them and told them to be fruitful and multiply. (Genesis 1:27, 28 KJV)

> But at the beginning of creation God "made them male and female: For this reason a man will leave his father and mother and be united to his wife, and the two will become one flesh"; so then they are no longer two, but one flesh. Therefore what God has joined together, let no man separate. (Mark 10:6–9)

> If a man also lie with mankind, as he lieth with a womankind, both of them have committed an abomination: they shall surely be put to death; their blood shall be upon them. (Leviticus 20:13 KJV)

> For whosoever shall commit any of these abominations, even the souls that commit them shall be cut off from among their

people. … Defile not yourselves therein: I am the Lord your God. (Leviticus 18:29, 30 KJV)

For this reason, God gave them up to vile passions. For even their women exchanged the natural use for what is against nature. Likewise, also the men, leaving the natural use of woman burned in their lust for one another, men with men committing what is shameful, and receiving in themselves the penalty of their error which was due. (Romans 2:26–27)

Dear people, I'm not here to judge anyone, but I must tell you the truth according to God's Word. We live in a fallen world with a sin nature. But in Jesus Christ we can be born again and become a new creation in Him. God loves you so very much. He knows your heart and your motives, He sees all that you are doing, and He hears your every thought and knows all your plans.

However, God cannot tolerate sin. And if He didn't spare the angels who sinned along with Satan, but cast them down into hell to be chained there until judgment; and if He didn't spare those who practiced immorality and unrighteousness in the days of Noah, but sent a flood and wiped everyone off the face of the earth (except Noah and his family and some animals); and if He destroyed those who practiced immoral sexual acts, men with men; and if He destroyed the wicked people (after two angels disguised as men led Lot and his family out) in Sodom and Gomorrah by fire (2 Peter 2:4–6; Genesis 19), then what makes you think that He will spare you (unless you repent)? (Read Jude 1:6–8; 1 Corinthians 6:9–10, 7:2; Romans 1:24–29; Revelation 22:15.)

God is a great counselor. Talk to Him about your concerns. Repent and turn from your wicked ways before it is too late! Call upon the name of the Lord, and He will save you from eternal death. For the wages of sin is death, but God wants to give you the gift of eternal life (Romans 6:23).

Satan has many counterfeiters in the world today, sometimes making it difficult for even the very elect people of God to recognize them. He can disguise or transform himself to look like an angel of light, and he's a good imitator. He is a liar and the father of lies. There is no truth (nor can there be) in him (John 8:44). So don't be so quick to believe everything you see and everything you hear. You must use spiritual discernment. We are warned in 1 John 4:1 to test the spirits to see if they are of God.

We're not to believe everyone and everything that sounds or look good. The grass may look greener on the other side, but looks can be deceiving. The ground or soil must be good for seeding, planting, and growing, and it must be cultivated. It must also be watered, nurtured, and cared for. So be very careful, watchful, and prayerful. Reject anyone whose preaching and teachings are different from those of Jesus Christ and are not in line with His Word. Remember, God loves us, but He hates sin and cannot, and will not, tolerate it. However, He can and will forgive us of our sins and cleanse us from all unrighteousness if we ask in sincerity.

False Prophets, Priests, Pastors (Shepherds), Preachers, and Teachers and Those with Titles such as Apostle, Bishop, Reverend, Pope, Rabbi, Elder, Minister, Evangelist, Deacon, Prophetess, Deaconess, and Missionary

God sends only true and honest men and women of God.

"And they shall teach my people the difference between the holy and profane [unholy]; and cause them to discern between the unclean and the clean" (Ezekiel 44:23–25 KJV).

Dear people, it doesn't matter whether you use a title in front of, behind, above, or underneath your name—or not—because God looks deep in the heart of a person, and what He sees there takes preference over everything else. Anyone can claim to be a Christian and say that they are called by God into a ministry to preach and teach the gospel of Jesus Christ. They will give themselves a title and also claim that they have been born again of the Spirit of God and have been baptized with the Holy Spirit. Maybe they have, and maybe they have not. God will be the judge.

But please listen to me carefully: if you are an impostor, untrue to your calling, using the name of Jesus and the people of God for your fame and riches, or if you are speaking and living a lie before God and His people, then God will surely expose you and punish you severely (unless you wholeheartedly ask Him to forgive you and repent). You will be judged and rewarded by Jesus Christ according to your deeds (as will I). All will be justified or condemned by their words. For every idle word people may speak, they will give an account of it; they will answer to God on Judgment Day (Matthew 12:36–37). Those who are false and deceitful, you will know them by their fruits and by the spirit of discernment. You must test the spirits today like never before. If you do not have the spirit of discernment, pray for it. God gives liberally as He wills and to those who are sincere.

> Beloved, do not believe every spirit, but test the spirits, whether they are of God, because many false prophets have gone out into the world. (1 John 4:1)

> Then many false prophets will rise up and deceive many. (Matthew 24:11)

> Woe unto you … hypocrites! For you are like whitewashed tombs which indeed appear beautiful outwardly, but inside are full of dead men's bones and all uncleanness. Even so you also outwardly appear righteous to men, but inside you are full of hypocrisy and lawlessness. (Matthew 23:27–28)

> But there were also false prophets among the people, even as there will be false teachers among you, who will secretly bring in destructive heresies, even denying the Lord who bought them, and bring on themselves swift destruction. And many will follow their destructive ways, because of whom the way of truth will be blasphemed. By covetousness they will exploit you with deceptive words. (2 Peter 2:1–3)

> Beware of false prophets who come to you in sheep's clothing [they merely look and act holy], but inwardly they are ravenous wolves. You will know them by their fruits; and by the spirit of discernment. (Matthew 7:15–16; 1 Corinthians 2:14)

> Do men gather grapes from thorn bushes or figs from thistles? Even so, every good tree bears good fruit, but a bad tree bears bad fruit. (Matthew 7:16–17)

> Thus says the Lord God: "Woe to the foolish prophets, who follow their own spirit and have seen nothing! … They have

envisioned futility and false divination, saying, 'Thus says the Lord!' But the Lord has not sent them; yet they hope that the word may be confirmed. Have you not seen a futile vision, and have you not spoken false divination? You say, 'The Lord says,' but I have not spoken." (Ezekiel 13:3, 6–7)

Therefore thus says the Lord God: "Because you have spoken nonsense and envisioned lies, therefore I am indeed against you," says the Lord God. "My hand will be against the prophets who envision futility and who divine lies; they shall not be in the assembly of My people, nor written in the record of the house of Israel. … Then you shall know that I am the Lord God." (Ezekiel 13:8–10)

Likewise, son of man, set your face against the daughters of your people, who prophesy out of their own heart [inspiration]; prophesy against them, and say, "Thus says the Lord God": And you have tested those who say they are apostles and are not; and have found them liars. (Revelation 2:2)

For such are false apostles, deceitful workers, transforming themselves into apostles of Christ. And no wonder! For Satan transforms himself into an angel of light. Therefore, it is no great thing if his ministers [those who serve him] also transform themselves into ministers [servants] of righteousness, whose end will be according to their works. (2 Corinthians 11:13–15)

An astonishing and horrible thing has been committed in the land: The prophets prophesy falsely, and the priests rule by their own power; and My people love to have it so. But what will you do in the end? (Jeremiah 5:30–31)

Thus, says the Lord of hosts: "Do not listen to the words of the prophets who prophesy to you. They make you worthless; they speak a vision of their own heart, not from the mouth of the Lord. They continually say to those who despise Me, 'The Lord has said, "You shall have peace"'; and to everyone who walks according to the dictates (stubbornness or imagination) of his own heart, they say, 'No evil shall come upon you.'" (Jeremiah 23:16–17)

The prophet that hath a dream, let him tell a dream; and he that hath my word, let him speak my word faithfully. What is the chaff to the wheat? saith the Lord. Is not my word like a fire? saith the Lord; and like a hammer that breaketh the rock in pieces? (Jeremiah 23:28–29 KJV)

"Therefore behold, I am against the prophets," says the Lord, "who steal My words everyone from his neighbor. Behold, I am against the prophets," says the Lord, "who use their tongues and say, 'He says.' "Behold, I am against those who prophesy false dreams," says the Lord, "and tell them, and cause My people to err by their lies and by their recklessness. Yet I did not send them or command them; therefore, they shall not profit this people at all," says the Lord. (Jeremiah 23:30–32)

I have not sent these prophets, yet they ran. I have not spoken to them, yet they prophesied." (Jeremiah 23:21)

But if they had stood in My counsel, and had caused My people to hear My words, then they would have turned from their evil way, and from the evil of their doings. "Am I a God near at hand," says the Lord, "And not a God afar off? Can anyone hide himself in secret places, so I shall not see him?" says the Lord; "Do I not fill heaven and earth?" says the Lord. (Jeremiah 23:22–24)

I have heard what the prophets have said who prophesy lies in My name, saying, "I have dreamed, I have dreamed!" How long will this be in the heart of the prophets who prophesy lies? Indeed, they are prophets of the deceit of their own heart. (Jeremiah 23:25–26)

But the prophet who presumes to speak a word in My name, which I have not commanded him to speak, or who speaks in the name of other gods, that prophet shall die. (Deuteronomy 18:20)

For every man's word shall be his own burden: for ye have perverted the words of the living God, of the Lord of hosts our God. (Jeremiah 23:36 KJV)

Here are other ways to test a prophet's authenticity:

And if you say in your heart, "How shall we know the word which the Lord has not spoken?" When a prophet speaks in the name of the Lord, if the thing does not happen or come to pass, that is the thing which the Lord has not spoken; the prophet has spoken it presumptuously; you shall not be afraid of him. (Deuteronomy 18:21–22)

"And now, O priests [pastors, all leaders in the church, and those who claim that they are called by God to do a special work for Him], this commandment is for you. If you will not hear, and if you will not take it to heart, to give glory to My name," says the Lord of hosts, "I will send a curse upon you, and I will curse your blessings. Yes, I have already cursed them, because you do not take it to heart. ... For the lips of a priest [pastor, minister, an ordained leader of the church] should keep knowledge, and people should seek the law [or the Word of God—true instructions] from his [or her] mouth; for he [or she] is the messenger of the Lord of hosts. But you have departed from the way; you have caused many to stumble at the law [or Word of God—true instructions]; you have corrupted the covenant of Levi [you refuse to live a holy and righteous life before God; you refuse to surrender your own glory and give all the glory to God]," says the Lord of hosts. "Therefore I also have made you contemptible and base before all the people, because you have not kept My ways, but have shown partiality in the law [or Word of God]." (Malachi 2:1–2, 7–9)

"A son honors his father, and a servant his master. If then I am the Father, where is My honor? And if I am a Master, where is My reverence?" says the Lord of hosts to you priests who despise My name. (Malachi 1:6)

"For both prophet and priest are profane; yes, in My house I have found their wickedness," says the Lord. (Jeremiah 23:11)

The priest and the prophet have erred through intoxicating drink; they err in vision, they stumble in judgment. (Isaiah 26:7)

God will cut off the names of the idolatrous priests with the pagan priests, those who worship anything or anyone other than God; and those who worship and swear oaths by the Lord, but at the same time worship other gods or pray to other idols. (Zephaniah 1:4–5)

There is a sound of wailing shepherds! For their glory is in ruins. (Zechariah 11:3)

For the shepherds have become dull-hearted and have not sought the Lord. (Jeremiah 10:21)

"Woe to the shepherds who destroy and scatter the sheep of My pasture!" says the Lord. Therefore, thus says the Lord God of Israel against the shepherds who feed My people: You have scattered My flock, driven them away, and not attended to them. "Behold, I will attend to you for the evil of your doings," says the Lord. (Jeremiah 23:1–2)

For the idols have spoken vanity, and the diviners have seen a lie, and have told false dreams; they comfort in vain: therefore they [the people] went their way as a flock, they were troubled, because there was no shepherd. (Zechariah 10:2 KJV)

Mine anger was kindled against the shepherds, and I punished the goats [leaders]: for the Lord of hosts visit His flock. (Zechariah 10:3 KJV)

Woe to the idol [or worthless] shepherd that leaveth the flock! the sword shall be upon his arm. (Zechariah 11:17 KJV)

Thus says the Lord God to the shepherds: "Woe to the shepherds ... who feed themselves! Should not the shepherds feed the flocks? You eat the fat and clothe yourselves with the wool; you slaughter the fatlings, but you do not feed the flock. The weak you have not strengthened, nor have you healed those who were sick, nor bound up the broken, nor brought back what was driven away, nor sought what was lost; but with force and cruelty you have ruled them. So, they were scattered because there was no shepherd; and they became food for all the beasts of the field when there were scattered. My sheep wandered. ... My sheep was scattered over the face of the earth, and no one was seeking or searching for them." (Ezekiel 34:2–6)

Therefore, you shepherds, hear the word of the Lord: "As I live," says the Lord God, "surely because My flock became a prey, and My flock became food for every beast of the field, because there was no shepherd, nor did My shepherds search for My flock, but the shepherds fed themselves and did not fed My flock"—therefore, O shepherds, hear the word of the Lord! Thus says the Lord God: "Behold, I am against the shepherds, and I will require My flock at their hand." (Ezekiel 34:7–10)

And as for my flock, they eat that which ye have trodden with your feet; and they drink that which ye have fouled with your feet. (Ezekiel 34:19 KJV)

For thus says the Lord God: "Indeed I Myself will search for My sheep and seek them out. ... I will feed them in good pasture." (Ezekiel 34:11, 14)

Wail, shepherds, and cry! Roll about in the ashes, you leaders of the flock! For the days of your slaughter and your dispersions are fulfilled; you shall fall like a precious vessel. And the shepherds will have no way to flee, nor the leaders of the flock to escape. A voice of the cry of the shepherds, and a wailing of the leaders to the flock will be heard. For the Lord has plundered their pasture, and the peaceful dwellings are cut down Because of the fierce anger of the Lord. (Jeremiah 25:34–37)

"Behold, you trust in lying words that cannot profit. Will you steal, murder, commit adultery, swear falsely, burn incense to Ba'al, and walk after other gods whom you do not know, and then come and stand before Me in this house which is called by My name, and say, 'We are delivered to do all these abominations'? Has this house, which is called by My name, become a den of thieves in your eyes? Behold, I, even I, have seen it," says the Lord. (Jeremiah 7:9)

For certain men have crept in unnoticed, who long ago were marked out for this condemnation, ungodly men, who turn the grace of our God into lewdness and deny the only Lord God and our Lord Jesus Christ. But I want to remind you, though you once knew this, that the Lord, having saved the people out of the land of Egypt, afterward destroyed those who did not believe. And the angels who did not keep their proper domain, but left their own abode, He has reserved in everlasting chains under darkness for the judgment of the great day; as Sodom and Gomorrah, and cities around them in a similar manner to these, having given themselves over to sexual immorality and gone after strange flesh, are set forth as example, suffering the vengeance of eternal fire. (Jude 1:4–7)

For there are many insubordinate, both idle talkers and deceivers, especially those of the circumcision, whose mouths must be stopped, who subvert whole households, teaching things which they ought not, for the sake of dishonest gain. (Titus 1:10–11)

Some will depart from the faith, giving heed to deceiving spirits and doctrines of demons, speaking lies in hypocrisy, having their own conscience seared with a hot iron. (1 Timothy 4:1–2)

"Because from the least of them even to the greatest of them, everyone is given to covetousness; and from the prophet even to the priest, everyone deals falsely. They have also healed the hurt of My people slightly, saying, 'Peace, peace!' When there is no peace. Were they ashamed when they had committed abomination? No! They were not at all ashamed; nor did they blush. Therefore, they shall fall among those who fall; at the time I punish them, they shall be cast down," says the Lord. (Jeremiah 6:13–15)

To the pure all things are pure, but to those who are defiled and unbelieving nothing is pure; but even their mind and conscience are defiled. They profess to know God, but in works they deny Him, being abominable, disobedient, and disqualified for every good work. (Titus 1:15–16)

Because, indeed, because they have seduced My people, saying, "Peace!" when there is no peace. (Ezekiel 13:10)

Now I urge you, brethren, note those who cause divisions and offenses, contrary to the doctrine which you have learned, and avoid them. For those who are such do not serve our Lord Jesus Christ, but their own belly, and by smooth words and flattering speech deceive the hearts of the simple. (Romans 16:17–18)

These are grumblers, complainers, walking according to their own lusts; and they mouth great swelling words, flattering people to gain advantage. (Jude 1:16)

But, beloved, remember … how they [the apostles of Lord Jesus Christ] told you that there would be mockers in the last time [days] who would walk according to their own ungodly lusts. These are sensual persons, who cause divisions, not having the Spirit. (Jude 1:17–19)

Shepherd the flock of God which is among you, serving as overseers, not for dishonest gain but eagerly; nor as being lords over those entrusted to you, but being examples to the flock; and when the Chief Shepherd appears, you will receive the crown of glory that does not fade away. (1 Peter 5:2–4)

Be diligent to know the state of your flocks and attend to your herd. For riches are not forever, nor does a crown endure to all generations. (Proverbs 27:23–24)

"Behold, the days are coming," says the Lord, "that I will raise to David a Branch of righteousness; a King shall reign and prosper and execute judgment and righteousness in the earth. … And Israel will dwell safely; now this is His name by which He will be called: the Lord our righteousness." (Jeremiah 23:5–6)

Fortune-Tellers, Palm or Tarot Readers, Sorcerers, and Witches

I'm talking not about storybook or television characters but about real people who worship, serve, and work for Satan. Some of these people will say even that they work for God, while others will say that they work for God and Satan. And then there are those who will flat out admit that they work for Satan alone. Whoever you are, if you think that you are getting away with your lies, evil ways, and tricks to seduce and get money from God's people, know that a horrible end awaits you, for the Lord thy God is against you. You will be rewarded according to your deeds, and your destination is a lake that burns forever with unquenchable fire and brimstone. You will burn there along with the one you serve, your master, Satan, unless you genuinely repent of your sins and ask Jesus Christ to forgive you and invite Him into your life.

> There shall not be found among you anyone who makes his son or daughter pass through the fire, or one who practices witchcraft, or a soothsayer, or one who interprets omens, or a sorcerer, or one who conjures spells, or a medium, or a spiritist, or one who calls up the dead. For all who do these things are an abomination to the Lord. (Deuteronomy 18:10–12)

> Woe to the women who sew magic charms on their sleeves and make veils for the heads of people of every height to hunt souls! Will you hunt the souls of My people, and keep yourselves alive? And will you profane Me among My people for handfuls of barley and for pieces of bread, killing people who should not

die, and keeping people alive who should not live, by your lying to My people who listen to lies? (Ezekiel 13:17–19)

Because with lies you have made the heart of the righteous sad, whom I have not made sad; and you have strengthened the hands of the wicked, so that he does not turn from his wicked way to save his life. Therefore, you shall no longer envision futility nor practice divination; for I will deliver My people out of your hand, and you shall know that I am the Lord. (Ezekiel 13:22–23)

But outside are dogs and sorcerers and sexually immoral and murderers and idolaters, and whoever loves and practices a lie. (Revelation 22:15)

You shall not permit sorceress to live. (Exodus 22:18)

We as born-again Christians are all called to serve God and His people and to be witnesses of the good news of Jesus Christ and win souls for His kingdom. However, those with specific titles who say that God has called and ordained them to a special office have a greater and stricter responsibility to God and His people. They are ordained by God and humankind to lead, teach, feed, nurture, and take care of the people of God; to equip the saints for the work of ministry; to win souls for His kingdom; and to build up His body—the church.

They are to tell the people about the love, mercy, and grace of God and Jesus Christ. They are to inform the people of what Jesus Christ did for us at Calvary and why He did it. They are to build up those who are torn down; give comfort and joy to those who mourn; heal the sick by/ through faith in Jesus Christ; raise the dead spiritually; and set free those who are captive by Satan in their minds and spirits with the Word of God. (For whom Jesus sets free is indeed free.)

Feed those who are hungry (physically and spiritually). Those are going down the wrong road, show them the road that will lead them to God, eternal life. It is true that you can't make them take that road or even stay on that road, but you have done what is required of you by God and as a born-again Christian. You showed them the right road and pointed them in the right direction. The final decision to repent, turn around, and change direction is solely up to them.

You are to tell the people about the love, mercy, and grace of God, but also you are to proclaim the acceptable year of the Lord, the day of vengeance, and the judgment of the Lord our God, because Judgment Day is coming! And God wants His people to know so that they can be prepared.

God says in His Word: "Vengeance is Mind, I will repay" (Romans 12:19). "And true and righteous are His judgments" (Revelation 19:2). All will be judged and rewarded according to their works. There will be no exceptions.

So, whatever your calling is, you must be sure and true to that calling. Don't you want God to find you worthy of your calling upon His return? I sure do!

With love and a compassionate spirit, they are to shepherd and serve the people or a flock in the church. (Read Matthew 9:36.) They are to minister to the spiritual, physical, and emotional needs of all people in any way that they possibly can. I don't care who they are, what the color of their skin is, where they were born, whether they are rich or poor, what they look like, or what they smell like. Jesus Christ is the Good Shepherd who gave His life for all sheep—for everyone (John 10:11–13). Your color or where you were born, whether a citizen of the USA or an immigrant from some other country—doesn't matter to God. We are all His creation.

> And He Himself gave some to be apostles, some prophets, some evangelists, and some pastors and teachers [why?], for the equipping of the saints for the work of the ministry, for the edifying of the body of Christ [for how long?], till we all come to the unity of the faith and of the knowledge of the Son of God, to a perfect man [or woman], to the measure of the stature of the fullness of Christ; that we should no longer be children, tossed to and fro and carried about with every wind of doctrine, by the trickery of men, in the cunning craftiness of deceitful plotting, but, speaking the truth in love, may grow up in all things into Him who is the head—Christ. (Ephesians 4:11–15)

Thank God for real men and women of God who are after God's own heart, who truly love and honor God, who are called, ordained, and commissioned by God. But on the other hand, there are impostors, those who say and pretend that they love God and that they have been called by God to preach the gospel of Jesus Christ, but they are hirelings. They do it for money, material things, and fame, and they care only about themselves (and maybe their families), not about God and His people. They're not concerned about the salvation of others, winning souls for Christ. They're not concerned about the hurt and brokenhearted or the homeless and less fortunate. They are too busy counting money and planning events to make more money. I think that Isaiah put it nicely when he said: "Yes, they are greedy dogs which never have enough. And they are shepherds who cannot understand; they all look to their own way, everyone for his own gain, from his own territory" (Isaiah 56:11).

As a shepherd, teacher, and leader of God's church, you have an even greater responsibility to the people of God. Our God sees, hears, and knows everything we say and do. He knows our thoughts before we can even think them. Yes, God loves us, but He can't and won't tolerate sin forever. His eyes are in every place, watching the good and the evil. One must repent of one's sins, ask God for forgiveness, and live a life that's pleasing and to Him and obedient to His Word.

Enjoy the time that you have now and the pleasures of this world, including material things, because all are temporary on this earth and will perish. But know this fact: your spirit will live forever, either with God or with Satan. It's just that simple.

For what does it profit you to gain the whole world now and then, when you die, to lose your soul and spend your eternal life in hellfire? Or what will you give in exchange for your soul or eternal life? Think about that for a moment. I pray that you will give your heart and your life to Jesus Christ in exchange for eternal life with Him. I promise you that you will never regret it and that your life will be filled with unexplainable joy and peace.

Everybody will answer to God one day and give an account for all that they have said and done, and for robbing and misleading the people of God. They will reap what they have sown. They think that they're getting away with their wickedness and wrongdoings. They do not realize that God sees them and that He knows their heart.

For if God did not spare the angels who sinned against Him but cast them down to hell and delivered them to chains of darkness to be reserved for judgment, and if He did not spare the ancient world but destroyed all in the world by a great flood except for Noah (a preacher of righteousness), his family, and two each of every kind of animal (read 2 Peter 2:4–5; Genesis 6–7), then neither will He spare you, me, or anyone else. Our God is a just God.

The cities (all but Zoar) of Sodom and Gomorrah and all the ungodly people were destroyed by fire because of their wickedness and unrighteousness, except Lot and his daughters. As they were leaving the city, Lot's wife turned into a pillar of salt because she turned and looked back at the cities as they were being destroyed by fire, although she had been told not to (Genesis 19).

(Zoar, which means "little or insignificant," was the city that Lot requested to live in and the place where the men [angels] favored him. However, Lot and his daughters went up out of Zoar and lived in the mountain because he was afraid to live in Zoar.)

"And turning the cities of Sodom and Gomorrah into ashes, condemned them to destruction, making them an example to those who afterward would live ungodly" (2 Peter 2:6).

It is for certain that you will not get away with anything, and you can be sure that your sin will find you out. There is no place to run or hide from an all-knowing, all-seeing God.

I implore you: repent of your sins, turn from your selfish wicked ways, and stop allowing the devil to use you before it is too late. He only wants to take you to hell with him. You know what you are doing wrong (and so does God). Ask God to forgive you right *now*. And if you have mistreated anyone or harbor unforgiveness in your heart for any reason, if you can, go to that person and ask them for forgiveness. If not, then tell God that you forgive them. Remember, God won't forgive you unless you forgive others. (Read Matthew 6:14–15.)

My friends, although many people (Christians and non-Christians) do this (in and out of the church), we should never seek to impress people, please humankind, or look for glory and pats on the back. Instead we must always seek to please God and give all the glory, honor, and praise for everything that we do to God the Father and Jesus Christ our Savior. To do anything less would be a dishonor, a slap in the face to our God:

"But as we have been approved by God to be entrusted with the gospel, even so we speak, not as pleasing men, but God who tests our hearts. For neither at any time did we use flattering words, as you know, nor a cloak for covetousness—God is witness. Nor did we seek glory from men, either from you or from others" (1 Thessalonians 2:4–6).

Your final judge will be God and not humankind.

"The boastful shall not stand in Your sight; You hate all workers of iniquity. You shall destroy those who speak falsehood; the Lord abhors the bloodthirsty and deceitful man" (Psalm 5:5–6).

Remember: "A true witness delivers souls, but a deceitful witness speaks lies" (Proverbs 14:25). "Take heed to yourself and to the doctrine. Continue in them, for in doing this you will save both yourself and those who hear you" (1 Timothy 4:16).

Preach the Gospel of Jesus Christ

But we preach Christ crucified
— 1 Corinthians 1:23

But as we were allowed of God to be put in trust with the gospel, even
so we speak; not as pleasing men, but God, which trieth our hearts.
—1 Thessalonians 2:4 (KJV)

For I am not ashamed of the gospel of Christ, for it is the
power of God to salvation for everyone who believes. For
in it the righteousness of God is revealed from faith to
faith; as it is written, "The just shall live by faith."
—Romans 1:16–17

And this gospel of the kingdom will be preached in all the world
as a witness to all nations, and then the end will come.
—Matthew 24:14

As born-again Christians (true believers in Jesus Christ), we are to testify, preach, and teach the Word of God to all people. We are to preach the gospel (good news) about Jesus Christ. Let the people know what we have in and through, and because of, Jesus. Tell why He came to earth; tell of His death on the cross for the sins of the world; and tell of His resurrection on the third day, His ascension back to the Father in heaven, and His second and final return to this earth, which is coming very soon.

Preach about things having to do with the kingdom of God and the name of Jesus Christ. Tell the world about His amazing love, grace, and mercy. Tell them that we have been reconciled to God, that we have been justified, that we have been put back into a right relationship with Him, and that we have been forgiven of our sins and are no longer under the power of sin or death or the power of Satan. Preach salvation through faith in Jesus Christ.

We now have the peace of God and have been set free by His Spirit. We now have the Spirit of God indwelling in us. We have been baptized with the Holy Spirit. We now speak in tongues and in heavenly language. We have been given the authority and power by God, in Jesus's name, to cast out devils, heal the sick, and raise the dead. And if we unknowingly eat or drink anything poisonous, it will not harm us. We are now the righteousness of God through Jesus Christ because of what He did at Calvary.

Those who are called, ordained, anointed, and appointed by God to be watchmen have a responsibility to God and the people to inform all people of physical and spiritual dangers. Whatever God reveals to a person relating to what is going to happen (what is coming upon the land), whether good or bad, is something that the person must warn other people about. If for any reason such a person refuses to obey God or fails to walk in their assignment, they will answer to God and Jesus Christ and will be held accountable.

Don't let the blood of the people be on your hands. Tell others what "sayeth the Lord" so that they will be without an excuse when they stand before God (i.e., so they can't say to God, "Nobody told me. I've never heard …"). I doing this you will have delivered your soul from hell, as it will now be up to the people to deliver their souls from hell by believing, repenting, and accepting God's Word.

> The Spirit of the Lord is upon Me, Because He has anointed Me to preach the gospel to the poor; He has sent Me to heal the brokenhearted, to proclaim liberty to the captives And recovery of sight to the blind. To set at liberty those who are oppressed; to proclaim the acceptable year of the Lord. (Luke 4:18–19)

> And He [Jesus] said to them, "Go into all the world and preach the gospel to every creature. He who believes and is baptized will be saved; but he who does not believe will be condemned.

And these signs will follow those who believe: In My name they will cast out demons; they will speak with new tongues; they will take up serpents; and if they drink anything deadly, it will by no means hurt them; they will lay hands on the sick, and they will recover." (Mark 16:15–18)

Dear people of God:

I charge you therefore before God and the Lord Jesus Christ, who will judge the living and the dead at His appearing and His kingdom: Preach the word! Be ready in season and out of season. Convince, rebuke, exhort, with all longsuffering and teaching. For the time will come when they will not endure sound doctrine, but according to their own desires, because they have itching ears, they will heap up for themselves teachers; and will turn their ears away from the truth, and be turned aside to fables. But you be watchful in all things, endure afflictions, do the work of an evangelist, fulfill your ministry. (2 Timothy 4:1–5)

And as you go, preach, saying, "The kingdom of heaven is at hand." Heal the sick, cleanse the lepers, raise the dead, cast out demons. Freely you have received, freely give. (Matthew 10:7–8)

To many people, the preaching or message of the cross—the gospel of Jesus Christ, the good news—doesn't make sense and is foolishness. (They just can't understand how someone can believe in someone they cannot see.) Because they can't believe, fail to believe, or choose not to believe in Jesus Christ and His works, they will perish. But we who do choose to believe (by faith, because we believe in Jesus and His works and we trust and believe in the Word of God) are saved, for we believe that it is the power of God. (Read 1 Corinthians 1:18.)

For the wrath of God is revealed from heaven against all ungodliness and unrighteousness of men, who suppress the truth in unrighteousness, because what may be known of God is manifest in them, for God has shown it to them. (Romans 1:18–19)

Then He [Jesus] said to His disciples, "The harvest truly is plentiful, but the laborers are few. Therefore, pray the Lord of the harvest to send out laborers into His harvest." (Matthew 9:37–38)

Some indeed preach Christ even from envy and strife, and some also from goodwill: The former preach Christ from selfish ambition, not sincerely, supposing to add affliction to my chains; but the latter out of love, knowing that I am appointed for the defense of the gospel. What then? Only that in every way, whether in pretense or in truth, Christ is preached; and in this I rejoice, yes, and will rejoice. (Philippians 1:15–18)

My friends, keep on believing and trusting in Jesus Christ. Don't ever let Satan or anyone else talk you into giving up on God. And many will—believe me.

Keep fighting a good fight, finish the race, and keep the faith. For the Lord, the righteous Judge has a crown of righteousness that He will give you, me, and everyone who believed and received Jesus Christ as Lord and Savior; and who have loved Him and is looking forward to His appearing on that great day. (2 Timothy 4:7–8)

Are you looking forward to His return any day now? I sure am!

Those Who Preach the Gospel of Jesus Christ for the Wrong Reasons

> No one can serve two masters; for either he will hate the one and
> love the other, or else he will be loyal to the one and despise the
> other. You cannot serve God and mammon [money, riches].
> —Matthew 6:24

Let me ask you two questions: Do you think that you're hiding from God and pulling the wool over His eyes? Do you think that Jesus isn't hip to you or that He doesn't know what's going on? You may be able to fool some people, but you can't fool God. You speak well, dress well, and say all the things that you know the people want to hear, especially about obtaining money and material things, but you're not genuinely concerned about others' spiritual well-being and long-term goal, which is to obtain eternal life. You're only concerned about yourself. You walk after your own ungodly lusts and desires. You say flattering big words just to impress others and take advantage of them and their trust in you. And you do it all for the sake of money and fame—in the name of Jesus!

How sad. I feel so sorry for you because you will give an account to God one day for your deeds. I wonder if then you will feel that it was all worth it, when God says, "Depart from Me, you who work iniquity. I do not know you," and you are cast into the lake of fire that burns with fire and brimstone forever and ever.

Just in case you don't believe, don't know, or have forgotten, or perhaps you just don't care anymore, God is omnipresent, omniscient, and omnipotent. He is the almighty God, and He is everywhere at the same time. He knows, sees, and hears all, so you're not getting away with anything. We are nothing without God, nor can we do anything without Him. We live, breathe, move, and have our being because of Him.

Hear the Word of Jesus:

I know your works, that you are neither cold nor hot. I could wish you were cold or hot. So then, because you are lukewarm, and neither cold nor hot, I will vomit you out of My mouth. (Revelation 3:15–16)

Because you say, "I am rich, have become wealthy, and have need of nothing"—and do not know that you are wretched, miserable, poor, blind, and naked—I counsel you to buy from Me gold refined in the fire, that you may be rich; and white garments, that you may be clothed; that the shame of your nakedness may not be revealed; and anoint your eyes with eye slave, that you may see. As many as I love, I rebuke and chasten. Therefore be zealous and repent. (Revelation 3:17–19)

But those who desire to be rich fall into temptation and a snare, and into many foolish and harmful lusts which drown men in destruction and perdition. For the love of money is a root of all kinds of evil, for which some have strayed from the faith in their greediness; and pieced themselves through with many sorrows. (1 Timothy 6:9–10)

For those who are such do not serve our Lord Jesus Christ, but their own belly, and by smooth words and flattering speech deceive the hearts of the simple. (Romans 16:18)

Useless wrangling's of men of corrupt minds and destitute of the truth, who suppose that godliness is a means of gain. From such withdraw yourself. Now godliness with contentment is great gain. For we brought nothing into this world, and it is certain we can carry nothing out. (1 Timothy 6:5–7)

But you, O man [or woman] of God, flee these things and pursue righteousness, godliness, faith, love, patience, gentleness. Fight the good fight of faith, lay hold on eternal life, to which you were called and have confessed in the presence of many witnesses. I urge you in the sight of God who gives life to all things, and before Christ Jesus … that you keep this commandment without spot, blameless until our Lord Jesus Christ's appearing, which He will manifest in His own time, He who is the blessed and only Potentate [Sovereign], the King of kings and Lord of lords, who alone has immortality, dwelling in unapproachable light, whom no man has seen or can see, to whom be honor and everlasting power. Amen. (1 Timothy 6:11–15)

Command those who are rich in this present age not to be haughty, nor to trust in uncertain riches but in the living God, who gives us richly all things to enjoy. Let them do good, that they may be rich in good works, ready to give, willing to share, storing up for themselves a good foundation for the time to come, that they may lay hold on eternal life. (1 Timothy 6:17–19)

Are you willing to lose your soul, be in eternal torment in the lake of fire with Satan, and be separated from the presence of God and all that He has prepared for us forever? Are you really willing to lose your soul for materialistic gain, knowing that this is only temporary, when what God has and offers you is eternal life with Him? Truly no amount of money or recognition in this world is worth being separated from God and all His glory for eternity—and it's surely not worth spending eternity in hellfire with Satan.

There are only two choices and two places. Choose today, right now, whom you will serve, whether God or Satan. Your decision will determine where you will spend your eternal life. Choose very carefully and wisely because it will be your final choice. You won't be able to buy your way out of this one.

In the end, it profits a person nothing to gain the whole world and yet lose their soul to the devil. Do not let Satan deceive you into adopting a temporary lifestyle that could cost you your eternal soul. Please, don't allow that devil to rob you of God's plans and purpose for your life while here on earth—and your eternal life with God our Father, and Jesus Christ our Savior.

"Be not deceived, God is not mocked; for whatever a man sows, that he will also reap. For he who sows to the flesh will of the flesh reap corruption, but he who sows to the Spirit will of the Spirit reap everlasting life" (Galatians 6:7–8). And reaping comes sooner than it used to.

Nevertheless, the solid foundation of God stands, having this seal: "The Lord knows those who are His" and "Let everyone who names the name of Christ depart from iniquity" (2 Timothy 2:19).

Don't let Satan fool you, and don't fool yourself. God knows and sees all. Do not compromise the Word of God for anyone, for anything, or for any reason, because it is not worth it. Your eternal life is at risk. All of this down here on this earth is just temporary. But what God has for you is for eternity, everlasting life. We can't imagine all that He has prepared for us in our beautiful new home where we will forever be in His presence. Glory to God!

Woe To …

Woe to unjust judges, police officers, politicians, law officials, and others who are *sworn* to uphold the law, protect people and our country, and do what's best for the people and our country, yet they break the law and are only concerned about what's best for themselves. You are someone who the people elected, put in office, and trusted to run our country for the good of its citizens, yet you are only concerned about you, yourself, and yours, not the poor or middle-class people.

"Thus says the Lord of hosts: 'Execute true justice, show mercy and compassion everyone to his brother. Do not oppress the widow or the fatherless, the alien, or the poor. Let none of you plan evil in his heart against his brothers [and sisters]'" (Zechariah 7:9–10).

Woe to those who break the law and thereby cause harm to others, those who desire and choose to walk in unrighteousness and do all kind of wickedness, those who know the right thing to do but will not do it for whatever reason, and those who have little or no regard for others. There are those who are prejudiced based on the color of people's skin, or their gender, or where they live or came from. These are the same people who have no love for others and have much hatred in their hearts. They are the ones who say that there is no God. Then there are those who believe there is a God but refuse to obey Him.

Woe to those who choose to do it their way instead of God's way, those who do not believe in God the Father and Jesus Christ His Son and do not accept Him as Lord and Savior. Woe unto you! What will be your final fate?

Know this one thing: what you do to others will eventually be done unto you. The seeds that you sow will be reaped someday, whether by you personally or someone you love very much. So respect people and treat them the way you want to be treated.

Almighty God sees all, knows all, and is everywhere at the same time. Therefore, there is nowhere that you can run to hide. And you can't block any sounds from God, as He hears your thoughts even before you whisper words or speak them out loud. Individually, we will all stand before God to be judged, and no one else can stand in our place. Therefore, each of us must work out our own salvation. You and you alone will be held accountable for yourself.

God's love, grace, and mercy is everlasting. He has given us more than enough time and countless chances to get our lives in order, to do the honest thing, and to choose life (Him) or death (Satan). And although He is a God of love, He is also a God of justice and wrath. It would not be fair if He were to allow the wicked to go unpunished. The unrighteous and the wicked and the righteous *cannot* and *will not* live together in God's kingdom, the New Jerusalem. It would be against God's will and plan for His children (the righteous).

So, there will be a separation of the two, and everyone will be judged and rewarded according to every idle word that they have spoken and everything that they have done (small or great, right or wrong). The righteous will reign with God forever, and the unrighteous will be cast into the lake that burns with fire and brimstone forever with Satan, his demons (fallen angels), the Antichrist, the false prophet, Satan's followers, and all the people who neither believed in nor accepted God the Father and His Son Jesus Christ.

Woe to those who refuse to admit and confess their sin, ask Jesus Christ for forgiveness, and accept Him into their lives as Lord and Savior. Jesus gave His life on the cross for the sins of the world, and God raised Him on the third day for our justification. Those who do not believe in His works or His Word now must face judgment and suffer the consequences for their sins, for the choices that they have made in this life.

> Woe unto them that call evil good, and good evil; that put darkness for light, and light for darkness; that put bitter for sweet, and sweet for bitter! (Isaiah 5:20 KJV)

Woe unto them that are wise in their own eyes, and prudent in their own sight! (Isaiah 5:21 KJV)

Woe unto them that are mighty to drink wine, and men of strength to mingle strong drink. (Isaiah 5:22 KJV)

Woe to those who seek deep to hide their counsel far from the Lord, and their works are in the dark: They say, "Who sees us?" and, "Who knows us?" (Isaiah 29:15)

"Woe to the rebellious children," says the Lord, "who takes counsel, but not of Me, and who devise plans, but not of My Spirit, that they may add sin to sin." (Isaiah 30:1)

Woe to you who plunder, though you have not been plundered; and you who deal treacherously, though they have not dealt treacherously with you! When you cease plundering, you will be plundered; when you make an end of dealing treacherously, they will deal treacherously with you. (Isaiah 33:1)

Woe to those who rise early in the morning, that they may follow intoxicating drink; who continue until night, till wine inflames them! (Isaiah 5:11)

Woe to those who draw iniquity with cords of vanity [emptiness or falsehood], and sin as if with a cart rope. (Isaiah 5:18)

Woe to men mighty at drinking wine, Woe to men valiant for mixing intoxicating drink. Who justify the wicked for a bribe and take away justice from the righteous man! (Isaiah 5:22–23)

Woe to them who are rebellious and have not obeyed the voice of the Lord God, have not received correction, have not trusted in Him, have not drawn near to Him, have not believed in Jesus Christ His Son, and have not accepted Him as their Lord and Savior. Woe to those who have walked away, have turned from following and serving the Lord, and have not sought Him or inquired of Him. (See Zephaniah 3:2.)

Woe to them, for they have fled from Me! Destruction to them, because they have transgressed against Me! Though I have redeemed them, yet they have spoken lied against Me. They did not cry out to Me with their whole heart when they wailed upon their beds. They rebel against Me; though I disciplined and strengthened their arms, yet they devised evil against Me. (Hosea 7:13–15)

But they do not regard the work of the Lord, nor consider the operation of His hands. (Isaiah 5:12)

For they being ignorant of God's righteousness, and seeking to establish their own righteousness, have not submitted to the righteousness of God. (Romans 10:3)

Therefore Sheol [hell] has enlarged itself and opened its mouth beyond measure; their glory and their multitude and their pomp, and he who is jubilant, shall descend into it. (Isaiah 5:14)

"I, the Lord, have spoken it; it shall come to pass, and I will do it; I will not hold back, nor will I spare, nor will I relent; according to your ways and according to your deeds they will judge you," says the Lord God. (Ezekiel 24:14)

For there is no respect of persons with God. (Romans 2:11 KJV)

Behold, all souls are mine; as the soul of the father, so also the soul of the son is mine: the soul that sinneth, it shall die. (Ezekiel 18:4 KJV)

"But if a man is just and does what is lawful and right …; if he has not oppressed anyone, but has restored the debtor his pledge; has robbed no one by violence, but has given his bread to the hungry and covered the naked with clothing; if he has not exacted usury nor taken any increase, but has withdrawn his hand from iniquity and executed true judgment between man and man; if he has walked in My statues and kept My judgments faithfully—he is just; he shall surely live!" says the Lord God. (Ezekiel 18:5, 7–9)

Yet you say, "The way of the Lord is not fair." Hear now ... is it not My ways which is fair, and your ways which are not fair? When a righteous man turns away from his righteousness, commits iniquity, and dies in it, it is because of the iniquity which he has done that he dies. Again, when a wicked man turns away from the wickedness which he committed, and does what is lawful and right, he preserves himself alive. Because he considers and turns away from all the transgressions which he committed, he shall surely live; he shall not die. (Ezekiel 18:25–28)

But we want to say that God isn't fair when in fact it is we ourselves who are not fair. We commit sin, *not* God. He didn't force us to commit sin; it was our choice. We knew the consequences because He has already told us that the wages of sin is death.

My dear friends, it appears to me that we are responsible for the choices that we make, and we have no right to blame God. It is our fault! We make the choice whether to live (forever with Jesus) or die (being eternally separated from God and spending eternity in hell, in torment, in a lake that burns with fire and brimstone forever and where there is total darkness and gnashing of teeth). God allows us to make our own choices in this life. He gave us free will. He will not force us to choose or even accept what He has chosen for us, nor will He force us to love Him, accept Him, or believe in Him or in Jesus Christ His Son. We will be held accountable for every choice and decision that we make, whether good or bad.

We must come to Him of our own free will, and out of love and respect for Him with appreciation and thanks for His loving us so much that He gave His only begotten Son, Jesus Christ, to die for our sins on the cross and rise from the grave on the third day, so that we could once again have fellowship and commune with Him and have a chance to live and not die.

We can choose to spend our eternal life with Him in that place that Jesus prepared for us well over two thousand years ago, or we can choose to spend our eternal life with Satan in hell, a place that has been prepared for Satan, his demons (fallen angels who rebelled against God in heaven), and the wicked. It is a place where the spirit will dwell in darkness in unquenchable fire in indescribable conditions, and in pain and torment forever. (Read Romans 4:24–25; John 14:3; Isaiah 5:14; Mark 9:44; Revelation 20:14.)

Believe in the Lord Jesus Christ, who gave His life to purchase our salvation; who rose from the grave for our justification, so we could once again be in right standing with God our Father and fellowship with Him; and who is coming back soon (as He said He would) to take us home to that place He has prepared for us.

Remember, we are a spirit, and we live in a body. Our spirit will never die. Our flesh (the body) will return to dust, and our spirit will return to Almighty God who gave it. Then He will determine where our spirit will reside for eternity. And that will be in one of two places—*heaven* or *hell*. There is *no in between.*

God our heavenly Father desires that all be saved and no one perish. That is why He sent His Son Jesus Christ to die on the cross for our sins. God raised Him from the grave on the third day for our justification, to reconcile us to Him, so that our relationship and fellowship with Him could be restored (as it was in the beginning with Adam and Eve when they were in the Garden of Eden, before they were thrown out because of their disobedience). Jesus is now seated at the right hand of God's throne, making intercession on our behalf, pleading our case.

And because He is a just God, He wants us to have a chance to choose of our own free will whom we will serve and where we would spend our eternal lives. He loves us, but He is a holy God and cannot and will not violate our right to choose. Nor will He tolerate sin. The wages of sin is death, but the gift of God is eternal life. I hope, and Jesus hopes, that you choose life.

Don't let Satan trick or fool you, because he wants to kill you, steal from you, and destroy you physically and spiritually. He doesn't care about you except to take your soul to hell, which will destroy you spiritually (resulting in total annihilation and permanent separation from God and Jesus Christ). That is his goal. (Read Romans 5:1, 2, 6–12; 23.)

"Jesus said: 'The thief does not come except to steal, and to kill, and to destroy. I have come that they may have life, and that they may have it more abundantly. I am the good Shepherd. The good shepherd gives His life for the sheep'" (John 10:10–11).

Jesus Christ, the Son of God, is the Good Shepherd. He gave Himself (His life) for our sins, so that He might deliver us from this present evil age (world), according to the will of God the Father (Galatians 1:4). He loves us so very much in spite of us. He desires for us to have a good and prosperous life here on earth, and He yearns for us to live our eternal life in happiness with joy unspeakable, full of His glory, in the place in heaven (or His kingdom) that He has prepared for us.

Satan's purpose and goal is to prevent us from believing in Jesus Christ, accepting Him as our Lord and Savior, and living with Him forever. From the day God kicked Satan and his demon angels out of heaven, Satan's vow and goal to get back at God has been to take you to hell along with him. He has already made a reservation for you. However, you can cancel that reservation right now, in the name of Jesus, by saying a short prayer with me. Satan can't win unless you let him. Jesus has already won, having defeated him over two thousand years ago, and He has purchased our salvation with His precious blood.

You have the power, privilege, and opportunity to choose at this very moment whom you will serve and where you will spend eternity. Will you serve God or humankind? Will you spend your eternal life with God our Father and Jesus Christ our Lord and Savior, along with our heavenly family, or will you spend eternity with Satan, demons, and all the wicked and unrighteous people who didn't believe in the gospel of Jesus Christ? Their eternity will be spent in a place called Hades (hell) that burns with unquenchable fire and brimstone forever, a place where there is darkness, indescribable constant pain, torture, maggots, and gnashing of teeth. There is no way out of this place. You will be totally separated from God. He will not hear your cries, and He won't be able to save you. It will be too late.

Whom do you choose? It's your choice, not the choice of your spouse, child, parents, friend, partner, enemy, or employer—no one! You can and must choose of your own free will, and you will be held responsible for the choice you make. I pray that it is the right choice because you will have to live with it forever. I hope that you choose Jesus Christ so that you can live in the place that He has prepared for us where there is joy unspeakable, full of His glory. For there is no other name given whereby you can be saved but the name of Jesus.

Prayer of Forgiveness

Will you pray the following prayer with your whole heart?

> Father God, I come to You right now in the name of Jesus Christ, asking You to forgive me of all my sins. I believe in my heart that Jesus died for my sins on the cross and rose from the grave on the third day. According to Your Word (Romans 10:9), if I confess with my mouth the Lord Jesus and believe in my heart that You raised Him from the dead, I will be saved. Father, I confess, and I believe. Thank You for salvation, for making me whole, and for delivering me out of darkness into Your marvelous light. Amen.

Dear brothers and sisters, the Word of God says: "For with the heart one believes unto righteousness, and with the mouth confession is made unto salvation; and whoever believes on Jesus Christ will not be put to shame" (Romans 10:10–11). "For whoever calls on the name of the Lord shall be saved" (Romans 10:13). So, if you said that prayer in all sincerity, then you are saved! Welcome to the family of God! I rejoice with you, along with God, the angels in heaven, and your new family on earth and in heaven. May you abide in Him and in His Words, and may He abide in you.

Thus Says the Lord

God wants you to know that He knows who you are, and He wants you to know who He is. He wants you to know that there is no other God and there is no one who can be compared to Him. Listen with your whole heart to what the Lord says. He who has an ear, let him hear:

Thus says the Lord, your Redeemer, and who formed you from the womb: "I am the Lord, who makes all things, who stretches out the heavens all alone, who spreads abroad the earth by Myself; who frustrates the signs of the babblers and drive the diviners mad; who turns wise men backward; and makes their knowledge foolishness; who confirms the word of His servant; and performs the counsel of His messengers." (Isaiah 44:24–26)

> Thus says the Lord: "Keep justice, and do righteousness, for My salvation is about to come, and My righteousness to be revealed. Blessed is the man who does this, and the son of man who lays hold on it. … And keeps his hand from doing evil." (Isaiah 56:1–2)

> Thus says the Lord: "Why, when I came, was there no man? Why, when I called, was there none to answer? Is My hand shortened at all that it cannot redeem? Or have I no power to deliver?" (Isaiah 50:2)

> "Listen to Me: Who have been upheld by Me from birth, who have been carried from the womb: Even to your old age, I am He, and even to gray hairs I will carry you! I have made, and I will bear; even I will carry, and will deliver you." (Isaiah 46:3–4)

Thus saith the Lord, "In an acceptable time have I heard thee, and in a day of salvation have I help thee: and I will preserve you." (Isaiah 49:8 KJV)

Can a woman forget her nursing child, and not have compassion on the son of her womb? Surely, they may forget, yet I will not forget you. See, I have inscribed you on the palms of My hands; your walls are continually before Me. (Isaiah 49:15–16)

For I know their works and their thoughts: it shall come, that I will gather all nations and tongues; and they shall come, and see my glory. (Isaiah 66:18 KJV)

The Lord God Almighty Is Saying to You, "Come to Me. Now Is the Accepted Time."

Come to Me, all you who labor and are heavy laden, and I
will give you rest. Take My yoke upon you and learn from Me,
for I am gentle and lowly in heart, and you will find rest for
your soul. For My yoke is easy and My burden is light.
—Matthew 11:28–30

Let not your heart be troubled; neither let it be afraid.
—John 14:27

Jesus loves you so very much and wants to save you from eternal destruction. God is calling you right now. Won't you please hear His voice and answer His call before it is too late, before He stops calling you (since you will not answer)? Put your faith and trust in Jesus Christ because He is the only one who can save you. You cannot save yourself, nor can humankind save you. Come to Jesus right now and be saved; don't be stubborn or worry about what someone may say about you or how they might feel about you, for the next second, or even the next moment, may be too late.

Do not negotiate with the devil. I don't care what he says, or what or whom he uses (money, fame, material things, spouse, children, parents, siblings, relative, friends, enemies, or even Satan himself), to hinder you and try to keep you from coming to Jesus and surrendering your life and heart to Him. Do not be intimidated by Satan. Resist him, give him no place in your life, and he will flee from you. The Word of God is your only weapon against Satan. So stay in the Word, stay in prayer, be watchful, stand in faith, be steadfast, and be unmovable.

Jesus Christ is saying the following things to you right now:

Ho! Everyone who thirsts, come to the waters; and you who have no money, Come, buy and eat. Yes, come, buy wine and milk without money and without price. Why do you spend money for what is not bread, and your wages for what does not satisfy? Listen carefully to Me, and eat what is good, and let your soul delight itself in abundance. Incline your ear, and come to Me. Hear, and your soul shall live; and I will make an everlasting covenant with you. (Isaiah 55:1–3)

Let not your heart be troubled: ye believe in God, believe also in me. (John 14:1 KJV)

I am the way, the truth, and the life: No man cometh unto the Father but by me. (John 14:6 KJV)

"Come now, and let us reason together," says the Lord. "Though your sins are like scarlet, they shall be as white as snow; though they are red like crimson, they shall be as wool. If you are willing and obedient, you shall eat the good of the land; but if you refuse and rebel, you shall be devoured by the sword"; for the mouth of the Lord has spoken. (Isaiah 1:18–20)

For He saith, I have heard thee in a time accepted, and in the day of salvation have I succoured thee: behold, now is the accepted time; behold, now is the day of salvation. (2 Corinthians 6:2 KJV)

"Wherefore come out from among them, and be separate," saith the Lord, "and touch not the unclean thing; and I will receive you, and will be a father unto you, and ye shall be my sons and daughters," saith the Lord Almighty. (2 Corinthians 6:17–18 KJV)

Jesus promised that He would always be with us and never leave us or forsake us. He wants to give you peace, happiness, blessings, unspeakable joy, and everlasting life. He wants to be your Lord and King and reign over your life—if you'll allow Him.

If you hear the voice of Jesus in your heart today, please answer and say yes to His will. Now is the right time, for the Groom (Jesus Christ) is coming for His bride (the church). Will you be prepared to meet your Groom? I pray that we all will be prepared.

Repent! Invite Jesus Christ into your Heart. Believe and Accept Him as Lord and Savior

Therefore be zealous and repent.
—Revelation 3:19

Repent, for the kingdom of heaven is at hand!
—Matthew 3:2

I [Jesus] tell you, no: … But unless you
repent you will all likewise perish.
—Luke 13:3, 5

Repent, and let every one of you be baptized in the name of Jesus Christ
for the remission of sins; and you shall receive the gift of the Holy Spirit.
—Acts 2:38

Now therefore, amend your ways and your doings, and obey
the voice of the Lord your God; then the Lord will relent
concerning the doom that He has pronounced against you.
—Jeremiah 26:13

The judgment of God is coming! Repent, turn to God now and
change your mind, your way of thinking. Call upon His name, and
He will save you; restore you, and pour out His Spirit upon you.
—Joel 2:1–2

Our God is merciful, gracious, kind, patient, and long-suffering, and His grace is amazing, but everyone must repent of their sins, ask for forgiveness, and accept Jesus Christ as Lord and Savior. And those who do not must suffer the consequences of rejecting God's Son who died for the sins of the world.

It doesn't matter who you are or what you have done. It doesn't matter if you're rich or poor. Your gender or race doesn't matter, or even where you live, for God is Lord over all people and offers salvation to everyone who calls upon Him in faith. We all must repent and ask God to forgive us of our sins. It doesn't matter if you go to church seven days a week, three hundred sixty-five days a year; give to the poor; visit the sick; visit those in prison; feed the hungry; set up foundations to help others; go on foreign missions; or even give your life for someone else. Although these things are good and honorable, your salvation is based not on works but on faith in Jesus Christ.

For the Son of man, Jesus Christ, has come to seek and to save them who are lost (Luke 19:10). He came to call sinners to repentance, to save their souls, to make them whole again, and to give them the chance to live forever with Him and share in His glory that the Father has bestowed upon Him from the foundation of the world—in the beginning.

Sin can't be hidden from God. He knows and sees everything. Acknowledge your faults and your sins (no one is perfect), confess them to Jesus, and ask Him for forgiveness. He is a forgiving God and Savior. He wants more than anything for us to be saved and live with Him forever in His kingdom. This is the reason Jesus came. It is the original plan of God.

> Perhaps everyone will listen and turn from his evil way that I may relent concerning the calamity which I purpose to bring on them because of the evil of their doings. (Jeremiah 26:3)

> For all have sinned and fall short of the glory of God, being justified freely by His grace through the redemption that is in Christ Jesus, whom God set forth as a propitiation [mercy seat] by His blood, through faith, to demonstrate His righteousness, because in His forbearance God has passed over the sins that were previously committed, to demonstrate at the present time His righteousness, that He might be just and the justifier of the one who has faith in Jesus. (Romans 3.23–26)

O God, You know my foolishness; and my sins are not hidden from you. (Psalm 69:5)

I acknowledge my sin to You, and my iniquity I have not hidden. I said, "I will confess my transgressions to the Lord," and You forgave the iniquity of my sin. Selah. (Psalm 32:5)

The soul who sins shall die. (Ezekiel 18:20)

The wages of sin is death, but the gift of God is eternal life. (Romans 6:23)

If you confess with your mouth the Lord Jesus and believe in your heart that God has raised Him from the dead, you will be saved. For with the heart one believes unto righteousness, and with the mouth confession is made unto salvation. (Romans 10:9–10)

For the Scripture says, "Whoever believes on Him will not be put to shame." (Romans 10:11)

For by grace you are saved through faith; and that not of yourselves: it is the gift of God: Not of works, lest any man should boast. (Ephesians 2:8–9)

But as many as received Him, to them He [Jesus] gave power to become the sons of God, even to them that believe on His name. (John 1:12)

Nor is there salvation in any other, for there is no other name under heaven given among men by which we must be saved. (Acts 4:12)

Jesus Christ is the only *name* and the only *way*.

Thus says the Lord God: "Repent, turn away from your idols, and turn your faces away from all your abominations." (Ezekiel 14:6)

"Therefore I will judge you ... everyone according to their ways," says the Lord God. "Repent, and turn from your transgressions, so that iniquity will not be your ruin. Cast away from you all the transgressions which you have committed and get yourselves a new heart and a new spirit. For why should you die? For I have no pleasure in the death of one who dies [in sin]," says the Lord God. "Therefore turn and live!" (Ezekiel 18:30–32)

And your covenant with death shall be disannulled, and your agreement with hell shall not stand. (Isaiah 28:18 KJV)

Thus saith the Lord of hosts, the God of Israel, Amend your ways and your doings, and I will cause you to dwell in this place. (Jeremiah 7:3 KJV)

For whosoever shall call upon the name of the Lord shall be saved. (Romans 10:13 KJV)

Therefore I abhor myself, and repent. (Job 42:6)

Break up the fallow ground of your heart. Jesus is standing and knocking at the door of your heart, waiting anxiously for you to open the door and invite Him into your heart and your life. Won't you please answer Him? I beg of you, on behalf of Jesus Christ, be reconciled to God. "For God the Father made Jesus Christ who knew no sin to be sin for us, that we might become the righteousness of God in Him" (2 Corinthians 5:21). He loves us so very much.

"For He says: 'In an acceptable time I have heard you, and in the day of salvation I have helped you.' Behold, now is the accepted time; behold, now is the day of salvation" (2 Corinthians 6:2). "The Lord was ready to save me" (Isaiah 38:20).

Jesus is always ready to save us. The question is, are you ready to be saved? Call upon the name of the Lord right now! Don't wait another second.

I say to you that likewise there will be more joy in heaven over one sinner who repents than over ninety-nine just persons who need no repentance. (Luke 15:7)

Those who are well have no need of a physician, but those who are sick. … For I did not come to call the righteous, but sinners, to repentance. (Matthew 9:12, 13)

Thus it is written, and thus it was necessary for the Christ to suffer and to rise from the dead the third day, and that repentance and remission of sins should be preached in His name to all nations. (Luke 24:46–47)

Repent therefore and be converted, that your sins may be blotted out, so that times of refreshing may come from the presence of the Lord, and that He may send Jesus Christ who preached to you before, whom heaven must receive until the times of restoration of all things, which God has spoken by the mouth of all of His holy prophets since the world began. (Acts 3:19–21)

And it shall come to pass, that whoever call on the name of the Lord shall be delivered. (Joel 2:32 KJV)

But as many as received him [Jesus Christ], to them gave he power to become the sons of God, even to them that believe on his name. (John 1:12 KJV)

And now why tarriest thou? Arise and be baptized, and wash away thy sins, calling on the name of the Lord. (Acts 22:16 KJV)

I, even I, am he that blotteth out thy transgressions for mine own sake, and I will not remember thy sins. (Isaiah 43:25 KJV)

He will turn again, he will have compassion upon us; he will subdue our iniquities; and thou wilt cast all their sins into the depths of the sea. (Micah 7:19 KJV)

My dear friends, our God has forgiven and forgotten your sins if you have sincerely repented of that sin. For all has been covered by the blood of Jesus Christ. If you truly believe in Jesus Christ and call on Him in all sincerity with your whole heart, you will be saved. It doesn't matter what you have done, He will still save you if you ask Him. Only God can forgive you of all your sins and give you the gift of salvation and eternal life with Him.

Salvation is in no other name but the name Jesus. Call upon Him right now and ask Him to circumcise the foreskin of your heart. Then obey and follow Christ. The plan of salvation is offered only through God's Son Jesus Christ. Please don't continue to let Satan deceive you.

Backslider, Return to God—Now! (It's Time for You to Come Back Home)

I will heal their backsliding, I will love them freely;
for mine anger is turned away from him.
—Hosea 14:4 (KJV)

For it is impossible for those who were once enlightened, and have tasted
the heavenly gift, and have become partakers of the Holy Spirit, and
have tasted the good word of God and the powers of the age to come,
if they fall away, to renew them again to repentance, since they crucify
again for themselves the Son of God and put Him to an open shame.
—Hebrews 6:4–6

The backslider in heart will be filled with his own ways,
but a good man will be satisfied from above.
—Proverbs 14:14

My people are bent on backsliding from Me. Though
they call to the Most High, none at all exalt Him.
—Hosea 11:7

Return, you backsliding children, and I will heal your backslidings.
—Jeremiah 3:22

Until we can truly with our whole hearts put Jesus Christ first and foremost,
before anything or anyone else, in our lives, we cannot totally fulfill God's
plan, purpose, and destiny for our lives. God our Father and Jesus Christ

His Son, our Lord and Savior, wants you to return home, to come back to Him, with your whole heart. He wants you to be fully committed to Him in every way, shape, and form. He wants you to renew your vows with Him. He is willing and ready to forgive, save, restore, heal, and cover you. He desires to be reconciled with you so that you can be in fellowship and have a personal relationship with Him once again.

Our God is full of mercy, love, grace, and kindness. He doesn't want anyone to perish but wants all to be saved. Come back home; return to Him now! Our heavenly Father is waiting for you with His loving arms wide open, longing to embrace you. He misses you, He loves you, and His heart pants for you. Won't you please return to Him now, right at this moment, while there is still time? For the next moment or second may not come for you.

> For if, after they have escaped the pollutions of the world through the knowledge of the Lord and Savior Jesus Christ, they are again entangled in them and overcome, the latter end is worse for them than the beginning. For it would have been better for them not to have known the way of righteousness, than having known it, to turn from the holy commandment delivered to them. But it has happened to them according to the true proverb: "A dog returns to his vomit, and a sow [pig], having washed, to her wallowing in the mire." (2 Peter 2:20–22)

> Therefore say to them, "Thus says the Lord of hosts: 'Return to Me,' says the Lord of hosts, 'and I will return to you,' says the Lord of hosts. "Do not be like your fathers, to whom the former prophets preached, saying, 'Thus says the Lord of hosts: "Turn now from your evil ways and your evil deeds." 'But they did not hear Me,'" says the Lord. (Zechariah 1:3–4)

> I have formed you, you are My servant; return to Me, for I have redeemed you. (Isaiah 44:21–22)

> "Return …," says the Lord; "I will not cause My anger to fall on you. For I am merciful," says the Lord; "I will not remain angry forever. Only acknowledge your iniquity, that you have

transgressed against the Lord your God, And have scattered your charms [ways]. ... And you have not obeyed My voice," says the Lord. "Return, O backsliding children," says the Lord; "for I am married to you." (Jeremiah 3:12–14)

Call un to me, and I will answer thee, and show thee great and mighty things, which thou knowest not. (Jeremiah 33:3 KJV)

"If you will return ...." says the Lord ..., "to Me; and if you will put away your abominations out of My sight, Then you shall not be moved." (Jeremiah 4:1)

Behold, I will bring health and cure, and I will cure them, and will reveal unto them the abundance of peace and truth. (Jeremiah 33:6 KJV)

And I will cleanse them from all their iniquity, whereby they have sinned against me; and I will pardon all their iniquities, whereby they have sinned, and whereby they have transgressed against me. (Jeremiah 33:8 KJV)

For thus says the Lord ...: "Break up the fallow ground, and do not sow among thorns. Circumcise yourselves to the Lord and take away the foreskins of your hearts. ... Lest My fury come forth like fire, and burn so that no one can quench it, Because of the evil of your doings. Wash your heart from wickedness, that you may be saved. How long shall evil thoughts lodge within you?" (Jeremiah 4:3–4, 14)

Wash yourselves, make yourselves clean; put away the evil of your doings from before My eyes. Cease to do evil, learn to do good; seek justice, rebuke the oppressor; defend the fatherless, plead for the widow. (Isaiah 1:16–17)

Now therefore, thus saith the Lord of hosts; Consider your ways. (Haggai 1:5 KJV)

Thus says the Lord: "Will one fall and not rise? Why has this people slidden back ...? They hold fast to deceit, they refuse to return. I listened and heard, but they do not speak aright. No man repented of his wickedness, saying, 'What have I done?' Everyone turned to his own course, as the horse rushes into the battle." (Jeremiah 8:4–6)

Remember therefore from where you have fallen; repent and do your first works, or else I will come to you quickly and remove your lampstand from its place—unless you repent. (Revelation 2:5)

"Now therefore," says the Lord, "turn to Me with all your heart, with fasting, with weeping, and with mourning." (Joel 2:12)

Come and let us return to the Lord; for He has torn; but He will heal us; He has stricken, but He will bind us up. (Hosea 6:1)

The Lord hath appeared of old unto me, saying, Yea, I have loved thee with an everlasting love: therefore with lovingkindness have I drawn thee. (Jeremiah 31:3 KJV)

And I will betroth thee unto me forever; yea, I will betroth thee unto me in righteousness, and in judgment, and in lovingkindness, and in mercies. I will even betroth thee unto me in faithfulness; and thou shalt know the Lord. (Hosea 2:19–20 KJV)

The Word of God tells us that if we confess our sins, God is faithful and just to forgive us of our sins, and will cleanse us from all unrighteousness (1 John 1:9). "And that if we confess with our mouth that Jesus Christ is Lord, and Savior of the world; and if believe in our heart that God the Father raised Him from the dead; we will be saved. For with the heart one believes unto righteousness, and with the mouth confession is made unto salvation. … Jesus said: Whoever calls on His name will be saved" (Romans 10:9–10, 13). Call upon His name for deliverance right now!

However, the Word of God also tells us that those who do not believe in Jesus Christ are condemned already because they have not believed and do not have faith in the name of God's only begotten Son (John 3:18). Everyone has sinned, and if we say that we have not sinned, we're only fooling ourselves. We are liars, we make God a liar (God cannot lie, for

He is the Truth, and He's not a human being that He should lie), and His Word is not in us, because all have sinned and fallen short of God's glory (1 John 1:8; Romans 3:23). We must ask God to forgive us of our sins and cleanse us from all unrighteousness. Don't wait until it's too late.

"Behold, all souls are mine. ... The soul who sins shall die" (Ezekiel 18:4).

Listen to what Jesus says in John 6:40: "And this is the will of him that sent me, that everyone which seeth the Son, and believeth on him, may have everlasting life: and I will raise him up at the last day" (KJV). Glory to God! Isn't that good news?

Dear friends, let us search our hearts and examine our ways and turn back to the Lord our God before it is too late. Let us lift up our hearts and hands to our God who is in heaven.

If you are sincere, and if you're seriously ready to return to Him, please say this short prayer with me now with your whole heart, and God will hear it and save you. Don't give up on Him, because He has not given up on you.

Father God, I return to You. Forgive me of my sins, forgive me for being disobedient, heal my backsliding, take away the foreskin of my heart, take away the stoniness of my heart and give me a heart of flesh. Baptize and fill me with Your Holy Spirit. Thank You for never leaving me or forsaking me, and thank You for never giving up on me, even when others gave up on me and I gave up on myself.

> I confess with my mouth that Jesus Christ is Your Son, that He is Lord and Savior, and that He died on the cross for my sins and for the sins of the whole world. I believe in my heart that You raised Jesus from the dead on the third day for my justification and that He is coming back to this earth any day for His people and to establish His kingdom.

> Thank You for reconciliation and salvation. Thank You for eternal life. Thank You for Your mercy and grace and for loving me unconditionally. I rededicate and surrender my life totally to You. In Jesus's name, I pray. Amen.

It Is Too Late for You to Repent or Ask for Forgiveness When You See Jesus Christ Coming from Heaven

He that is unjust, let him be unjust still: and he which is
filthy, let him be filthy still: and he that is righteous, let him
be righteous still: and he that is holy, let him be holy still.
—Revelation 22:11 (KJV)

God has given you and me more than enough time to get ourselves ready, to prepare for the day of His return, that day when He will take us to live in our new and eternal home. He gave us His only begotten Son, Jesus Christ, that whosoever believes in Him would not perish but have everlasting life. He gave us His mercy, grace, love, long-sufferingness, kindness, and graciousness; countless chances to change the way we are living; and protection from our enemies and from dangers seen and unseen. He has comforted us in our times of sorrow, He has supplied our needs, and He has taken care of and protected us and our family.

Jesus Christ gave His life on the cross and shed His precious blood. He was wounded for our transgressions, bruised for our iniquities. He was mocked, spit upon, beaten, and whipped with a strap that ripped flesh out of His back as He was struck thirty-nine times. A crown of thorns was pressed on His head as blood ran down His face. Christ's face was barely recognizable to His loved ones and friends. Yet He never said or mumbled a word of complaint against His enemies. Instead He said, "Father, forgive them. They do not know what they're doing." What kind of love is this that the Father would give His Son and that His Son would give His life for humankind?

I could go on and on about what He went through for us, about His goodness and all that He has done and is doing for us. But what you need to know and must believe right now is that Jesus Christ is about to return to this earth. You must be ready and prepared to meet Him. For this time He will come as Judge to judge all people, and He will reward everyone according to their works (deeds). There will be *no* exceptions, and *no* excuses will be accepted.

All of us will spend our eternal lives someplace, for our spirits will never die. The question is, where will you spend your eternal life? There are only two places, and you must choose one:

(1) Heaven, where you will have eternal life with God the Father and Jesus Christ His Son, our Lord and Savior, along with the angels and family of God, in the place that He prepared for us, a paradise of sheer indescribable beauty that shall be called the kingdom of God, the New Jerusalem. It is a place where there is no more sickness, pain, or physical or mental suffering, no more crying, dying, hunger, loneliness, child abuse, domestic abuse, elder abuse, suicidal thoughts, robbery, prejudice, killings, violence, or crime of any kind. It is a place of unspeakable and indescribable joy, peace, and happiness where we will be in the presence of our Father God and our Lord, Savior, and King Jesus Christ, worshipping and praising Him forever, along with our loved ones and friends who made it, the angels, and the whole family of God. You can read about your new eternal home in the book of Revelation 21:1–27; 22:1–5.

(2) Hell, where you will spend your eternal life with Satan, demons (fallen angels), the Antichrist, false prophets, the wicked and unrighteous, and those who rejected and did not believe in God or His Son Jesus Christ, in a place with indescribable and constant torment that burns with unquenchable fire and brimstone. It is a place where there is weeping, gnashing of teeth, darkness, cries of sorrow and pain, worms that crawl over you, and the most terrible unbearable odor. You will suffer physically, mentally, and emotionally, and you will be spiritually separated from God forever. (He will not hear you when you call upon Him to help you.) You don't want to go to this place that was purposely prepared for Satan and

his demons only. You can read about your new eternal home in Revelation 19:20; 20:10, 14, 15; 21:8.

Dear sisters and brothers, now is the time to get yourselves ready to meet with the Creator and Savior of the world. Don't wait until it is too late or until you see Him coming in the clouds. Call upon His name right now.

When you look up and see Jesus Christ coming, it will be too late for you to suddenly want to live a holy life. It will be too late to repent, too late to ask Him to forgive you of your sins, and too late to get things right with Him. We are now in the final stage: no exchanges, no refunds, no excuses, and no forgiveness. God will now be silent; He will not hear you.

"So, my friends, seek the Lord while He may be found, call upon Him while He is near. Let the wicked forsake his way, and the unrighteous man his thoughts; let him return to the Lord, and His will have mercy on him; and to our God, for He will abundantly pardon" (Isaiah 55:6–7).

If you hear His voice today (in your heart, in your spirit), do not harden your heart. Open the door of your heart and let Jesus in. He loves you so very much and has a wonderful plan for your life. How much more does He have to do to prove His love for you?

"Jesus said: 'Behold, I stand at the door and knock. If anyone hears My voice and opens the door, I will come in to him and dine with him, and he with Me'" (Revelation 3:20).

My dear friend, only *you* can answer the call, and only *you* can open the door. I pray that you will hear Him knocking, hear His voice, and open the door of your heart. The choice is yours.

Every one of us has a personal responsibility to work out our own salvation with fear and trembling, for it is God who works in you both to will and to do for His good pleasure (Philippians 2:12–13). Each one of us will personally be held accountable for the things that we say and do. We will not be able to point a finger at or blame anyone else for our actions. Excuses will not be accepted or tolerated on the day of judgment.

"Therefore you are inexcusable, O man [or woman], whoever you are" (Romans 2:1). "But he who does wrong will be repaid for what he has done, and there is no partiality" (Colossians 3:25).

Reconciled to God

Now all things are of God, who has reconciled us to Himself through
Jesus Christ, and has given us the ministry of reconciliation, that is, that
God was in Christ reconciling the world to Himself, not imputing their
trespasses to them, and has committed to us the word of reconciliation.
Now then, we are ambassadors for Christ, as though God were pleading
through us: we implore you on Christ's behalf, be reconciled to God.
—2 Corinthians 5:18–20

It is because of the death and shed blood of Jesus Christ on the cross that
we have been reconciled to God. We have been changed; our relationship
with God has been restored; and we can once again coexist in harmony.
Any problems that had previously separated us that were caused by
Adam and Eve's disobedience have now been forever resolved and settled
by Jesus Christ. We can once again have communion and fellowship
with God because the middle wall of separation that was between us
(due to sin) was broken down when Jesus died on the cross for our sins.
Jesus never sinned, yet He became sin for us so that we could have the
opportunity to become the righteousness of God through Him and
obtain eternal life.

When Jesus purchased our salvation, He made the ultimate sacrifice
and paid a ransom for us that no one else could pay. He gave His life and
paid with His precious blood. He did something that no one else could
do, all because He loves us and wants us to live with Him forever. God
desires to prosper us and fulfill His plan and purpose for our life. But we
have to obey and allow Him.

For if, when we were enemies, we were reconciled to God by the death of his Son, much more, being reconciled, we shall be saved by his life. And not only so, but we also joy in God through our Lord Jesus Christ, by whom we have now received the atonement [reconciliation]. Wherefore, as by one man [Adam] sin entered into the world, and death through sin; and so death passed upon all men, for that all have sinned. (Romans 5:10–12 KJV)

But the free gift is not like the offense. …For if by the one man's offense death reigned through the one, much more those who receive abundance of grace and the gift of righteousness will reign in life through the One, Jesus Christ. Therefore, as through one man's offense judgment came to all men, resulting in condemnation, even so through one Man's [Jesus Christ] righteous act the free gift came to all men, resulting in justification of life. For as by one man's disobedience many were made sinners, also by one Man's obedience many will be made righteous. (Romans 5:15, 17–19)

Moreover the law entered that the offense might abound. But where sin abounded, grace abounded much move, so that as sin reigned in death, even so grace might reign through righteousness to eternal life through Jesus Christ our Lord. (Romans 5:20–21)

Now if we died with Christ, we believe that we shall also live with Him, knowing that Christ, having been raised from the dead, dies no more. Death no longer has dominion over Him. For the death that He died, He died to sin once for all; but the life that He lives, He lives to God. (Romans 6:8–10)

Sin, my friends, no longer has dominion over us because of what Jesus did for us at the cross. And we should not continually live in or commit sin. We are no longer under the law but are under God's grace. And where sin abounds, grace abounds even more.

Remember, every single person on planet Earth, underneath the earth, and on any other planet will have to stand before God on the day of judgment and give an account of their deeds and faith in Jesus Christ. And you will be rewarded accordingly: eternal life with God or eternal death and torment, living in total darkness with Satan, his demons, and all the evil, wicked, and unrighteous people.

And, yes, you will be fully aware and conscious of those around you, of your eternal suffering and horrible pain, of the darkness, of the weeping and gnashing of teeth, of the worms and things crawling over your body, of the constant torment, and of the unquenchable fire and brimstone that burns forever and ever. There will be no end to your torment, no escape, no peace, no love, no presence of God, and no mercy.

Satan, that old devil, will have you right where he wants you. Having fought so hard to get you, he will keep you. He will have won your soul, your spirit, and your eternal life. Don't let him win; don't let him rob you of eternal life with God! Jesus has already paid the ransom for your life with His life; that price was paid in full with His precious blood, through which we have been redeemed—we belong to Him. Therefore, Satan no longer has any claim or dominion over our lives. We have the victory through Jesus Christ our Lord, Savior, and soon-coming King.

Repent and be reconciled to God now before it is too late.

> For it pleased the Father that in Him all the fullness should dwell, and by Him to reconcile all things to Himself, by Him, whether things on the earth or things in heaven, having made peace through the blood of His cross. And you, who once were alienated and enemies in your mind by wicked works, yet now He has reconciled in the body of His flesh through death, to present you holy, and blameless, and above reproach in His sight—if indeed you continue in the faith, grounded and steadfast, and are not moved away from the hope of the gospel which you heard, which was preached to every creature under heaven. (Colossians 1:19–23)

> If you have not invited Jesus Christ into your heart and life, would you please ask Jesus to forgive you of your sins? Tell Him that you believe that He is the Son of God, that He died on the cross for your sins and those of the world, that He rose from the grave on the third day, and that He is now seated at the right hand of God the Father in heaven. Invite Him into your heart as Lord and Savior. Tell Him that you want to be prepared for His soon return for His children.

To All Christians, Born-Again Believers in Jesus Christ

Because you have kept My command to preserve, I will also keep
you from the hour of trial which shall come upon the whole
world, to test those who dwell on the earth. Behold, I am coming
quickly! Hold fast what you have, that no one may take your
crown. He who overcomes, I will make him a pillar in the temple
of My God, the New Jerusalem, which comes out of heaven
from My God. And I will write on him My new name. He who
has an ear, let him hear what the Spirit says to the churches.
—Revelation 3:10–13

What a promise! God is awesome, true to His Word, and He is truly
amazing. As true believers in Jesus Christ, we are born again of the Spirit
of God. We are new creations in Him. We now have a new way of thinking
and living, which is God's way. When you are saved, there must be a
change in your heart and your life: the way you act, talk, think, and believe
after you accept Jesus Christ as your Lord and Savior. As Christians, we
are the salt of the earth and the light of the world; therefore, we should
live a holy life, bless others, and do good works. We should let our light
shine so that others can see our good works and glorify God. Let us not
lose our saltiness or flavor, and let not our light go out, because then we
would be of no use to anyone.

Jesus told a ruler of the Jews named Nicodemus, "Most assuredly, I
say to you, unless one is born again, he cannot see the kingdom of God,
unless one is born of water and the Spirit, he cannot enter the kingdom
of God. That which is born of the flesh is flesh, and that which is born

of the Spirit is spirit. Do not marvel that I said to you, 'You must be born again'" (John 3:5–7).

> But to as many as received Him [Jesus], to them He gave the right to become children of God, to those who believe in His name: who were born, not of blood, nor of the will of flesh, nor of the will of man, but of God. (John 1:12–13)

> Therefore, if anyone is in Christ, he is a new creation; old things have passed away; behold, all things have become new. (2 Corinthians 5:17)

> Or do you not know that as many of us as were baptized into Jesus Christ were baptized into His death? Therefore we were buried with Him through baptism into death, that just as Christ was raised from the dead by the glory of the Father, even so we also should walk in newness of life (Romans 6:3–4) … are buried with Christ in baptism, in which you also were raised with Him through faith in the working of God, who raised Him from the dead. (Colossians 2:12)

When we are baptized by water, it symbolizes our faith in Jesus Christ and His work at the cross. We take part in His death and resurrection through water baptism. We go down into the water and therefore die to the old person and the old life. And when we come up out of the water, we are raised with Jesus Christ through faith and resurrected into His likeness. Therefore, we are a new creation and we walk in a spiritual newness of life.

After the completion of water baptism and spiritual baptism (with the Holy Spirit), we're telling God and the world that the old person has been crucified with Jesus, that we too have been raised from the dead by the glory of the Father, that we have been reborn by His Spirit, and that He will transform our lives and our minds as we study His Word, pray, live, and walk according to His Word in a spiritual new life, a life of holiness and righteousness. We must be born again (spiritually) if we are to enter the kingdom of God. There has got to be a change in our life.

"I indeed baptize you with water unto repentance, but He who is coming after me is mightier than I. … He will baptize you with the Holy Spirit and fire" (Matthew 3:11).

"Go therefore, and make disciples of all nations, baptizing them in the name of the Father and of the Son and of the Holy Spirit, teaching them to observe all things that I have commanded you; and lo, I am with you always, even to the end of the age. Amen" (Matthew 28:19–20).

For more on water baptism and spiritual baptism and rebirth, you may read in the King James Version Acts 2:38, 16:33, 22:16; 1 Corinthians 12:13; Luke 12:50; Mark 16:16; Matthew 3:16; Ephesians 4:5; and Hebrews 6:2.

God searches deep into the heart. He sees all, He knows all, and He is everywhere. Jesus loves us and wants you and me to be prepared and ready when He comes. As true believers in Jesus Christ, we have been imbued with power (the Holy Spirit) from God. We have been baptized and filled with the Holy Spirit and have the power to live according to God's Word, serve God, and do the work He has called us to do, which is to witness and minister to all people.

"But you shall receive power when the Holy Spirit has come upon you; and you shall be witnesses to Me … to the end of the earth" (Acts 1:8).

"And these signs shall follow them that believe; In my name shall they cast out devils; they shall speak with new tongues; They shall take up serpents; and if they drink any deadly thing, it shall not hurt them; they shall lay hands on the sick, and they shall recover" (Mark 16:17–18 KJV).

We as Christians must hold on tight to our faith, to what and whom we believe in, and to what we have in Jesus Christ. We are to love one another, be truthful, show kindness and tender mercies, pray for one another, and bear with and forgive one another. We will be known by our fruits. God knows our heart. God wants us to obey Him and be strong no matter the trials or tests we are faced with. We are to trust and rely only on Him. As children of God, we all have an assignment and responsibility to win souls for His kingdom.

To start a race isn't the real challenge—anyone can do that. The challenge is to endure the race and overcome all obstacles until you reach the finish line. The real challenge is staying in the race and giving it all you've got, determined not to give up. At our finish line, God has waiting for us the greatest reward that anyone can receive, which is *eternal life*!

We are to be Christlike and Christ-minded according to God's Word, for we are now children of the Most High God. We are to look like Jesus, walk like Him, and talk like Him (according to His Word). We are to be loving and forgiving. We are to be concerned and have a heart and compassion for others and to pray for them. We are to love, trust, and obey God (and His Word) and fellowship with Him.

> If then you were raised with Christ, seek those things which are above, where Christ is, sitting at the right hand of God. Set your mind on things above, not on things on the earth, for you died, and your life is hidden with Christ in God. When Christ who is our life appears, then you also will appear with Him in glory. (Colossians 3:1–4)

> Therefore, put to death your members which are on earth: fornication, uncleanness, passion, evil desire, and covetousness, which is idolatry. Because of these things the wrath of God is coming upon the sons of disobedience, in which you yourselves once walked when you lived in them. (Colossians 3:5–7)

> But now you yourselves are to put off all these: anger, wrath, malice, blasphemy, filthy language out of your mouth. Do not lie to one another, since you have put off the old man with his deeds; and have put on the new man who is renewed in knowledge according to the image of Him who created him, where there is neither Greek nor Jew … slave or free, but Christ is all and in all. (Colossians 3:8–11)

My brothers and sisters, we as Christians must remember to be subject to rulers and authorities; to pray and obey; to be ready for every good work; and to speak evil of no one. We are to be peaceable, gentle, polite, kind, and thoughtful, showing humility to all people. For we ourselves were also once foolish, disobedient, and deceived, serving various lusts and pleasures, living in malice and envy, and hating one another. We had no love or compassion for anyone other than those extremely close to us.

> But when the kindness and the love of God our Savior toward humankind appeared, not by works of righteousness which we have done, but according to His mercy He saved us, through the washing of regeneration and renewing of the Holy Spirit, whom He poured out on us abundantly through Jesus Christ

our Savior, that having been justified by His grace we should become heirs according to the hope of eternal life. (Titus 3:4–7)

Let us try as much as is in us to avoid: foolish disputes, questions you can't answer, theological ideas, genealogies, contentions, arguing about the Word of God, and strivings about the law; for all of these things are unprofitable and useless. There is no spiritual inspiration nor edification. Do not cause division and reject, or do not associate with a divisive person who insists on being right about everything; even though he knows that he is not perfect, and is living sinful life. (Titus 3:9–11)

Therefore, as the elect of God, holy and beloved, put on tender mercies, kindness, humility, meekness, longsuffering; bearing with one another, and forgiving one another. And if anyone has a complaint against another; even as Christ forgave us, so we must do also. But above all these things put on love, which is the bond of perfection. Love binds and keep everything else together. (Colossians 3:12–14)

My dear brothers and sisters in Christ, remember that Satan is after your anointing because he knows that it is the anointing of God that can and will destroy his works. I want to encourage you to hold onto God's unchanging and strong hands as you hold onto your faith. Jesus Christ is coming soon, the one our hearts have so long panted and waited for, the one we long to see face-to-face, our Lord, Savior, and High Priest, the bishop of our souls, our King.

We have said that we believe in Jesus and have accepted Him as Lord and Savior. We have declared His name and said that we love Him. We pray to Him; preach, teach, witness to, and pray for others; sing, dance, and lift up our hands to Him; and worship and praise His holy name. We're in church for every service; we perform our duties in church; we pay our tithes and offerings and give to charities; we obey and respect our pastor and the leaders placed in our church; and we help our community and others.

Even though all these things are good, none of them matter if you do not truly trust and have faith in Jesus Christ. You must have a personal relationship with Him and love Him with all your heart, soul, and mind. Don't just put on a show and go through the motions, because then you are only fooling yourself and wasting precious time. Do not play games with your eternal life, because Satan and hell are real, and he's playing for your eternal life.

> Therefore, let us lay aside every weight, and the sin which so easily ensnares us, and let us run with endurance the race that is set before us, looking unto Jesus, the author and finisher of our faith, who for the joy that was set before Him endured the cross, despising the shame, and has sat down at the right hand of the throne of God. For consider Him who endured such hostility from sinners against Himself, lest you become weary and discouraged in your souls. (Hebrews 12:1–3)

> Stand fast therefore in the liberty by which Christ has made us free, and do not be entangled again with a yoke of bondage. (Galatians 5:1)

> You ran well. Who hindered you from obeying the truth? This persuasion does not come from Him who calls you. (Galatians 5:7–8)

> I say then: Walk in the Spirit, and you shall not fulfill the lust of the flesh. For the flesh lusts against the Spirit, and the Spirit against the flesh; and these are contrary to one another, so that you do not do the things that you wish. But if you are led by the Spirit you are not under the law. (Galatians 5:16–18)

> If you do those things, then the flesh will not have dominion over you.

> Some of the works of the flesh are evident, which are: adultery, fornication, uncleanness, lewdness, idolatry, sorcery, hatred, contentions, jealousies, outbursts of wrath, selfish ambitions, dissentions, heresies, envy, murders, drunkenness, revelries, and the like; of which I tell you beforehand … that those who practice such things will not inherit the kingdom of God. (Galatians 5:19–21)

> All who practice these works of the flesh will be judged by God.

Please take a moment and read the book of Titus. It is a short letter written to Titus by the apostle Paul, who talks about proper conduct for Christians, among a number of other things. In this epistle, there is a lot of spiritual food to eat, digest, and appropriate into our lives.

In Paul's letter to the Corinthians, he lets us know clearly who will not enter into God's kingdom, and he warns us not to be deceived in our thinking and behavior:

> Do you not know that the unrighteous will not inherit the kingdom of God? Do not be deceived. Neither fornicators, nor idolaters, nor adulterers, nor homosexuals, nor sodomites, nor thieves, nor covetous, nor drunkards, nor revilers, nor extortioners will inherit the kingdom of God. Paul reminded us that some of us were in the same state; but we were washed, we were sanctified, and we were justified in the name of Jesus Christ our Lord, and by the Spirit of our God. (1 Corinthians 6:9–11)

> Brothers and sisters: We are to *flee* sexual immorality. Do you realize that every sin that a man or woman does is outside the body; but if one commits sexual immorality, they sin against their own body? Or do you not know that our body is the temple of the Holy Spirit who is in us; whom we have from God; and we are not our own? For we were redeemed, bought, purchased at a very high price—the sacrifice and blood of Jesus Christ. Therefore, we should glorify God in our body and in our spirit, which are God's. (1 Corinthians 6:18–20)

> Our body is God's temple where the Spirit of God dwells. If anyone defiles the temple of God [our bodies], God will destroy them. For the temple of God is holy, which temple you [we] are. (1 Corinthians 3:16–17)

> We, too must be holy, for our Lord God commands it. (See Hebrews 12:14.)

> Nevertheless, if one does not have self-control or dominion over your flesh, and because of sexual immorality [fornication,

adultery], then each man should have his own wife, and let each woman have her own husband. (1 Corinthians 7:2)

Apostle Paul wrote to the church in Corinth concerning his personal views on those who are unmarried (single), and those whose husbands are deceased: "Say to the unmarried and to the widows: It is good for them if they remain even as I am [single]; but if they cannot exercise self-control [in the flesh—sexual desires], let them marry. For it is better to marry than to burn with passion" (1 Corinthians 7:8–9).

He wrote to Timothy: "Flee also youthful lusts; but follow righteousness, faith, charity, peace, with them that call on the Lord out of a pure heart" (2 Timothy 2:22 KJV).

To the Galatians, he said, "As born again Christians, and children of the Most High God, we are to walk in the fruit of the Spirit which is: Love, joy, peace, longsuffering, kindness, goodness, faithfulness, gentleness, and self-control. Against such there is no law" (Galatians 5:22–23). "And those who are Christ's have crucified the flesh with its passions and desires. If we live in the Spirit, let us also walk in the Spirit. We should not be conceited, provoking and envying one another" (Galatians 5:24–26). And do not think that you are better than anyone else. Remember, God is watching!

Keep your flesh under control, and don't let your flesh keep you under control and have dominion over you. God has given us the power to handle our flesh if we so choose. Our sinful nature has been broken, and sin no longer has dominion or power over our flesh. Don't allow your fleshly desires to be the cause of your eternal destruction. Don't let Satan trick you. Tell me, which would you choose if given the choice: to commit fornication or adultery for a few minutes of fleshly pleasure and spend eternity in a lake of fire in hell with Satan, or resist temptation and the lust of the flesh and spend eternity in the kingdom of God? Well, which one do you choose? *It is your choice.*

"I beseech you therefore, brethren, by the mercies of God, that you present your bodies a living sacrifice, holy, acceptable to God, which is your reasonable service" (Romans 12:1). It is the fair and right thing to do. We are not being asked to do the impossible.

"A servant of the Lord should not quarrel but be gentle, kind to all people, able to teach, patient, in humility correcting those who are in opposition, if God perhaps will grant them repentance, so that they may know the truth, and that they may come to their senses and escape the snare of the devil, having been taken captive by him to do his will" (2 Timothy 2:24–26).

"Brothers and sisters, be strong in the Lord and in the power of His might. Put on, and keep on the whole armor of God, that you may be able to stand against the wiles, or stratagems of the devil. Know that we do not wrestle against flesh and blood, but against principalities, against powers, against the rulers of the darkness of this age, against spiritual hosts of wickedness in the heavenly places" (Ephesians 6:10–12).

And they are all running rampantly on this earth because they know that their time is running out.

But don't be dismayed, for our God has equipped and provided us with armor to protect us from the power of darkness, temptations, evil, and anything that Satan throws at us or uses to try to trip us up. But we must keep this armor on all the time and accompany it with praying in the Spirit.

> We put on the whole armor of God so that we may be able to withstand in the evil day, and having done all, to stand. We must stand having girded our waist with truth; having put on the breastplate of righteousness; having shod our feet with the preparation of the gospel of peace; and above all, taking the shield of faith with which we will be able to quench all the fiery darts of the Satan and his demons. We are to put on the helmet of salvation, and the sword of the Spirit, which is the Word of God; praying always with all prayer and supplication in the Spirit, being watchful to this end with all perseverance, and supplication for all the saints, and all people. (Ephesians 6:13–18)

We should always respect and pray for our spiritual leaders and our church family who are in the faith.

"Brethren, if anyone among you wanders from the truth, and someone turns him back, let him know that he who turns a sinner from the error of his way will save a soul from death and cover a multitude of sins" (James 5:19–20).

God's got us covered, and He will do just what He said and promised in His Word.

> For as the rain comes down, and the snow from heaven, and do not return there, but water the earth, and make it bring forth and bud, that it may give seed to the sower and bread to the eater, so shall My word be that goes forth from my mouth; it shall not return to Me void, but it shall accomplish what I please, and it shall prosper in the thing for which I sent it. (Isaiah 55:10–11)

> Indeed I have spoken it; I will also bring it to you. I have purposed it; I will also do it. (Isaiah 46:11)

> For God did not call us to uncleanness, but in holiness. (1 Thessalonians 4:7)

> God told us that we must be holy [live according to His Word] because He is holy. (1 Peter 1:16)

> Do not lay hands on anyone hastily, nor share in other people's sins; keep yourself pure. (1 Timothy 5:22)

> And even to your old age I am he; and even to hoar [gray] hairs will I carry you; I have made, and I will bear; even I will carry, and will deliver you. (Isaiah 46:4 KJV)

> I will go before thee, and make the crooked places straight: I will break in pieces the gates of brass; and cut in sunder the bars of iron. (Isaiah 45:2 KJV)

> I am He who searches the minds and hearts. And I will give to each one of you according to your works. (Revelation 2:23)

> Beloved, do not imitate what is evil, but what is good. He who does good is of God, but he who does evil has not seen God. (3 John 1:11)

> I want you to be wise in what is good, and simple concerning evil. … And the God of peace will crush Satan under your feet shortly. The grace of our Lord Jesus Christ be with you. Amen. (Romans 16:19, 20)

> For many deceivers have gone out into the world who do not confess Jesus Christ as coming in the flesh. This is a deceiver and an antichrist. Look to yourselves, that we do not lose those things we worked for, but that we may receive a full reward. (2 John 1:7–8)

> We are to be an example to believers in word, in conduct, in love, in spirit, in faith, in purity. (1 Timothy 4:12)

> These be they who separate themselves, sensual, having not the Spirit. But you, beloved, building up yourselves on your most holy faith, praying in the Holy Ghost [Spirit], keep yourselves in the love of God, looking for the mercy of our Lord Jesus Christ unto eternal life. and of some have compassion, making a difference: and others save with fear, pulling them out of the fire, hating even the garment spotted [defiled] by the flesh. (Jude 1:17–23 KJV)

> Whoever transgresses and does not abide in the doctrine of Christ does not have God. He who abides in the doctrine of Christ has both the Father and the Son. If anyone comes to you and does not bring this doctrine, do not receive him into your house nor greet him; for he who greets him shares in his evil deeds. (2 John 1:9–11)

Dear brothers and sisters, aren't you tired of playing church? Who do you think you are fooling? Remember, what happens in the dark will eventually come to light.

"For, the time has come for judgment to begin at the house of God; and if it begins with us first, what shall be the end of those who do not obey the gospel of God? Now if the righteous one is scarcely saved, where will the ungodly and the sinner appear? Therefore let those who suffer according to the will of God commit their souls to Him in doing good, as to a faithful Creator" (1 Peter 4:17–19).

It is time for church people to get real, get right, and get serious with God. Live a holy life so that God can use us to do His work in these last days and find us to be worthy and prepared to go back with Jesus when He returns.

Lift up your eyes to the heavens and look on the earth beneath. For the heavens will vanish away like smoke, the earth will grow old like a garment, and those who dwell in it will die in like manner; but My salvation will be forever, and My righteousness will not be abolished. (Isaiah 51:6)

"Listen to Me, you who know righteousness, you people in whose heart is My law; do not fear the reproach of men, nor be afraid of their insults. For the moth will eat them up like a garment, and the worm will eat them like wool; but My righteousness will be forever, And My salvation from generation to generation. (Isaiah 51:7–8)

Now, brethren, concerning the coming of our Lord Jesus Christ and our gathering together to Him, we ask you, not to be soon shaken in mind or troubled, either by spirit or by word or by letter. ... Let no one deceive you by any means; for *that Day will not come* unless the falling away comes first, and the man of sin is revealed, the son of perdition, who opposes and exalts himself above all that is called God or that is worshiped, so that he sits as God in the temple of God, showing himself that he is God. (2 Thessalonians 2:1–4, emphasis added)

Do you not remember that when I was still with you I told you these things? And now you know what is restraining, that he may be revealed in his own time. For the mystery [hidden truth] of lawlessness is already at work; only He who now restrains will do so until He is taken out of the way. And then the lawless one will be revealed whom the Lord will consume with the breath of His mouth and destroy with the brightness of His coming. (2 Thessalonians 2:5–8)

The coming of the lawless one [who will soon be revealed to the world] is according to the working of Satan, with all power, signs, and lying wonders, and with all unrighteous deception among those who perish, because they did not receive the love of the truth, that they might be saved. And for this reason, God will send them strong delusion, that they should believe the lie, that they all may be condemned who did not believe the truth but had pleasure in unrighteousness. (2 Thessalonians 2:9–12)

Who is this lawless one? He is the antichrist. This man of sin, this lawless one will be given power by Satan to perform signs, miracles, and lying wonders which will cause people to believe in him. This total deception will lead numerous people away from God, into everlasting hellfire with Satan, the Antichrist, demons, and all those who rejected; and did not believe in the love of the truth, who did not believe in Jesus Christ that they might be saved. (1 Thessalonians 2:9–10)

However, this deception will not mislead or blind the eyes of true believers in Jesus Christ. For they know the truth and abide in the truth, and the truth—the Spirit of God—abides in them. And greater is He who lives (abides, dwells) in them (believers in Jesus Christ) than he who lives in the world or according to the world's system. The children of God know the voice of God the Father; they know the voice of Jesus Christ, the Good Shepherd, our Lord and Savior; and they will not follow the voice of a stranger (Satan).

And Jesus answered and said to them: "Take heed that no one deceives you. For many will come in My name, saying, 'I am the Christ,' and will deceive many.'" (Matthew 24:4–5)

And the sheep hear his voice; and he calls his own sheep by name and leads them …. He goes before them; and the sheep follow him; for they know his voice. Yet they will by no means follow a stranger but will flee from him. (John 10:3, 4–5)

That they all may be condemned who did not believe the truth but had pleasure in unrighteousness. (2 Thessalonians 2:12)

He who sins is of the devil, for the devil has sinned from the beginning. For this purpose the Son of God was manifested, that He might destroy the works of the devil. (1 John 3:8)

Whoever has been born of God does not sin, for His seed remains in him; and he cannot sin, because he has been born of God. (1 John 3:9)

Beloved, let us love one another, for love is of God; and everyone who loves is born of God and knows God. (1 John 4:7)

In this the children of God and the children of the devil are manifest: Whoever does not practice righteousness is not of God, nor is he who does not love his brother. (1 John 3:9–10)

Whoever hates his brother is a murderer, and you know that no murderer has eternal life abiding in him. He who does not love his brother abides in death. (1 John 3:15–14)

We know that we are of God, and the whole world lies under the sway of the wicked one. And we know that the Son of God has come and has given us an understanding, that we may know Him who is true, and we are in Him who is true, in His Son Jesus Christ. This is the true God and eternal life. (1 John 5:19–20)

Beloved, now we are children of God; and it has not yet been revealed what we shall be, but we know that when He is revealed, we shall be like Him, for we shall see Him as He is. And everyone who has this hope in Him purifies himself, just as He is pure. (1 John 3:2–3)

Dear brothers and sisters, be very mindful, and spiritually discern all voices when related to the things of God. And always remember: greater is He who is in you than he who is in the world. Consider all that God our Father and Jesus Christ His Son, our Lord and Savior, have done for us as we give thanks to the Father who has qualified us to be partakers of the inheritance of the saints in the marvelous light.

God loved us so much that He gave His only begotten Son, that whoever believes in Him should not perish but have eternal life. (John 3:16)

Holy God sent His Son, Jesus Christ so that the world, you and I, through Him might be saved. Jesus lovingly, willingly, and obediently humbled Himself, even to the death of the cross; and took on the form of flesh in the likeness of men and a bondservant; and for a while laid aside His deity, and divine glory; and gave His life for all mankind so that they would have a chance to live forever in that place He has prepared for us; and just as God had planned in the beginning. (Philippians 2:6–8)

Jesus Christ was obedient to the Father, even to the death of the cross. He was temporary separated from His Father. He was lied upon, despised, and rejected by men. He was spit on, mocked, and beaten beyond recognition. He was oppressed, and He was afflicted for us, yet He did not open His mouth in His defense. He was a man of pain, sorrows, and well acquainted with griefs. He has borne our griefs [sicknesses] and carried our sorrows. He was wounded for our transgressions, and He was bruised for our iniquities; the chastisement for our peace was upon Him, and by His stripes [the bloody wounds that He received on His body] we are healed. (Isaiah 53:3–5)

Jesus Christ, God only Son, suffered, shed His precious blood, died on the cross, and rose from the dead for us; and is now seated at the right hand of God the Father in heaven making intercession for you and me, and where angels and authorities and powers have been made subject to Him. (1 Peter 3:22)

Jesus Christ knew no sin, yet because of His love for us, He became sin for us so that we might become the righteousness of God in Him. (2 Corinthians 5:21)

Who committed no sin, nor was deceit found in His mouth; who, when He was reviled, did not revile in return; when He suffered, He did not threaten, but committed Himself to Him [God] who judges righteously; who Himself bore our sins in His own body on the tree, that we, having died to sins, might live for righteousness—by whose strips you were healed. (1 Peter 2:21–24)

For Christ also suffered once for sins, the just for the unjust, that He might bring us to God, being put to death in the flesh but made alive by the Spirit, by whom also He went and preached to the spirits in prison, who formerly were disobedient. (1 Peter 3:18–20)

God has given us the Holy Spirit—the Spirit of truth—to dwell inside of us to comfort us, help us, lead us, guide us, teach us, bring things to our remembrance, and enable us to live a Christian or Christlike life pleasing to God according to His Word. (Read John 14:16–17, 26; Romans 5:5.)

God has delivered us from the power of darkness and conveyed [transferred] us into the kingdom of the Son of His love, in whom we have redemption through His blood, forgiveness of sins. He [Jesus] is the image of the invisible God, the firstborn over all creation. For by Him all things were created that are in heaven and that are on earth, visible and invisible, whether thrones or dominions or principalities or powers. All things were created through Him and for Him. And He is before all things, and in Him all things consist. (Colossians 1:13–17)

And He [Jesus Christ] is the head of the body, the church, who is the beginning, the firstborn from the dead, that in all things He may have the preeminence. For it pleased the Father that in Him all the fullness should dwell, and by Him to reconcile all things to Himself, by Him, whether things on earth or things in heaven, having made peace through the blood of His cross. (Colossians 1:18–20)

The mystery [secret or hidden truth] which has been hidden from ages and from generations, but now has been revealed to His saints. To them God willed to make known what are the riches of the glory of this mystery among the Gentiles: which is Christ in you, the hope of glory. Him we preach, warning every man and teaching every man in all wisdom, that we may present every man perfect in Christ Jesus. (Colossians 1:26–28)

I thank God for loving me so much that He gave His only begotten Son, Jesus Christ, and I thank Jesus Christ for being obedient to our

Father, even to the point of death on the cross, and for loving me so much that He was willing to sacrifice His life for me so that I would be reconciled to God the Father, have a chance to have eternal life, and reign with Them for eternity.

Beloved, be extremely careful who you allow to feed you spiritually. Read the Word (the Bible) for yourself, and ask God for wisdom, knowledge, and understanding. Don't just take humankind's word or their interpretation if it doesn't line up with God's Word. There are many who say they are a Christian, or a pastor, preacher, bishop, teacher, prophet, minister, or deacon—this, that, and the other thing (frankly, titles means very little to me)—but have only a form of godliness. Many want to feel important in other people's eyes or think that they have crossed all their *t*'s and dotted all their *i*'s.

Their main interest and focus is popularity, money, and more money. They are more concerned about the type and number of cars that they have or hope to get than they are about people. They are concerned with materialistic things and with who lives in the biggest house, where, and in what neighborhood. For they all care about and seek their own glory. They are not sincere, and they don't care about the things of God or His people.

They always have their hands out, but they never give a hand out to the people. They never extend their hands to help and bless the people in their church and community. They are always counting the number of people in church while counting the amount of money they will receive in tithes and offerings. They rarely do anything for the children, young adults, or seniors in their church. Nor do they give back to their neighborhood. What a shame, and how sad this is.

The food programs provided by the city or state cost them nothing out of their funds. And many churches won't even take the time to participate in such programs, which otherwise would be a great blessing to many people in their church and community.

"For many walk, of whom I have told you often, and now tell you even weeping, that they are the enemies of the cross of Christ: whose end is destruction, whose god is their belly, and whose glory is in their shame—who set their mind on earthly things" (Philippians 3:18–19).

Be mindful and careful not to fall into such a trap—set by Satan himself.

"For our citizenship is in heaven, from which we also eagerly wait for the Savior, the Lord Jesus Christ, who will transform our lowly body that it may be conformed to His glorious body, according to the working by which He is able even to subdue all things to Himself" (Philippians 3:20–21).

Saints of God, my brothers and sisters in Jesus Christ our Lord and Savior: we as children of God should make sure that our works reflect the truthfulness and sincerity of our faith. Regardless of trials and tribulations, let us continually offer the sacrifice of praise to God our Father, that is, the fruit of our lips giving thanks to and confessing His almighty name. Let Jesus handle all of our haters, the evil and wicked ones (influenced by and working for Satan). They will all be punished one day soon.

> And whatever we do, we must do it heartily, as unto the Lord and not to men, knowing that from the Lord we will receive the reward of the inheritance; for we serve the Lord Jesus Christ. But those who does what is wrong will be repaid for what he or she has done, and there is no partiality. (Colossians 3:23–25)

> Therefore gird up the loins of your mind, be sober, and rest your hope fully upon the grace that us to be brought to you at the revelation of Jesus Christ; as obedient children, not conforming yourselves to the former lusts, as in your ignorance; but as He who called you is holy, you also be holy in all your conduct, because it is written: "You shall be holy, for I the Lord your God am holy." (Leviticus 19:2)

> And if you call on the Father, who is without partiality judges according to each one's work, conduct yourselves throughout the time of your stay here in fear; knowing that you were not redeemed with corruptible things, like silver or gold, from your aimless conduct received by tradition from your fathers, but with the precious blood of Christ, as a lamb without blemish and without spot. He indeed was foreordained before the foundation of the world but was manifest in these last times for you who through Him believe in God, who raised Him from the dead and gave Him glory, so that your faith and hope are in God. (1 Peter 1:13–21)

For to this end we both labor and suffer reproach, because we trust in the living God, who is Savior of all humankind, especially of those who believe. (1 Timothy 4:10)

For Jesus Christ is the only door to salvation.

My family of God let nothing, nor no one separate you from the love of Jesus Christ. Do not allow anyone or anything that Satan throws at you, turn you around: *Not tribulation, stress, persecution, relationships, finances, hatred, or bigotry.* And even though we may go through all of these things including dangers, trials, tests, mighty storms, and heartaches; we are still more than conquerors through Jesus Christ who love us. (Romans 8:37, emphasis added)

Believe me, my friends, nothing and no one is worth spending eternity in hellfire. Everyone has the same opportunity to be saved and to choose eternal life.

For I am persuaded that neither death nor life, nor angels nor principalities nor powers, nor things present nor things to come, nor height nor depth, nor any other created thing, shall be able to separate me [us] from the love of God which is in Christ Jesus our Lord. (Romans 8:38)

But as it is written: "Eye has not seen, nor ear heard, not have entered into the heart of man the things which God has prepared for those who love Him." (1 Corinthians 2:9)

Now my family of God; unto Him who's able to keep you from stumbling, and to present you faultless before the presence of His glory with exceeding joy. To God our Savior, who alone is wise, be glory and majesty, dominion and power, both now and forever. Amen. (Jude 1:24–25)

Until we meet again, stay with God, keep the faith, and believe and trust in Jesus Christ His Son for He is coming soon!

I ... saw under the sun that the race is not to the swift, nor the battle to the strong, nor riches to men of understanding, nor favor to men of skill; but time and chance happen to them all. For man also does not know his time: Like fish taken in a cruel net, like birds caught in a snare, so the sons of men are snared in an evil time, when it falls suddenly upon them. (Ecclesiastes 9:11)

Let us hear the conclusion of the whole matter: Fear God and keep His commandments, for this are man's all. For God will bring every work into judgment, including every secret thing, whether good or evil. (Ecclesiastes 12:13–14)

Wait on Our Lord Jesus Christ for He Is Surely Coming

Truly my soul silently waits for God; from Him comes my salvation.
—Psalm 62:1

Therefore be patient, brethren, until the coming of the Lord. See
how the farmer waits for the precious fruit of the earth, waiting
patiently for it until it receives the early and latter rain. You also
be patient. Establish your hearts, for the coming of the Lord is
at hand. Do not grumble against one another, brethren, lest you
be condemned. Behold, the Judge is standing at the door!
—James 5:7–9

But the end of all things is at hand; therefore, be
serious and watchful in your prayers.
—1 Peter 2:7

There are many people who don't believe that Jesus Christ is coming again
(or that He came a first time for that matter), but the day will come when
they will see for themselves. Meanwhile, you who do believe, don't worry
about the negativity and disbelief of people who speak against Jesus's
coming. Just continue to believe, serve, trust, and obey Him. Stand firm
upon God's Word, and keep the faith. His Word is true and will stand
forever. He loves you, and He is not slack concerning His promises. The
wicked and those who do not fear, serve, believe, have faith in, or obey God
the Father and His Son Jesus Christ will stand before Him one day to be
judged and rewarded according to their deeds and their belief.

Satan will do anything and use anyone (who will allow him) to discourage them while they're waiting, and he will try to make them lose hope and their faith. But we should hold on to hope, our confession, and our faith in Jesus Christ and all of His promises. For He who made the promises is faithful and will keep and fulfill every promise He has made to you personally and in His Word. For His Word cannot return to Him void but will accomplish all that He sends it out to do. So don't you worry about what others may say; don't give up; and don't faint. Stay true to God and meditate on His Word day and night. Let no one separate you from His love.

Make sure that your name is written in the book of remembrance and the Lamb's book of life (Revelation 20:12, 15, 21:27; Luke 10:20). Stay meek and humble, and love one another. Continue to reverently fear, respect, love, serve, trust, obey, believe, and have faith in God and His Word. Tell others about His awesome love, mercy, grace, and power. Jesus Christ wants everyone to be saved, for He died on the cross at Calvary and rose from the grave for the whole world. Whosoever will come to Him with a sincere heart, He will not turn them away.

Jesus will give you eternal life to live with Him *if* that is what you desire and what you choose. He is sitting at the right hand of God the Father right now as our High Priest, Advocate, Mediator, and Intercessor, pleading to the Father on our behalf and interceding for us. God sees, hears, and knows everything. Nothing is hidden from Him; His memory fails not. No one will get away with doing evil and wicked things, and the righteous shall be rewarded.

> Then those who feared the Lord spoke to one another, and the Lord listened and heard them; so a book of remembrance was written before Him For those who fear the Lord and who mediate on His name. "They shall be Mine," says the Lord of hosts, "on the day that I make them My jewels. And I will spare them as a man spares his own son who serves him." Then you shall again discern between the righteous and the wicked, between one who serves God And one who does not serve Him. (Malachi 3:16–18)

> For they themselves shew of us what manner of entering in we had unto you, and how ye turned to God from idols to serve

the living and true God; and to wait for his Son from heaven, whom he raised from the dead, even Jesus, which delivered us from the wrath to come. (1 Thessalonians 1:9–10 KJV)

Then you will know that I am the Lord, for they shall not be ashamed who wait for Me. (Isaiah 49:23)

"Your words have been harsh against Me," says the Lord. "Yet you say, 'What have we spoken against You?' You have said, 'It is useless to serve God; what profit is it that we have kept His ordinance, and that we have walked as mourners Before the Lord of hosts? So now we call the proud blessed, for those who do wickedness are raised up; they even tempt God and go free.'" (Malachi 3:13–15)

I will stretch out My hand against … those who have turned back from following the Lord, and have not sought the Lord, nor inquired of Him. (Zephaniah 1:4, 6)

Scoffers will come in the days, walking according to their own lusts, and saying, "Where is the promise of His coming? For since the fathers fell asleep, all things continue as they were from the beginning of creation." For this they willfully forget: that by the word of God the heavens were of old, and the earth standing out of water and in the water, by which the world that then existed perished, being flooded with water. But the heavens and the earth which are now preserved by the same word, are reserved for fire until the day of judgment and perdition (destruction) of ungodly men. (2 Peter 3:3–7)

But, beloved, do not forget this one thing, that with the Lord one day is as a thousand years, and a thousand years as one day. The Lord is not slack concerning His promise, as some count slackness, but is longsuffering toward us, not willing that any should perish but that all should come to repentance. (2 Peter 3:8–9)

Dear people, God loves you, and He has been waiting on you to come to Him. However, He can't continue to wait much longer. Time is running out, the oil in the lamp is running very low, and the light is about to go out. Jesus Christ's Second Coming is near. Won't you please call upon the name of the Lord? He cares so much for you and is waiting to help you. He wants to reign in and over your life. He wants to endow you with His Holy Spirit to lead and guide you.

> Therefore the Lord will wait, that He may be gracious to you; and therefore He will be exalted, that He may have mercy on you. For the Lord is a God of justice; blessed are all those who wait for Him. (Isaiah 30:18)

> You also be patient. Establish your hearts, for the coming of the Lord is at hand. Do not grumble against one another, brethren, lest you be condemned. Behold, the Judge is standing at the door! (James 5:8–9)

> Nevertheless we, according to His promise, look for new heavens and a new earth in which righteousness dwells. (2 Peter 3:13)

> Remember my brothers and sisters in our Lord Jesus Christ: They that wait on the Lord our God, their strength shall be renewed; they shall mount up with wings as eagles; they shall run and not get tired or be weary; and they shall walk and not faint. (Isaiah 40:31)

> Wait patiently on Him. Jesus Christ is coming soon!

> Therefore wait ye upon me, saith the Lord, until the day I rise up to the prey: for my determination is to gather the nations, that I may assembly the kingdoms, to pour upon them mine indignation, even all my fierce anger: for all the earth shall be devoured with the fire of my jealousy. (Zephaniah 3:8 KJV)

> He will swallow up death in victory; and the Lord God will wipe away tears from off all faces; and the rebuke of his people shall he take away from all the earth: for the Lord hath spoken it. (Isaiah 25:8 KJV)

And it shall be said in that day, Lo, this is our God; we have waited for him, and he will save us: this is the Lord; we have waited for him; we will be glad and rejoice in his salvation. (Isaiah 25:9 KJV)

Look to yourselves, that we do not lose those things we worked for, but that we may receive a full reward. (2 John 1:8)

As many as I love, I rebuke and chasten. To him who overcomes I will grant to sit with Me on My throne, as I also overcame and sat down with My Father on His throne. He who has an ear, let him hear what the Spirit says to the churches. (Revelation 3:19, 21–22)

We give You thanks, O Lord God Almighty, the One who is and who was and who is to come, because You have taken Your great power and reigned. The nations were angry, and Your wrath has come, and the time of the dead, that they should be judged, and that You should reward Your servants the prophets and the saints, and those who fear Your name, small and great, and should destroy those who destroy the earth. (Revelation 11:17–18)

Surely Jesus Christ is coming, and woe to those who have not believed, trust, obeyed Him; and have not prepared for His coming. For, there is no escape from His wrath. It is a fearful thing to fall into the hands of the living God. (Hebrews 10:31)

Therefore, my beloved brethren, be steadfast, immovable, always abounding in the work of the Lord, knowing that your labor is not in vain in the Lord. (1 Corinthians 15:58)

One day soon, we are all going to have a new body. And when our corruptible body puts on incorruption and our mortal body has put on immortality, we shall be forever changed in the likeness of our God. Death will then be swallowed up in victory. We will no longer fear death, or the grave, or hell.

"O Death, where is your sting? O Hades [the grave, hell], where is your victory" (1 Corinthians 15:54–55)? I thank God for giving us the victory through our Lord and Savior, Jesus Christ.

Dear friends, may God's choice blessings, kindness, grace, and mercy rest upon you and your family. May you have peace, be found worthy upon Christ's return, and rest in His love and fellowship and the communion of the Holy Spirit.

God Is God, the Alpha and the Omega, the Great I Am, the Creator of Heaven and Earth

In the beginning God created the heavens and the earth. The earth was without form, and void; and darkness was on the face of the deep. And the Spirit of God was hovering over the face of the waters. Then God said, "Let there be light"; and there was light. And God saw the light was good; and God divided the light from the darkness. God called the light Day, and the darkness He called Night. So, the evening and the morning were the first day.
—Genesis 1:2–5

And God said, Let us make man in our image, after our likeness. …
So God created man in his own image; in the image of God created he him; male and female created he them. And God blessed them, and God said unto them, Be fruitful, and multiply, replenish the earth, and subdue it: and have dominion over the fowls of the air, and over all the earth, and over everything that moveth upon the earth.
—Genesis 1:26–28 (KJV)

Wow! Look and see what God has given to us, His children: dominion over the earth and everything in and on it, even the fowls and whatever else that flies in the air. What an almighty God we love and serve. There's no one like Him, and no one can compare with Him.

The Lord by wisdom hath founded the earth; by understanding hath he established the heavens. By his knowledge the depths are broken up, and clouds drop down the dew. (Proverbs 3:19–20 KJV)

By faith we understand that the worlds were framed by the word of God, so that the things which are seen were not made of things which are visible. (Hebrews 11:3)

By the word of the Lord the heavens were made, and all the host of them by the breath of His mouth. … Let all the earth fear the Lord; let all the inhabitants of the world stand in awe of Him. For He spoke, and it was done; He commanded, and it stood fast. (Psalm 33:6, 8)

Behold, the heaven and the heaven of is the Lord's thy God, the earth also, with all that therein is. (Deuteronomy 10:14 KJV)

Let me start by saying that God is Spirit, and those who worship Him, must worship in spirit and truth. (John 4:24)

God created (made, spoke into existence) heaven and earth and all that is in it in six days, and on the seventh day He rested from all His work. And all that He created and made was good—actually very good. God spoke what was nothing into existence, and a whole universe was born. Time and matter did not exist prior to God creating it. Only God who has no beginning or ending, His Son Jesus Christ, and the Holy Spirit existed.

You can read about the history of God's creation (how, when, what, etc.) in Genesis 1–2. Continue reading Genesis 3, which speaks about the serpent (Satan) who deceived Eve into eating the fruit from the tree in the Garden of Eden that God had specifically said not to eat. Adam and Eve were created sinless and indeed perfect, but God also gave them a free will (the freedom of choice).

You know the story: Eve was influenced and deceived by the serpent (Satan) because of what he told her she would gain by eating the apple. She liked what she'd heard and saw, and she hoped to gain what Satan had promised her. (Satan has not changed and continues to deceive the minds and wills of human beings. Both men and women seek for knowledge, wisdom, power, riches, and wealth.)

Satan, that old serpent, said to Eve: "You will not surely die. For God knows that in the day you eat of it your eyes will be opened, and you will be like God, knowing good and evil" (Genesis 3:4–5). So she took the fruit from the tree, choosing to disobey God. Then, knowing full well what she had done, she gave the fruit to Adam. Now I truly do not know what story she told him as far as which tree the fruit had come from or if she even mentioned her conversation with the serpent regarding the tree of the knowledge of good and evil (which sat in the midst of the garden). Maybe Adam just assumed the fruit was from one of the trees that they were permitted to eat from in the garden. Or perhaps Adam knew precisely that the fruit came from the one tree God had told him not to eat from, but he was influenced by Eve, his wife, and just couldn't say no to her—and the fruit did look good to eat. In his defense (not that it matters), he blamed the woman (his wife, whom he later named Eve), saying to God: "The woman whom You gave me, she gave me of the tree, and I ate" (Genesis 3:12). And Eve blamed the serpent, saying to God: "The serpent deceived me, and I ate" (Genesis 3:13).

Just like today, no one wants to tell the truth or assume responsibility and face up to the consequences for their own errors and/or mistakes. Satan has his own agenda. Given that he desires to kill, steal from, and destroy us, he continues to attack God's Word and His trustworthiness, and he tries to make God's Word serve him. But Satan, that old serpent, that devil, is a deceiver, a liar, and the father of lies.

Adam and Eve knew of God's love and power. He supplied their needs and visited them in the garden every day. Yet they chose to listen to and obey the wrong voice (Satan's), and they allowed their curiosity (to be like God or a god) to result in a death sentence and separation from the very presence and communion of God. However it happened, they both ate the fruit, and as a result their eyes were opened. Thus the fall of humankind—humanity's first sin and the results as they relate to sin.

"And the Lord God commanded the man, saying, 'Of every tree of the garden thou mayest freely eat: But of the tree of the knowledge of good and evil, thou shalt not eat of it: for in the day that thou eatest thereof you eat of it thou shalt surely die'" (Genesis 2:16–17 KJV).

Sin and the desire or inclination to do wrong and disobey God entered into human nature (and the world) because of their disobedience. Death now has a sting, and the grave has victory. Sickness, pain, and suffering would now be like an incurable infectious disease from one generation to another all because Adam and Eve disobeyed God—all because they wanted to have it their way. They desired to be like God, so they listened to and obeyed the wrong voice, which was Satan's. God cursed Adam, Eve, and the serpent (Satan) (Genesis 3:14–19). Now, instead of the blessing that God had planned for humankind (the human race) whom He made in His image, a curse came upon man and woman.

But glory be to God, He came up with another plan of salvation, a plan of redemption for humankind through the obedience of another Man, His Son Jesus Christ, so that we might obtain the blessing of fellowship with Him and gain eternal life, just as He had planned for us in the beginning.

"For since by man came death, by Man also came the resurrection of the dead. For as in Adam all die, even so in Christ all shall be made alive" (1 Corinthians 15:21–22).

Jesus took the sting out of death, and He took the victory from the grave:

"Death is swallowed up in victory. O Death, where is your sting? O Hades (grave, hell) where is your victory?" (1 Corinthians 15:54–55).

We thank God for giving us the victory through Jesus Christ our Lord and Savior. We have been redeemed by His blood, the blood of the Lamb of God. My friends, children of God, do you have any concept of whom you serve, of whom you belong to, and of who God and Jesus are?

Now hear the voice of God, the one and only true God, as He Himself bears proof of and witnesses to His own identity. Why? Because He is God. I pray that the Holy Spirit will spiritually open your eyes, ears, and heart so that you can see, hear, and receive Him. If you do, you will never be the same again. And I promise that you will be forever changed for the good.

Hear ye the Word of the Lord our God:

Listen to Me. … I Am Who I Am. (Exodus 3:14)

Listen to Me …: I am He, I am the First, I am also the Last. Indeed, My hand has laid the foundation of the earth, and my right hand has stretched out the heavens; when I call to them, they stand up together. (Isaiah 48:12–13)

I am the Lord, your Holy One, the Creator of Israel, your King. (Isaiah 43:15 KJV)

For I, the Lord your God, will hold your right hand, saying to you, "Fear not, I will help you." (Isaiah 41:13)

For I am God, and not man, the Holy One in your midst. (Hosea 11:9)

"For I am a great King," says the Lord of hosts, "and My name is to be feared among the nations." (Malachi 1:14)

I am the Lord, that is my name: and my glory will I not give to another, neither my praise to graven images. (Isaiah 42:8 KJV)

Before Me there was no God formed, nor shall there be after Me. I, even I, am the Lord, and besides Me there is no savior. I have declared and saved, I have proclaimed, and there was nor foreign god among you. (Isaiah 43:10–12)

Indeed before the day was, I am He; and there is no one who can deliver out of My hand; I work, and who will reverse it? (Isaiah 43:13)

For I am God, and there is none else; I am God, and there is none like me, declaring the end from the beginning, and from ancient times the things that are not yet done, saying, my counsel shall stand, and I will do all my pleasure. (Isaiah 46:9–10 KJV)

Behold, I am the Lord, the God of all flesh. Is there anything too hard for Me? (Jeremiah 32:27)

I, the Lord, speak righteousness, I declare things that are right. (Isaiah 45:19 KJV)

I have spoken it, I will also bring it to pass: I have purposed it, I will also do it. (Isaiah 46:11 KJV)

And there is no God else beside me; a just God and a Saviour; there is none besides me. (Isaiah 45:21 KJV)

To whom will you liken me, and make me equal, and compare me, that we should be alike? (Isaiah 46:5)

"To whom then will you liken Me; or to whom shall I be equal?" says the Holy One. Lift up your eyes on high, and see who has created these things, who brings out their host by number; He calls them all by name, by the greatness of His might and the strength of His power; no one is missing. (Isaiah 40:25–26)

Who has performed and done it, calling the generations from the beginning? I, the Lord, am the first; and with the last I am He. (Isaiah 41:4)

Yet I am the Lord thy God, and thou shalt know no god but me; for there is no Saviour beside me. (Hosea 13:4 KJV)

"Am I a God near at hand," says the Lord, "and not a God afar off? Can anyone hide himself in secret places, so I shall not see him?" says the Lord. "Do I not fill heaven and earth?" says the Lord. (Jeremiah 23:23–24)

For thus saith the Lord, that created the heavens; God himself that formed the earth and made it; he hath established it, he created it not in vain, he formed it to be inhabited: I [am] the Lord; and [there is] none else. (Isaiah 45:18 KJV)

For Thus saith the Lord, who created the heavens and stretched them out, who spread forth the earth and that which comes from it, who gives breath to the people on it, and spirit to those who walk on it: I, the Lord, have called You in righteousness, and will hold Your hand. (Isaiah 42:5–6)

Thus, says the Lord, the King of Israel, and His Redeemer, the Lord of hosts: "I am the first, and I am the Last; besides Me there is no God. And who can proclaim as I do? Then let him declare it and set it in order for Me, since I appointed the ancient people. And the things that are coming and shall come, let them show these to them. 'Is there a God besides Me? Indeed, there is no other Rock; I know not one.'" (Isaiah 44:6–8)

That they may know from the rising of the sun to its setting that there is none besides Me. I am the Lord, and there is no other; I form the light and create darkness, I make peace and create calamity; I, the Lord, do all these things. (Isaiah 45:6–7)

Thus, says the Lord, your Redeemer, and He who formed you from the womb: I am the Lord, who makes all things, who stretches out the heavens all alone, Who spreads abroad the earth by Myself; who frustrates the signs of the babblers; and drive diviners mad; who turns wise men backward, and make their knowledge foolishness; who confirms the word of His servant, and performs the counsel of His messengers. (Isaiah 44:24–26)

Thus, says the Lord, the Holy One of Israel, and his Maker: … I have made the earth and created man on it. I—My hands— stretched out the heavens, and all their host I have commanded. (Isaiah 45:11–12)

I beheld the earth, and indeed it was without form, and void; and the heavens, they had no light. (Jeremiah 4:23)

I beheld, and indeed there was no man, and all the birds of the heavens had fled. (Jeremiah 4:25)

I, even I, am He who comforts you. Who are you that you should be afraid of a man who will die, and of the son of a man who will be made like grass? And you forget the Lord your Maker, who stretched out the heavens and laid the foundations of the earth; you have feared continually every day because of the fury of the oppressor, when he has prepared to destroy. And where is the fury of the oppressor? (Isaiah 51:12–13)

But I am the Lord your God, who divided the sea whose waves roared—the Lord of hosts is His name. And I have put My words in your mouth; I have covered you with the shadow of My hand, that I may plant [establish] the heavens, lay the foundations of the earth, and say to Zion, "You are My people." (Isaiah 51:15–16)

Look to Me, and be saved, all you ends of the earth! For I am God, and there is no other. I have sworn by Myself; the word has gone out of My mouth in righteousness, and shall not return, that to Me every knee shall bow, every tongue shall take an oath. (Isaiah 45:22–23)

Listen, everybody! Have you not known? Have you not heard? Has it been told you from the beginning? Have you not understood from the foundations of the earth? It is He who sits above the circle of the earth, and its inhabitants are like grasshoppers, who stretches out the heavens like a curtain, and spreads them out like a tent to dwell in. He brings the princes to nothing; He makes the judges of the earth useless. (Isaiah 40:21–23)

I'm talking about God Almighty, who is great and awesome!

"Have you not known? Have you not heard? The everlasting God, the Lord, The Creator of the ends of the earth, neither faints nor is weary. His understanding is unsearchable. He gives power to the weak, and to those who have no might He increases strength" (Isaiah 40:28–29).

What a mighty powerful God we are so honored to serve. He is our heavenly Father. What an honor!

Ah, Lord God! behold, thou hast made the heaven and the earth by thy great power and outstretched arm, there is nothing too hard for thee. (Jeremiah 32:17 KJV)

For behold, He who forms mountains, and creates the wind, who declares to man what his thought is, and makes the morning darkness, who treads the high places of the earth—the Lord God of hosts is His name. (Amos 4:13)

You are worthy, O Lord, to receive glory and honor and power; for You created all things, And by Your will they exist and were created. (Revelation 4:11)

Lord God of Israel, there is no God in heaven above or on earth below like You, who keep Your covenant and mercy with Your servants who walk before You with all their hearts. (1 Kings 8:23)

That all the people peoples of the earth may know that the Lord is God; there is no other. Let your heart therefore be loyal to the Lord our God, to walk in His statures and keep His commandments ... this day. (1 Kings 8:60–61)

Dear friends, our God is not a man that He should lie, nor a son of man that He should repent. What has He said that He will not do? What has He spoken of that He will not make good? God will do just what He says and what He has promised, for He is a God of truth.

Give praise, honor, and glory to the Lord, our awesome and almighty God. Let all people around the world, in the heavens, and underneath the earth give glory to God the Father and Jesus Christ His Son, the Lamb of God, Lord, Savior, Redeemer, High Priest, and King, who sits at the right hand of God on His throne and lives forever and ever, who always existed and will always exist, who is Alpha and Omega, the Beginning and the End, the First and the Last, Creator and Ruler with all power.

O Lord, You created heavens and earth and beneath the earth; and all that is in it. You laid the foundations of the earth so that it should not be moved forever. ... You appointed the moon for seasons; the sun knows it's going down. You make darkness and its night; in which the beast of the forest creep about. ... And when the sun rises man goes out to his work and to his labor until the evening. O Lord how manifold are Your works! In wisdom You have made them all. The earth is full of Your possessions. ... Father God, if You hide Your face from us, we are troubled; if You take away the air we breathe—our breath—we die, and our body return to dust; our spirit returns to You who gave it. You send forth Your Spirit, we are created; and You renew the face of the earth. May You rejoice in all Your works, and may Your glory endure forever, and ever. (Psalm 104:5, 19–20, 22–24, 29–31)

For You, Father, have provided us the ultimate deliverance in Christ Jesus Your Son. By the sacrifice that He made on the cross for us, we have been redeemed by the precious blood of Jesus and are delivered from eternal death in hellfire. We now have a chance for eternal life with God the Father and Jesus Christ His Son. Glory to God!

For the Lord your God is God of gods and Lord of lords, the great God, mighty and awesome, who shows no partiality nor takes a bribe. (Deuteronomy 10:17)

To you it was shown, that you might know that the Lord Himself is God; there is none other besides Him. … Therefore, know this day, and consider it in your heart, that the Lord Himself is God in heaven above and on earth beneath; there is no other. (Deuteronomy 4:35, 39)

Therefore, You are great, Oh Lord. For there is none like You, nor is there any God besides You, according to all that we have heard with our ears. … So, let Your name be magnified forever. (2 Samuel 7:22, 26)

Do you still have some doubts as to who God is? You shouldn't! Who wouldn't love, worship, praise, appreciate, and serve a God such as this? Glory to our Lord God Almighty!

Jesus Christ Is the Son of God the Father; He Is Lord, Savior of the World, Lamb of God, High Priest, Alpha and Omega, Creator of the Universe (and All Things in It), and King of Kings Who's Coming Very Soon

And we have seen and testify that the Father has sent
the Son [Jesus Christ] as Savior of the world.
—1 John 4:14

And without controversy great is the mystery [hidden truth]
of godliness: God was manifested in the flesh, justified in the
Spirit, seen by angels, preached among the Gentiles [non-Jews,
unbelievers], believed on in the world, received up in glory.
—1 Timothy 3:16

God, who at various times and in various ways spoke in time past
to the fathers by the prophets, has in these last days spoken to us
by His Son [Jesus], whom He has appointed heir of all things,
through whom also He made the worlds; who being the brightness
of His glory and the express image of His person, and upholding
all things by the word of His power, when He had by Himself
purged our sins, sat down at the right hand of the Majesty on
high, having become so much better than the angel, as He has
by inheritance obtained a more excellent name than they.
—Hebrews 1:1–4

> But when the fullness of the time had come, God sent forth
> His Son, born of a woman, born under the law, to redeem those
> who were under the law, that we might receive the adoption as
> sons. And because you are sons, God has sent forth the Spirit
> of His Son into your hearts, crying out, "Abba, Father!"
> —Galatians 4:4–6

We are now heirs of God through Jesus Christ.

> For unto us a Child is born, unto us a Son is given; and the
> government will be upon His shoulder. And His name will be
> called Wonderful, Counselor, Mighty God, Everlasting Father,
> Prince of Peace. (Isaiah 9:6)

> Behold, the virgin shall be with child, and bear a Son, and shall
> call His name Immanuel, which is translated, "God with us."
> (Matthew 1:23; Isaiah 7:14)

> And the angel answered and said to her [Mary]. "The Holy
> Spirit will come upon you, and the power of the Highest [God]
> will overshadow you; therefore, also, that Holy One who is to
> be born will be called the Son of God." (Luke 1:35)

> And she will bring forth a Son, and you shall call His name
> Jesus, for He will save His people from their sins. (Matthew
> 1:21)

The apostles were witnesses, and they physically saw Jesus Christ, the Son of God, representing God the Father in the flesh. Today we have His Holy Spirit living and abiding in us as our witness, confirming that He is who He says He is. We believe and have faith in Him.

In the following scriptures, Jesus Christ (the Messiah, the Christ, the Anointed One, the Son of God) clearly identifies Himself and indicates who He is and His relationship with God the Father. He speaks of, speaks to, and prays to God His Father. In the Gospel of John (the Baptist), John represents and speaks about Jesus in His deity (John was sent specifically by God to bear witness that Jesus Christ was, and is, the Son of God and to prepare the way of our Lord, making straight paths for Him to walk), while Luke (the physician) portrays Jesus's humanity as the Son of God.

Jesus has always been with the Father since the beginning of time. The triunity (Trinity) of God the Father, God the Son, and the Spirit of God (the Holy Spirit) has always existed. No, not as three Gods, but *one* God existing as three persons. Jesus said that He and His Father are *one*, which means that they are of the same substance and essence. All three—the Father, the Son, and the Holy Spirit (Holy Ghost)—are coequal persons existing as God (who is the one and only God).

Jesus said: "I and My Father are one." (John 10:30)

In the beginning God created the heavens and the earth. … Then God said, "Let Us make man in our image, according to Our likeness." (Genesis 1:1, 26)

For there are three that bear witness in heaven: the Father [God], the Word [Jesus, the Son], and the Holy Spirit; and these three are one. (1 John 5:7)

In the beginning was the Word [Jesus], and the Word was with God, and the Word was God. All things were made through Him, and without Him nothing was made that was made. In Him was life, and the life was the light of men. And the light shines in the darkness, and the darkness did not comprehend it. That was the true Light which gives light to every man, woman, boy, and girl coming into the world. He was in the world [when Jesus first walked among human beings over two thousand years ago], and the world was made through Him. And the world did not know Him. He came to His own [the Jews], and His own did not receive, nor believed in Him. (John 1:1–11)

But as many [that includes you, me, and everybody] as received Him, to them He gave the right [authority, power] to become children of God, to those who believe in His name: who were born, not of blood, nor of the will of the flesh, nor of the will of man, but of God. And the Word became flesh and dwelt among us and we beheld His glory, the glory as of the only begotten of the Father, full of grace and truth. ... No one has seen God at any time. The only begotten Son, who is in the bosom of the Father, at His side, He has declared Him. (John 1:12–14, 18)

For God so loved the world that He gave His only begotten Son [Jesus Christ], that whoever believes in Him should not perish but have everlasting life. For God did not send His Son into the world to condemn the world, but that the world through Him might be saved. He who believes in Him is not condemned; but he who does not believe is condemned already, because he has not believed in the name of the only begotten Son of God. (John 3:16–18)

In this love of God was manifested toward us that God has sent His only begotten Son [Jesus] into the world that we might live through Him. In this love, not that we loved God, but that He loved us and sent His Son to be the propitiation for our sins. (1 John 4:9–10)

God was in Christ reconciling the world to Himself. (2 Corinthians 5:19)

He who believes in the Son of God has the witness in himself; he who does not believe God has made Him a liar, because he has not believed the testimony that God has given of His Son. And this is the testimony: *that God has given us eternal life, and this life is in His Son.* He who has the Son has life; he who does not have the Son of God does not have life. (1 John 5:10–12, emphasis added)

So, also Christ did not glorify Himself to become High Priest, but it was He who said to Him: "You are My Son, Today I have begotten You." As He also says in another place: "You are a priest forever According to the order of Melchizedek." ... Though He was a Son, yet He learned obedience by the things which He suffered. And having been perfected, He became the author of eternal salvation to all who obey Him. (Hebrews 5:5–6, 8–9)

Hear ye the Word of our Lord Jesus Christ, and may your faith come, and be increased by hearing: "No one has ascended to heaven but He who came down from heaven, that is, the Son of Man who is in heaven. And as Moses lifted up the serpent in the wilderness, even so must the Son of Man be lifted up." (John 3:13–14)

Jesus said, "I am the way, the truth, and the life. No one comes to the Father except through Me." (John 14:6)

I am the First and the Last. I am He who lives, and was dead, and behold, I am alive forevermore. Amen. And I have the keys of Hades and of Death. (Revelation 1:17–18)

If you had known Me, you would have known My Father also; and from now on you know Him and have seen Him. (John 14:7)

For as the Father has life in Himself, so He has granted the Son to have life in Himself, and has given Him authority to execute judgment also, because He is the Son of Man. Do not marvel at this: for the hour is coming in which all who are in the graves will hear His voice and come forth—those who have done good, to the resurrection of life, and those who have done evil, to the resurrection of condemnation. I can of Myself do nothing. As I hear, I judge; and My judgment is righteous, because I do not seek My own will but the will of the Father who sent Me. (John 5:26–30)

All things have been delivered to Me by the Father, and no one knows the Son except the Father. Nor does anyone know the Father except the Son, and the one to whom the Son wills to reveal Him. (Matthew 11:27)

A voice came out of the cloud, saying, "This is My beloved Son, in whom I am well pleased. Hear Him!" (Matthew 17:5)

Behold! The Lamb of God [Jesus] who takes away the sin of the world! (John 1:29)

The Father loves the Son and has given all things into His hand. He who believes in the Son has everlasting life; and he who does not believe the Son shall not see life, but the wrath of God abides on him. (John 3:35–36)

For as the Father raises the dead and gives life to them, even so the Son gives life to whom He will. (John 5:21)

For the Father judges no one, but has committed all judgment to the Son, that all should honor the Son just as they honor the Father. He who does not honor the Son do not honor the Father who sent Him. (John 5:22–23)

Most assuredly, I [Jesus] say to you, he who hears My word and believes in Him [God the Father] who sent Me has everlasting life, and shall not come into judgment, but has passed from death to life. (John 5:24)

And He [Jesus] said to them, "You are from beneath; I am from above. You are of this world; I am not of this world. Therefore, I said to you that you will die in your sins; for if you do not believe that I am He, you will die in your sins." (John 8:23–24)

For I have come down from heaven, not to do My own will, but the will of Him who sent Me. This is the will of the Father who sent Me, that all He has given Me I should lose nothing; but should raise it up at the last day. (John 6:38–39)

And this is the will of Him who sent Me, that everyone who sees the Son and believes in Him may have everlasting life; and I will raise him up at the last day. (John 6:40)

For the Father Himself loves you, because you have loved Me, and have believed that I came forth from God. I came forth from the Father and have come into the world. Again, I leave the world and go to the Father. (John 16:27–28)

My Father, who has given them to Me, is greater than all; and no one is able to snatch them out of My Father's hand. (John 10:29)

And the Father Himself, who sent Me, has testified of Me. You have neither heard His voice at any time, nor seen His form. (John 5:37)

As the Father knows Me, even so I know the Father, and I lay down My life for the sheep. (John 10:15)

Therefore, My Father loves Me, because I lay down My life that I may take it again. No one takes it from Me, but I lay it down Myself. I have power to lay it down, and I have power to take it again. This command I have received from My Father. (John 10:17–18)

Jesus said to them, "If God were your Father, you would love Me, for I proceeded forth and came from God; nor have I come of Myself, but He sent Me." (John 8:42)

Jesus said to her [Martha]: "I am the resurrection and the life. He who believes in Me, though he may die, he shall live. And whosoever lives and believes in Me shall never die. Do you believe this?" She said to Him, "Yes, Lord, I believe that You are the Christ, the Son of God, who is come into the world." (John 11:25–27)

[Jesus was about to raise Lazarus (Martha and Mary's brother), who had been dead now for four days, from the grave.] Then Jesus lifted up His eyes and said, "Father, I thank you that you have heard Me. And I know that You always hear Me, but because of the people who are standing by I said this, that they may believe that You sent me." (John 11:41–42)

At that time Jesus answered and said, "I thank You, Father, Lord of heaven and earth, that You have hidden these things from the wise and prudent, and have revealed them to babes. Even so, Father, for so it seemed good in Your sight." (John 11:25–26)

Then Jesus cried out and said, "He who believes in Me, believes not in Me but in Him who sent Me. And he who sees Me sees Him who sent Me." (John 12:44–45)

He who have seen Me has seen the Father; so how can you say, "Show us the Father"? Do you not believe that I am in the Father, and the Father in Me? The words that I speak to you I do not speak on My own authority; but the Father who dwells in Me does the works. Believe Me that I am in the Father and the Father in Me, or else believe Me for the sake of the works themselves. (John 14:9–11)

Whoever denies the Son does not have the Father either; he who acknowledges the Son has the Father also. (1 John 2:23)

At that day you will know that I am in My Father, and you in Me, and I in you. (John 14:20)

He who has My commandments and keeps them, it is he who loves Me. And he who loves Me will be loved by My Father, and I will love him and manifest Myself to him. (John 14:21)

Jesus answered and said to him, "If anyone loves Me, he will keep My word; and My Father will love him, and We will come to him and make our home with him." (John 14:23)

You have heard me say to you, "I am going away and coming back to you." If you loved Me, you would rejoice because I said, "I am going to the Father," for My Father is greater than I. (John 14:28)

Nathanael answered and said to Him [Jesus], "Rabbi, You are the Son of God! You are the King of Israel!" (John 1:42)

Whoever confesses that Jesus is the Son of God, God abides in him, and he in God. (1 John 4:15)

The woman said to Him, "I know that Messiah is coming" (who is called Christ). "When He comes, He will tell us all things." Jesus said to her, "I who speaks to you am He." (John 4:25)

Again the high priest asked Him [Jesus] …, "Are You the Christ, the Son of the Blessed?" Jesus said, "I am. And you will see the Son of Man sitting at the right hand of Power and coming with the clouds of heaven." (Mark 14:61–62)

Jesus said to them, "My food is to do the will of Him [God the Father] who sent Me, and to finish His work." (John 4:34)

So Jesus said to him, "Why do you call Me good? No one is good but one, that is, God." (Mark 10:18)

He [Jesus] went a little farther and fell on His face, and prayed, saying: "O My Father, if it is possible, let this cup pass from Me; nevertheless, not as I will, but as You will." (Matthew 26:39)

Again, a second time, He went away and prayed, saying, "O My Father, if this cup cannot pass away from Me unless I drink it, Your will be done." (Matthew 26:42)

In that hour Jesus rejoiced in the Spirit and said: "I thank You, Father, Lord of heaven and earth, that You have hidden these things from the wise and prudent and revealed them to babes. Even so, Father, for so it seemed good in Your sight." (Luke 10:21)

All things have been delivered to Me by My Father, and no one knows who the Son is except the Father, and who the Father is except the Son, and the one to whom the Son wills to reveal Him. (Luke 10:22)

And when they had come to the place called Calvary, there they crucified Him, and the criminals, one on the right hand and the other on the left. ... Then he [one of the criminals] said to Jesus, "Lord, remember me when You come into Your kingdom. And Jesus said to him, "Assuredly, I say to you, today you will be with Me in Paradise." (Luke 23:33, 42–43)

Then Jesus said, "Father, forgive them, for they do not know what they do." (Luke 23:34)

And when Jesus had cried out with a loud voice, He said, "Father, into Your hands I commit My spirit." Having said this, He breathed His last. (Luke 23:46)

And about the ninth hour Jesus cried out with a loud voice, saying, "Eli, Eli, Lama' sabach'thani" that is: "My God, My God, why have You forsaken Me?" ... And Jesus cried out again with a loud voice and yielded up His spirit. (Matthew 27:46, 50)

So. when the centurion and those with him, who were guarding Jesus, saw the earthquake and the things that had happened, they feared greatly, saying, "Truly this was the Son of God!" (Matthew 27:54)

But the angel answered and said to the women [Mary Magdalene and the other Mary], "Do not be afraid, for I know that you seek Jesus who was crucified. He is not here; for He has risen, as He said. ... He is risen from the dead." (Matthew 28:5–7)

Jesus said to her [Mary Magdalene], "Do not cling to Me, for I have not yet ascended to My Father; but go to My brethren and say to them, 'I am ascending to My Father and your Father, and to My God and your God.'" (John 20:17)

"He [Jesus] is not here but is risen! Remember how He spoke to you when He was still in Galilee, saying, 'The Son of Man must be delivered into the hands of sinful men, and be crucified, and the third day rise again.'" And they remembered His words. (Luke 24:7–8)

But God raised Him [Jesus] from the dead, releasing Him from the agony of death, because it was impossible for Him to be held in its clutches. (Acts 2:24)

But that the world may know that I love the Father, and as the Father gave Me commandment, so I do. Arise, let us go from here. (John 14:31)

Jesus Christ came to reconcile us to God. He came to give us eternal life with Him and God the Father. Jesus came as the incarnate Son of God to do the will of God. He is a member of the Trinity (Father, Son,

Holy Spirit), and coequal with God the Father. Upon Jesus's return to earth, God will put all things under Him. Then Jesus Christ will bring all—everything, everyone—to God the Father so that God may be all in all. All creation will be reconciled to God (as it was in the beginning), and our redemption and salvation will be complete.

It is a fact that not everyone will believe that Jesus Christ is the Son of God, or who the Bible says He is, because they can't believe beyond their five senses. For them to believe and/or have faith in someone or something, they must be able to see, feel, touch, hear, or taste it. These people certainly have no faith to believe in the impossible or believe in God's Word. And Christians walk by faith (from start to finish) in God's Word, and not by sight or our five senses.

In John 10:24–28 the Jews said to Jesus: "How long do You keep us in doubt? If You are the Christ [Messiah, Anointed One], tell us plainly." Jesus answered them:

"I told you, and you do not believe. The works that I do in My Father's name, they bear witness of Me. But you do not believe, because you are not of My sheep, as I said to you. My sheep hear My voice; and I know them, and they follow Me. And I will give them eternal life, and they shall never perish; neither shall anyone snatch them out of My hand."

What a promise! I feel like praising Him as I shout with joy right now for the gift of salvation and eternal life in His kingdom. We hear and know His voice because we have faith in Him. We believe, love, trust, obey, and abide in Him, and therefore He has given us His Spirit, who dwells in us. Glory to God! We have the same Spirit, and there we connect with each other.

Read what Jesus said to Thomas in John 20:29 after He appeared to His disciples, after He had risen from the grave and had ascended to the Father (Thomas wasn't with the disciples when Jesus had first appeared to them): "Thomas, because you have seen Me, you have believed. Blessed are those who have not seen and yet have believed."

My dear friends, I am one of those blessed people. I believe although I have not seen Jesus Christ physically as Thomas did. I have seen Him spiritually instead. I can feel His awesome presence and power because His Holy Spirit dwells inside of me. I have not touched Jesus physically, but I have been touched by Him spiritually, and I have been transformed by the renewing of my mind by His Word. For His Word abides in me, and my whole life (physical, moral, spiritual, and mental) has been changed forever.

I am a new creation in Him. I have been born again spiritually and now walk in a newness of life. I have been baptized with the Holy Spirit. It is no longer "I, me, myself," but Jesus Christ, who loves me, lives in me, died for me, and rose for me. And He is coming back for me to take me to my eternal home that He has prepared for me and all who believe in Him.

I would not want to live without Him in my life, and I'm so thankful that I don't have to. He is everything to me. Taste Him for yourself, for He is good, sweeter than honey, and full of love, grace, and mercy. He is faithful, and you can always depend upon Him. He will never leave you or forsake you, and He will never give up on you, even if we give up on yourself. He will supply your needs. He will endow you with spiritual gifts and the gift of the Holy Spirit. Jesus may not take you out of every storm in your life, but He will walk with you through the storm, and if need be He will carry you. His grace is sufficient and is truly amazing.

Jesus Christ is the Son of God. He is Lord of Lords, Emmanuel (meaning God with us), Savior, Redeemer, Everlasting God, Almighty God, King of Kings, High Priest, the Way, the Truth, and the Life. He is the Light of the World and my salvation, the True Vine, the Lamb of God, the Chief Cornerstone, the Prince of Peace, the Prince of Life, the Bright and Morning Star, and our Shepherd. He is the Author and Finisher of our faith, the bishop of our soul, the Bread of Life, the door to salvation, Advocate, Intercessor, and Mediator. He is a healer, protector, and comforter, a light in the darkness, Counselor, Friend, Shield, Rock, Water, and shelter in the time of storms. He is waymaker, provider, sustainer, guiding light, and everything else. He is all that we need.

I believe without a shadow of doubt (along with Brother Philip and trillions of others) that Jesus Christ is the Son of God (Acts 8:37).

> And this is He who came by water and blood—Jesus Christ; not only by water, but by water and blood. And it is the Spirit who bears witness because the Spirit is truth. For there are three that bear witness in heaven: The Father, the Word (Jesus), and the Holy Spirit; and these three are one. (1 John 5:6–7)

> If we receive the witness of men, the witness of God is greater; for this is the witness of God which He has testified of His Son [Jesus Christ]. He who believes in the Son of God has the witness in himself; he who does not believe God has made Him a liar, because he has not believed the testimony that God has given of His Son. And, this is the testimony: that God has given us eternal life, and this life is in His Son. He who has the Son has life; he who does not have the Son of God does not have life. (1 John 5:9–12)

> These things I have written to you who believe in the name of the Son of God, that you may know that you have eternal life, and that you may continue to believe in the name of the Son of God. (1 John 5:13)

And, dear friends, that name is Jesus. For He is the Son of God. I will never let anyone or anything separate me from Him or His love.

I will close this chapter with one of the most beautiful intercessory prayers that I have ever read or heard. This is a prayer that Jesus Christ prayed (just before He was arrested and crucified) to the Father for His disciples and for everyone who believed, asking that still others would come to believe in Him in the future, which means that Jesus prayed this prayer for you and me also. He prayed to the Father as a Son, as a man, and as an intercessor and mediator for us.

> And Jesus spoke these words, lifted His eyes to heaven, and said: "Father, the hour has come. Glorify Your Son, that Your Son also may glorify You, as You have given Him authority over all flesh, that He should give eternal life to as many as You have given Him. And this is eternal life, that they may know You, the only true God, and Jesus Christ whom You have sent. I have glorified You on the earth. I have finished the work which You have given Me to do. And now, O Father, glorify Me together with Yourself, with the glory which I had with You before the world was. I have manifested Your name to the men whom You have given Me out of the world. They were Yours, You gave them to Me, and they have kept Your word. Now they have known that all things which You haven Me are from You. For I have given them the words which You

have given Me; and they have received them, and have known surely that I came forth from You; and they have believed that You sent Me. I pray for them. I do not pray for the world but for those whom You have given Me, for they are Yours. And all Mine are Yours, and Yours are Mine, and I am glorified in them. Now I am no longer in the world, but these are in the world, and I come to You. Holy Father keep through Your name those whom You have given Me, that they may be one as We are. While I was with them in the world, I kept them in Your name. Those whom You gave Me I have kept; and none of them lost except the son of perdition, that the Scriptures might be fulfilled. But now I come to You, and these things I speak in the world, that they may have My joy fulfilled in themselves. I have given them Your Word, and the world has hated them because they are not of the world, just as I am not of the world. I do not pray that You should take them out of the world, but that You keep them from the evil one. They are not of the world, just as I am not of this world. Sanctify them by Your truth. Your Word is truth. As You sent Me into the world, I also have sent them into the world. And for their sakes I sanctify Myself, that they also may be sanctified by the truth. I do not pray for these alone, but also for those who will believe in Me through their word; that they all may be one, as You, Father, are in Me, and I in You; that they may also be one in Us, that the world may believe that You sent Me. And the glory which You gave Me I have given them, that they may be one just as We are one: I in them, and You in Me; that they may be made perfect in one, and that the world may know that You have sent Me, and have loved them as You have loved Me. Father, I desire that they also whom You gave Me may be with Me where I am, that they may behold My glory which You have given Me; for You loved Me from the foundation of the world. O righteous Father! The world has not known You, but I have known You; and these have known that You sent Me. And I have declared to them Your name, and will declare it, that the love with which You loved Me may be in them, and I in them." (John 17:1–26)

Let us say amen!

There are many other scriptures concerning Jesus and His Father, but I hope that I have provided enough here. I hope that you now believe, that your faith has grown stronger, and that all your doubts have faded away as to who Jesus Christ is. I pray that He will baptize you with His Holy Spirit and reveal Himself to you personally as you pray to Him and study His Word. I pray that you will draw closer to Him as He draws closer to you. Jesus's grace has been given to us to forgive us of our sins and to cleanse us from all unrighteousness, and this is made possible only through the work of Christ on the cross with God raising Him from the dead for our justification. Jesus Christ took our punishment upon Himself. He who knew no sin took our sins upon His body. If you have faith in Him, you are justified and are once again in right standing with God. We have been reconciled to God through Jesus our Lord. Praise the name of Jesus!

For we have been redeemed, purchased by the blood of Jesus Christ (the Lamb of God); we are no longer our own. We have been forgiven of our sins and transformed by God's Word (giving us a heart of flesh rather than of stone; renewing our minds), and we have been born again (a spiritual new birth) by the Spirit of God, who now dwells in us. And guess what? Our names have now been written in the book of life. We now have eternal life through Jesus Christ our Lord and Savior. I surely thank God for Jesus, for loving us so much, and for giving us the chance to have eternal life. And I thank Jesus for His love for us and obeying His Father, even to His death on the cross, and God for raising Him from the grave on the third day for our justification.

My brothers and sisters, I pray that our heavenly Father, the God of hope, fills you with all joy, faith, and peace in believing, so that you may abound in hope by the power of the Holy Spirit. May God's love and mercy, the grace of Jesus Christ our Lord and Savior, and the communion and fellowship of the Holy Spirit be with you all. In Jesus's name. Amen.

Just imagine, one day soon we will see Him face-to-face. We will see Him as He is, and we will be just like Him.

"Beloved, now we are children of God; and it has not yet been revealed what we shall be, but we know that when He is revealed we shall be like Him, for we shall see Him as He is" (1 John 3:2).

A New Heaven and a New Earth—the New Jerusalem

> I am in hope of eternal life, which God, that cannot
> lie, promised before the world began.
> —Titus 1:2

> Nevertheless we, according to His promise, look for a new
> heavens, and a new earth in which righteousness dwells.
> —2 Peter 2:13

In Revelation chapters 21 and 22, John gives us a descriptive view of what Jesus Christ revealed to him about our new home, the New Jerusalem, and the indescribable beauty of it. This place of paradise was prepared for us, God's children, as our eternal home by Jesus Christ. In John 14:2, Jesus told us not to allow our hearts to be troubled and not to worry, because in His Father's house there are mansions. He said that He would go and prepare a place for us and then return for us so that we would be with Him forever.

> Now I saw a new heaven and a new earth, for the first heaven
> and the first earth had passed away. Also, there was no more
> sea. Then I, John, saw the holy city, New Jerusalem, coming
> down out of heaven from God, prepared as a bride adorned
> for her husband. And I heard a loud voice from heaven saying,
> "Behold, the tabernacle of God is with men, and He will dwell
> with them, and they shall be His people. God Himself will
> be with them; and be their God. And God will wipe away
> every tear from their eyes; there shall be no more death, nor

sorrow, nor crying. There shall be no more pain, for the former things have passed away." Then He who sat on the throne said, "Behold, I make all things new." And He said to me "Write, for these words are true and faithful." (Revelation 21:1–5)

"For as the new heavens and the new earth which I will make shall remain before Me," says the Lord. (Isaiah 66:22)

And they sang a new song, saying: "You are worthy to take the scroll, and to open its seals; for You were slain and have redeemed us to God by Your blood out of every tribe and tongue and people and nation; and have made us kings and priests to our God; and we shall reign on the earth." (Revelation 5:9–10)

My dear friends, indeed eyes have not seen and ears have not heard, and we can't fully imagine, all that God has prepared and has waiting for us. But we do know that it is glorious.

You can read all about our new eternal home, the New Jerusalem, in Revelation chapters 4, 21, and 22. It is awesome! There are not enough words to describe the beauty and joy of it. Who wouldn't want to live in a place like that? However, sad to say, not everyone will. Of course, this is no fault of God or Jesus Christ. It is the fault of the person who, with freedom of choice, chose not to believe in Jesus Christ.

There will be new heavens and a new earth. All flesh will worship God, and those who do not accept Jesus Christ will be doomed forever. (Isaiah 66:22–24)

But there shall be no means enter it anything that defiles, or causes an abomination or a lie, but only those who are written in the Lamb's Book of Life. (Revelation 21:27)

So, precious people of God, continue to abide in His love, have faith, and be rooted and grounded in Him. And be steadfast, unshakable, unmovable. Obey the Lord and do His work; this way your work is not in vain. Keep doing what you're doing for Jesus and His kingdom because He is coming to take us to our new and eternal home to reign with Him forever.

And now: To Him who loved us and washed us from our sins in His own blood and has made us kings and priests to His God and Father, to Him be glory and dominion forever and ever. Amen. (Revelation 1:6)

For: Behold, He is coming with clouds, and every eye will see Him, even those who pierced Him. And all the tribes of the earth will mourn because of Him. Even so. Amen. (Revelation 1:7)

Even so, come, Lord Jesus! (Revelation 22:20)

Believe it or not, and whether you are prepared or not, Jesus Christ is coming! Go and prepare.

The Lord's Prayer

Jesus Christ taught His disciples how to pray in Matthew 6:5–13. He told them not to use vain repetitions and not to say a lot of words, because God already knew their needs and desires before they asked. I believe we can also use this model prayer in our prayer life today.

> In this manner, therefore pray:
> Our Father in heaven, hallowed be Your name,
> Your kingdom come,
> Your will be done on earth as it is in heaven.
> Give us this day our daily bread,
> And forgive us our debts, as we forgive our debtors.
> And do not lead us into temptation,
> But deliver us from the evil one.
> For Yours is the kingdom,
> And the power, and the
> Glory forever. Amen.

> (This prayer was given to me in my dreams, September 18, 1989 and January 13, 1991.)

Salvation Repentance Prayer

Father God, I acknowledge that I am a sinner. I have sinned against You and You only. I ask You to forgive me of all sins and cleanse me from all unrighteousness. Wash me in the blood of Jesus and make me whiter than snow. I repent and turn away from my old way of living, my old sinful life, and I now make You Lord of my life. I embrace a new way of living—Your way of living. Make me a new creation in You.

You said in Your Word that if I confess my sins, You are faithful and just to forgive me of my sins and will cleanse me from all unrighteousness (1 John 1:9). You said in Your Word that if I confess with my mouth the Lord Jesus and believe in my heart that You raised Jesus from the dead, I will be saved. For with the heart one believes unto righteousness, and with the mouth confession is made unto salvation. I confess with my mouth and I believe in my heart (Romans 10:9–10).

Thank You for delivering me from sins and eternal damnation and for giving me the gift of eternal life with You in Your kingdom. Thank You for Your Son Jesus Christ, who purchased my salvation with His blood on the cross. In Him I put my faith. Thank You for Your love, mercy, and grace. Thank You for saving my soul, and thank You for making me whole.

In the name of Jesus, I pray. Amen.

"Nor is there salvation in any other [than Jesus Christ], for there is no other name under heaven given among men by which we must be saved" (Acts 4:12).

My Prayer for You after You Have Received Jesus Christ as Savior

Father God, thank You for hearing the prayers of my brothers and sisters who have opened the door of their hearts to You. You said in Your Word that You will forgive their sins and remember those sins no more (Hebrews 8:12). According to Your Word, they will be saved if they confess with their mouths the Lord Jesus and believe in their hearts that You have raised Him from the dead. For with the heart one believes unto righteous, and with the mouth confession is made unto salvation (Romans 10:9–10).

You also said that whoever calls upon the name of the Lord shall be saved (Romans 10:13). Father, we are calling upon You right now in the name of Jesus. So, along with You and the angels in heaven, I rejoice with them for their salvation. You save to the uttermost, and whom Your Son Jesus Christ sets free is free indeed.

And Father, I pray that You will fill them with Your Holy Spirit to enable them to do the work You have called them to do and to live a holy life while here on this earth. I pray that their minds will be transformed as they renew them with Your Word. As they pray, fast, and study Your Word to show themselves approved and to hear from You, they will draw closer to You, as You will to them. I pray that You will reveal Yourself to them in a special and real way. Let them feel Your awesome love, presence, and power in their lives. When they are weak, show Yourself strong in and through them.

Bless Your children and their families. Keep Your covering over them, protecting them wherever they go from the clutches of the enemy and from all danger, seen and unseen. Thank You for Your love, Your mercy, and Your amazing grace that You have bestowed upon us all. I love You. I pray in the name that is above every name in heaven, on earth, and beneath the earth. Thank You for saving their souls, making them whole, and making them a new creation in You.

In the name of Jesus, I pray. Amen.

A Soldier's Prayer

Almighty God, first I ask You to forgive me of my sins and cleanse me from all unrighteousness. Deliver me from the hand of Satan and all my enemies. You are my strength, my rock, my fortress, my shield, and my deliverer. I will always trust in You. You are my shelter in the time of storms, my stronghold and my refuge, my Savior, my Lord, and my best friend. I will call upon You, for I know that You hear me and You will deliver me.

When the sound and waves of death confronts and surrounds me and I feel overwhelmed, oppressed, and afraid, I will keep my faith and trust in You. I will call upon You in my sadness, sorrow, distress, pain, affliction, and trouble. I will cry out to You, for I know that You will answer me from Your tabernacle. You will rescue me and deliver me from those who hate me and from all enemies. For You are my God, Lord, and Savior.

I believe that You, O Lord my God, are in the center of my situation. And in all that I do, and whatever the outcome, You work it out for my good. Whenever I am afraid, no matter what problem lies ahead, I will not doubt Your love and faithfulness for me. I have no fear of humankind or of what they can do to me. For only You have the power to destroy my body and soul; You hold my eternal destiny. Therefore, it is You, O Lord, that I fear.

Thank You for Your love, mercy, grace, and faithfulness and for forgiving me of all my sins. You are an awesome God! My soul trusts in You. In the shadow of Your mighty wings I will make my refuge, until these calamities have passed by. Please guide my footsteps, be my compass, and be a light unto my path. Do not allow any weapon contrived by my enemies against me or my fellow brethren to be successful, and condemn every tongue that revolts or comes against me in judgment. Shield me with Your buckler and against the fiery darts of Satan, terrorist attacks, and weapons of destruction. Though hundreds may fall before me, please protect my brothers and sisters as we stand and fight this war together. For we are Your children; we are more than conquerors, and we have the victory through Jesus Christ Your Son, our Lord, Savior, and King. Let no weapon formed against me, my family, my friends, or my colleagues prosper. In Jesus's name I ask these things.

> And they cried out to the Lord in their trouble, and He saved them out of their distresses. He bought them out of darkness and the shadow of death; and broke their chains in pieces. (Psalm 107:13–14)

> The Lord my God lives! Blessed be my rock; and let the God of my salvation be exalted. It is You Lord God who avenges me; and subdues the peoples under me; and You deliver me from my enemies; and You also lift me up above those who rise against me. You have delivered me, from the violent man, and you have not forsaken me. I will praise Your holy name forever. (Psalm 18:46–48)

> Let it be done. In Jesus's name, I pray. Amen.

My Prayer for All Soldiers

Most gracious and merciful Father, I pray for the brave and courageous men and women in the US Armed Forces (every branch) all around the world who are willing to sacrifice their lives, fighting for and serving their country with honor, pride, and dignity, trying to keep it safe, protect it, and make it a better place for all people to live. I ask You to protect them from their enemies as they face the forces of evil and darkness, hatred, and violence and weapons of mass destruction. Keep them covered with the blood of Jesus and under Your mighty wing. Let Your favor, mercy, and grace be upon them. Be a lamp unto their feet and a light unto their path as You lead and guide them wherever they may go. Be their refuge and fortress.

Father God, go before them and make the crooked places straight; destroy their enemies and their plots and schemes. Any trap that their enemy has set for them, let their enemies fall into it. Let no weapon or plan that the enemy devises against them be successful. Let Your blessings of goodness, mercy, and grace be upon them (and their families); give them a long and abundant life. Strengthen their weak hands and make firm and strong their body.

When they are afraid, when troubles arise all around them, embrace them with Your love, endow them with the power of Your Holy Spirit, and let them know that You will never leave them alone. Even in the midst of all that's going on with and around them, You are there. You're still in control of everything, and they can call on You and trust You in their time of need. Encourage them, comfort them, give them Your peace, heal them mentally, physically, and emotionally, and make them whole in body and mind. Let Your grace be sufficient for them.

Father, I pray that You will show Yourself strong in their lives; answer them when they call upon You; and fulfill their petitions (according to Your will). Do a new thing in their lives. For You have demonstrated Your love for them and everyone else in that while we were still sinners, Jesus Christ died for us all. And You raised Him from the grave on the third day so that we could once again be in right standing with You. You gave us Your Son Jesus, and He gave His life for us. Father, please protect their families and supply them with their needs. Let Your Holy Spirit minister to them and their families, and bless them as they and their families wait for their safe return home.

In the name of Jesus Christ, I say to those whose hearts are fearful: "Be strong, be courageous, be bold, and do not fear! For behold, your God will come with a vengeance, with the recompense of God; He will come and save you" (Isaiah 35:4). Just put and keep your trust in God our Father and Jesus Christ your Savior.

Father, please return them home whole, sound in mind, body, and soul. In Jesus's name. Amen.

My dear brothers and sisters: if you who have not accepted Jesus Christ as your Savior and Lord, please say the few words below with me and mean them with all your heart. For the Word of God says: "If you hear My voice today, do not harden your heart as in rebellion" (Hebrews 3:15). Jesus Christ is coming again to this earth very soon. Will you be prepared?

Let us pray:

Lord Jesus, I repent of my sins and ask You to forgive me. Come into my heart and my life, and make me a new creation in You. I believe in my heart, and I confess with my mouth, that You are the Son of God; You died on the cross for my sins; and God raised You from the grave on the third day for my justification. Lead me, guide me, and fill me with the Holy Spirit. Thank You for my salvation. In Your name I pray. Amen.

My Prayer for You

Lord Jesus, thank You for saving my brothers and sisters. You said that whosoever believes in You and calls upon Your name would be saved and that You would not turn them away. Prove Yourself to them in a mighty way, and remind them that You will never leave them or forsake them—no matter what Satan throws at them. For they have the victory in You, and they have already won the fight. Holy Spirit, fill them, comfort them, and give them a peace that surpasses all understanding. Keep them and their families safe and covered by the blood of Jesus as they believe, trust, and keep their faith in You. In Your name, I pray. Amen.

Trust God and have faith in Him and in Jesus Christ, for He knows better than anyone—yes, even you—what is best for you (and your family). He loves you, He knows all about you, and He cares about you.

Psalm 12: Prayer for Help in Perilous Times

Help, Lord, for the godly man ceases! For the faithful disappear from among the sons of men. They speak idly everyone with his neighbor; with flattering lips and a double heart they speak.

May the Lord cut off all flattering lips, and the tongue that speaks proud things, who have said, "With our tongue we will prevail; our lips are our own; who is lord over us?"

"For the oppression of the poor, for the sighing of the needy, Now I will arise," says the Lord; "I will set him in the safety for which he yearns."

The words of the Lord are pure words, like silver tried in a furnace of earth, purified seven times. You shall keep them, O Lord, You shall preserve them from this generation forever.

O Lord, help me to be faithful and loyal to You and to others. Let me not harbor pride and deception in my heart.

The wicked prowl on every side, when vileness is exalted among the sons of men.

(This Psalm given to me in a dream, December 9, 2009.)

Psalm 39: O Lord, Hear My Prayer. My Hope Is in You

I said, "I will guard my ways, lest I sin with my tongue; I will restrain my mouth with a muzzle, while the wicked are before me." I was mute with silence; I held my peace even from good; and my sorrows were stirred up. My heart was hot within me; while I was musing [meditating], the fire burned.

Then I spoke with my tongue; "Lord, make me to know my end, and what is the measure of my days, that I may know how frail I am. Indeed, You have made my days as handbreadths, and my age is as nothing before You; certainly every man at his best state is but vapor. Selah.

"Surely every man walks about like a shadow; surely, they busy themselves in vain [make an uproar for no reason]; he heaps up riches and does not know who will gather them.

"And now, Lord, what do I wait for? My hope is in You. Deliver me from all my transgressions; do not make me the reproach of the foolish. I was mute, I did not open my mouth, because it was You who did it.

"Remove Your plague from me; I am consumed by the blow of Your hand. When with rebukes You correct man for iniquity, You make his beauty melt away like a moth; surely every man is vapor. Selah.

"Hear my prayer, O Lord; and give ear to my cry; do not be silent at my tears; for I am a stranger with You, a sojourner, as all my fathers were. Remove Your gaze from me that I may regain strength before I go away and am no more."

(This psalm was given to me in a dream, March 22, 2017.)

Psalm 43: Deliver Me, O God, for You Are My Strength

Vindicate me, O God, and plead my cause against an ungodly nation; oh, deliver me from the deceitful and unjust man! For You are the God of my strength; why do You cast me off? Why do I go mourning because of the oppression of the enemy?

Oh, send out Your light and Your truth! Let them lead me; let them bring me to Your holy hill and to Your tabernacle. Then I will go to the altar of God, to God my exceeding joy; and on the harp, I will praise You, O God, my God.

Why are you cast down, O my soul? And why are you disquieted within me? Hope in God; for I shall yet praise Him, the help of my countenance and my God.

(This psalm was given to me in a dream, January 24, 2017.)

Psalm 71: Senior's Prayer for Deliverance

In You, O Lord, I put my trust; let me never be put to shame. Deliver me in Your righteousness and cause me to escape; incline Your ear to me and save me. Be my strong refuge, to which I may resort continually; You have given the commandment to save, for You are my rock and my fortress. Deliver me, O my God, out of the hand of the wicked, out of the hand of the unrighteousness and cruel man. For You are my hope. O Lord God, You are my trust from my youth. By You I have been upheld from birth; You are He who took me out of my mother's womb. My praise shall be continually of You. I have become a wonder to many, but You are my strong refuge. Let my mouth be filled with Your praise, and with Your glory all the day.

Do not cast me off in the time of old age; do not forsake me when my strength fails. For my enemies speak against me; and those who lie in wait for my life take counsel together, saying, "God has forsaken him [or her]; pursue and take him [or her], for there is none to deliver him [or her]." O God, do not be far from me; O my God, make haste to help me! Let them be confounded and consumed who are my adversaries of my life; let them be covered with reproach and dishonor who seek my hurt. But I will hope continually and will praise You yet more and more. My mouth shall tell of Your righteousness and Your salvation all the day; for I do not know their limit. I will go in the strength of the Lord God; I will make mention of Your righteousness, of Yours only. O God, You have taught me from my youth; and to this day I declare Your wondrous works. Now also when I am old and grey headed, O God, do not forsake me, until I declare Your strength to this generation, Your power to everyone who is to come.

Also Your righteousness, O God, is very high, You who have done great things; O God, who is like You? You, who have shown me great and severe troubles, shall revive me again, and bring me up again from the depths of the earth. You shall increase my greatness, and comfort me on every side. Also, with the lute I will praise You and Your faithfulness, Oh my God! To You I sing with the harp, O Holy One of Israel. My lips shall greatly rejoice when I sing to you, and my soul, which You have redeem. My tongue also shall talk of Your righteousness all the day long; for they are confounded, for they are bought to shame who seek my hurt.

Psalm 103: Bless the Lord! Never Forget His Benefits and All He's Done

Bless the Lord, O my soul; and all that is within me, bless His holy name! Bless the Lord, O, my soul, and forget not all His benefits. Who forgives all your iniquities, who heals all your diseases, who redeems your life from destruction, who crowns you with loving-kindness and tender mercies, who satisfies your mouth with good things, so that your youth is renewed like the eagle's. The Lord executes righteousness and justice for all who are oppressed. He made known His ways to Moses, His acts to the children of Israel.

The Lord is merciful and gracious, slow to anger, and abounding in mercy. He will not always strive with us, nor will He keep His anger forever. He has not dealt with us according to our sins, nor punished us according to our iniquities. For as the heavens are high above the earth, so great is His mercy toward those who fear Him; as far as the east is from the west, so far has He removed our transgressions from us. As a father pities his children, so the Lord pities those who fear Him.

For He knows our frame; He remembers that we are dust. As for men, his days are like grass; as a flower of the field, so he flourishes, for the wind passes over it, and it is gone, and its place remembers it no more. But the mercy of the Lord is from everlasting to everlasting on those who fear Him, and His righteousness to children's children to such as keep His covenant, and to those who remember His commandments to do them. The Lord has established His throne in heaven, and His kingdom rules over all. Bless the Lord, you His angels, who excel in strength, who do His Word, heeding the voice of His Word. Bless the Lord, all you His hosts, you ministers [servants] of His, who do His pleasure. Bless the Lord, all His works, in all places of His dominion. Bless the Lord, O my soul!

(This psalm was given to me in a dream, March 11, 1982.)

Let Us Pray for Spiritual Wisdom and Blessings

Blessed be the God and Father of our Lord Jesus Christ, who has blessed us with every spiritual blessing in the heavenly places in Christ His Son, just as He chose us in Him before the foundation of the world, that we should be holy and without blame before Him in love, having predestined us to adoption as sons by Jesus Christ to Himself, according to the good pleasure of His will, to the praise of the glory of His grace [His favor, blessing, kindness], by which He made us accepted in the Beloved.

In Him [Jesus Christ] we have redemption through His blood, the forgiveness of sins, according to the riches of His grace which He made to abound toward us in all wisdom and prudence [understanding], having made known to us the mystery of His will, according to His good pleasure which He purposed in Himself, that in the dispensation of the fullness of the times He might gather together in one all things in Jesus Christ, both which are in heaven and which are on earth—in Him.

We pray that the God of our Lord and Savior Jesus Christ, the Father of glory, give to us the spirit of wisdom and revelation in the knowledge of Him; and the eyes of our understanding being enlightened; that we may know what is the hope of His calling; what are the riches of the glory of His inheritance in the saints; and what is the exceeding greatness of His power toward us who believe; according to the working of His mighty power which He worked in Jesus Christ when He raised Him from the dead and seated Him at His right hand in the heavenly places; far above all principality [rule]; and power [authority]; and might [power] and dominion; and every name that is named; not only in this age but also in that which is to come.

We pray and that we have confidence in knowing that God, who has begun a good work in us, will complete it until the day of Jesus Christ return to this earth. We pray that our love abounds even the more in knowledge and all discernment, that we may approve the things that are excellent and good, that we may be sincere and truthful; and without offense till the day of Christ return, being filled with the fruits of righteous which are by Jesus Christ our Lord, to the glory and praise of God our Father.

Spiritual blessings and wisdom, and peace to all who are faithful in Jesus Christ, and sincerely love Him. May the grace of our Lord and Savior Jesus Christ; the love of God our Father; and the fellowship of the Holy Spirit be with us all.

In Jesus's name we pray. Amen.

—Ephesians 1:3–10, 17–21; Philippians 1:6, 9–11

The Beatitudes

Blessed are the poor in spirit: for theirs is the kingdom of heaven.

Blessed are they that mourn: for they shall be comforted.

Blessed are the meek: for they shall inherit the earth.

Blessed are they which do hunger and thirst after righteousness: for they shall be filled.

Blessed are the merciful: for they shall obtain mercy.

Blessed are the pure in heart: for they shall see God.

Blessed are the peacemakers: for they shall be called the children of God.

Blessed are they which are persecuted for righteousness' sake: for theirs is the kingdom of heaven.

Blessed are ye, when men shall revile you, and persecute you, and say all manner of evil against you falsely, for My sake.

Rejoice, and be exceeding glad: for great is your reward in heaven: for so they persecuted the prophets which were before you.

—Matthew 5:3–12 (KJV)

Intercessory Prayer for Those Who Are Suicidal

Dear families, loved ones, friends, prayer warriors, the church of God, Christians: it is high time that we all unite and intercede in prayer on behalf all people around the world against suicidal spirits. People of all ages, but especially our children and young people, are committing suicide, taking their own lives because they have lost all hope and they feel like they can't cope with or in this life anymore. Their minds have become a battlefield, and the enemy has taken control. They see death as the only answer, the only way out to escape from it all.

We must be more concerned about our loved ones and friends and talk to and listen to them. We also need to spend quality time with our children. We need to talk more to our children; we need to listen to our children; and we need to pray for our children. We need to treat them with respect and let them know that we love them and value their opinions. Regardless of their age, we need to take the time to sit down with them, ask them how their day was, and listen. We must give them our undivided attention—really listen to them and look at them. Do they sound or look different? Has their behavior or personality changed? Are they withdrawn and seem not to feel like being around family? We can read our children better than anyone else, that is, when we do spend quality time with them.

They are not exempt from everyday problems just because they are children or young adults. Life is not all carefree or problem-free for them. They too are pressured with the cares of this world. They may be going through peer pressure, emotional abuse, physical abuse, sexual abuse, verbal abuse, bullying, gang-related violence, coercion, intimidation, threats, neglect, drug addiction, or sexual trauma (especially children), may feel unloved or unwanted, and may have low self-esteem.

They may have thoughts and feelings of anxiety, hopelessness, depression, humiliation, shame, and unhappiness with themselves, and they may not fully know how to express their feelings or how to deal with their emotions. They may feel too embarrassed and believe that you don't really care. Remember, they too (regardless of age) can feel overwhelmed, afraid, hurt, confused, broken, and like they're suffocating. They may feel like they're sinking in quicksand, and the more they fight against it in order to stay alive, the deeper they sink. They look around for someone to throw them a lifeline, someone or something to pull them out of this death trap (of Satan), but no one is there to help pull them to safety. No one is around who can speak the Word of God (life) into their lives and hearts. So they give up; they succumb to death and what it has to offer, which they think is peace and freedom from the cares of this world. How sad and disillusioned.

Parents, please pray for and with your children. Communicate with your children. Listen to them, for they may be trying to tell you something, something that may not seem important to you but that is a matter of life and death for them. Cherish and love them because they desperately need you. Maybe they just need a smile or a hug or to hear you say, "I love you, and I'm always here for you no matter what."

Take time to talk to them, and let them know that they can talk to you about anything, anytime. Let them know that you will not judge them but that you will listen to them, advise them, and help them in any way that you can. Don't wait for them to approach you; go to them. You're their mom or dad; you are their strength. They trust you with their lives, and they believe that you, more than anyone else, can provide the answers to their questions and problems. And even if they have a relationship with Christ, they still need you; they still need to feel your love and see Christ in and through you. Satan's goal is to kill, steal from, and destroy all he can, but especially our young people.

Your children didn't ask to be born, nor were they given a choice of parents. But God chose you, and you will be held responsible by Him for their well-being. We *must* fight for our children's souls. We cannot allow Satan to destroy them. Please, don't let him win.

Dear friends, we are in the midst of spiritual warfare. This fight is spiritual; it is not of flesh and blood. Therefore, we must wear the whole armor of God and fight with the sword of the Spirit, which is the Word of God. Read your Bible and pray as never before.

Take your children to Sunday school and Bible study so that they can learn about God and be taught the gospel of Jesus Christ and how to fight spiritual battles (they're not too young for this). Teach them how to pray, and pray with them. Tell them that God loves them and that they can trust Him. Raise them in the love and admonition of the Lord our God.

Spiritual Warfare against Demon Spirits

Calling *all* prayer warriors, the body of Jesus Christ, and people of God. It is time that we come together as the church of God, as true Christians, as the children of God, as the body of Christ, and as a people to intercede and to cry out of our hearts to Abba, Father, our God, and Jesus Christ, our Lord and Savior, on behalf of *all* people (regardless of their race, faith, gender, or age) around the world who are being tormented by suicidal demonic spirits that have been released by Satan upon the earth. It is high time for us to stand together and fight against Satan and the powers of darkness. We can't just do nothing! We can't continue to let Satan win. It's time for us to suit up in our spiritual armor and join the fight in this spiritual war.

For information about suicide and vital statistics, please visit the following websites: Centers for Disease Control and Prevention (CDC); American Foundation for Suicide Prevention (AFSP); American Association of Suicidology; and SAVE (Suicide Awareness Voice of Education) / Worldwide Health. There are many other websites where you can find information on suicide. Thousands of people—from the very young to as old as eighty-five—commit suicide every year. According to the CDC, suicide is the tenth leading cause of death in the US for all ages.

Can you imagine that? The statistics regarding suicide victims in every state and across the global are astounding and unbelievable. When I read them, it nearly took my breath away. I hate Satan and his demons even more for the part that they have played in shortening the lives of these people and the life of my nephew. Church, we need to pray like never before!

One day in May 2017, someone who was like a son to me, whom I loved very much, *committed suicide*. It was a terrible shock to our family.

I could not believe what happened. It stills lingers in my heart. I had so many questions. Why did he take his own life? What made him want to take his life? Why didn't he talk to me? I thought, *Why didn't God show me, or give me a sign concerning this? What had happened that he felt that taking his life was the only solution? Why?* He believed in God, and he was raised in church, so what happened?

He had no reason to take his life. And the way that he took it hurt me even more. He had a good job for twenty-plus years and was manager of his department. He had a lovely apartment; he had people he thought were his friends; he had a family who loved, adored, respected him; and he had money in the bank. He was very handsome, was a good dresser, and was very intelligent. So, why did he take his life? Why did he commit suicide? I felt like I was about to explode with too many thoughts, too much pressure, too many questions, and no answers. I couldn't sleep for twenty-four hours when I first heard about his death.

About two weeks after his death, one night I just couldn't sleep because I was thinking about him. For the first time, I talked to God, trying to understand why this had happened. I heard clearly within my spirit a voice calmly say: "A suicidal demon spirit. Pray against suicidal demon spirits." I received the answer to my questions and a solution for dealing with the enemy's causing so many people to commit suicide. I knew that my new assignment from God was to prepare myself and others for spiritual warfare specifically against suicidal demon spirits.

This is a spiritual fight. We the church and family of God *must* stand together and fight it. We will need to put on (and keep on) the whole armor of God; fast; be watchful; pray together; and be of one accord with the same mind. We need to stay in the Word of God, memorize scriptures, keep our minds and eyes focused on Jesus, and keep our faith rooted and grounded in Him.

We are God's army; we are to stand and fight against the enemies together as one body. For this fight will take all of us. And we will win because greater is He who is within us than he who is in the world. We have the Holy Spirit, the power and authority of God the Father, and Jesus Christ our Lord and Savior. And since Jesus is for us, He is more than Satan and his demons against us.

Satan, that old devil, has released a demonic attack—an army of suicidal demon spirits—upon the earth to kill, steal from, and destroy everyone that they can: the weak and the strong, the saved and the unsaved, the young and the old, the rich and the poor. It's war for Satan, and his attack is on humanity because he knows that his time is just about up. His goals have not changed; they are to destroy those who believe in God the Father and His Son Jesus Christ.

Satan wants to take as many as he can to spend their eternal lives in hell (in a lake that burns with unquenchable fire and brimstone) with him and his demons. The evil, the wicked, the unrighteous, and false worshippers have a form of godliness and holiness, but they deny the power of God and do not truly believe, trust, or obey God. These people reject Jesus Christ as Lord and Savior.

You see, Satan knows exactly just how bad the end will be for him and his followers, and there's nothing he can do to stop it. Hell is his destiny. However, he wants hell to be your destiny too. I detest him (and his buddies) because of who he is, and what he does. He's a murderer, thief, destroyer, false accuser of the people of God, and liar.

He knows that Jesus Christ is soon to return to this earth, so he must hurry to prevent anyone from believing in Jesus and accepting Him as Lord and Savior. And for those who already believe, have faith, and have Jesus in their lives, Satan's job is to make them curse God, blame Him for everything that they're going through right now, and lose faith and hope in Him.

Satan (the devil) wants you, me, and everybody else to give up on life and die. He wants our souls. He tells people that suicide is the best and only way out. Don't believe him or listen to him, because he is a liar. Satan is the father of lies, a deceiver, an accuser, an imitator, a tempter, a thief, a killer, and a destroyer. And he's always seeking whom he can devour. He hates us and everything about us that represents God and Jesus Christ.

We as Christians, children of the Most High God, and born-again believers in the gospel of Jesus Christ must stand up and fight for those who can't (whatever the reason) or who don't know how to fight this demonic spiritual war. We must stand *in* faith because we live and walk by faith—*not* by sight. And with faith we totally believe (in the spirit) and have complete confidence that whatsoever we say (according to God's Word and will) has happened and will materialize in God's own time. Don't believe everything that you see in the natural.

We must stand united, fearless, firm, and strong. We must stand together in prayer, stand together in love, and stand up for Jesus Christ. We must pray for one another, pulling down strongholds with the Word of God and its truth; our faith in His Word and in Jesus Christ; and the power of the Holy Spirit. We must show the devil, our enemies, and the world that we are not ashamed of the gospel of Jesus Christ because it is the power of God to save everyone who believes and has faith in His Word and His Son Jesus Christ.

The Word of God tells us that one believer in Jesus Christ "can chase a thousand [enemies, demons], and two can put ten thousand [enemies, demons] to flight" (Deuteronomy 32:30); and "five of us shall chase a hundred [enemies, demons] and a hundred of us shall put ten thousand [enemies, demons] to flight" (Leviticus 26:8).

God assures us that He is with and for us. He said, "No weapon [of Satan, demons, or any person] formed against us [the body of Jesus Christ, His children] shall prosper, and every tongue which rises against us in judgment will be condemn. This is the heritage of the servants of the Lord, and their righteous is from Me" (Isaiah 54:17).

Also, Jesus said that where two or three of His children are gathered together for prayer, praise, and worship in His name, He is in their midst (Matthew 18:20). And whatever things we ask in prayer, believing, we will receive (Matthew 21:22). How awesome is that?! So, when we pray in unity and in agreement, our prayers are more powerful.

Jesus is coming back soon, and we will have to give an account and be judged by all that we have said and done. When God asks you if you prayed for His people who were considering suicide and if you prayed against the enemies of those who became suicidal victims of Satan, what will your response be?

We are our brethren's keeper in that we should be concerned and have compassion for one another, should pray for one another, should encourage one another, and should be helpful and assist those who ask for (and truly need) help in any way that we can. You know what you have and what you can do, and so does Your heavenly Father, for all that you have belongs to Him. He blessed you to obtain it for you and your family and to be a blessing to others.

Saints, children of God, we are the army of the almighty God, Creator of heaven, earth, the area underneath the earth, everyone, and everything. We are more than conquerors in Jesus Christ. We have been given the privilege, authority, dominion, and power to fight against Satan and his demons. The Holy Spirit lives in us, and the Word of God abides in us. His Word is our weapon; it is our sword.

We must wear the whole armor that God has provided us with to fight and stand against Satan's schemes, trickery, lies, and fear and all that he throws at us to try to block and stop us. We only need to open our mouths and speak the Word of God in faith. Do not fear or be intimidated by Satan. Remember, our fight is spiritual; we are not fighting against flesh and blood, but against powers of darkness: Satan, demons (fallen angels), those who are spiritually wicked and evil, and demonic forces.

Satan wants to keep our spiritual eyes blinded and our ears closed so that we can't see God or hear His voice. He wants to keep us oppressed and depressed, without hope, and prevent us from growing spiritually and nearer to God our Father and Jesus Christ our Lord and Savior. Get in God's Word and stay there no matter what Satan says; meditate on it both day and night.

"For the word of God is living and powerful, and sharper than any two-edged sword, piercing even to the division of soul and joints and marrow, and is a discerner of the thoughts and intents of the heart. And there is no creature hidden from His sight; but all things are naked and open to the eyes of Him to whom we must give account" (Hebrews 4:12–13).

We have been given power and authority by Almighty God and Jesus Christ with the anointing of the Holy Spirit to live a holy life, pull down strongholds, cast down everything that exalts itself against God's knowledge, stand and fight against powers and rulers of darkness and against spiritual hosts of wickedness in heavenly places, cast out demons, and do the work that God has assigned us to do while here on earth. We can't let Satan continue to get away with murder.

Remember, we have been endowed with the power of the Holy Ghost; we are armed and dangerous, a force to be reckoned with. Satan knows this. He fears our anointing because he knows that the anointing will destroy his work. He knows that we are covered by the blood of Jesus and that the Holy Spirit dwells inside of us. And none of his strategies, tactics, or weapons he forms against us will be useful; they will not work—in the name of Jesus! Satan can't win because he has already lost. Remember, Jesus won over two thousand years ago!

But you shall receive power when the Holy Spirit has come upon you, and you shall be witnesses to Me. (Acts 1:8)

Behold, I send the Promise of My Father upon you … until you are endued with power from on high. (Luke 24:49)

This is He who baptizes with the Holy Spirit. And I have seen and testified that this is the Son of God. (John 1:33–34)

But the Helper [Comforter], the Holy Spirit, whom the Father will send in My name, He will teach you all things, and bring to your remembrance all things that I said to you. My peace I give you; not as the world gives. Let not your heart be troubled, neither let it be afraid. (John 15:26–27)

And they were all filled with the Holy Spirit and began to speak with other tongues, as the Spirit gave them utterance. (Acts 2:4)

And these signs will follow those who believe. In My name they will cast out demons; they will speak with new tongues; they will take up serpents; and if they drink anything deadly, it will by no means hurt them; they will lay hands on the sick, and they will recover. (Mark 16:17–18)

Heal the sick, cleanse the lepers, raise the dead, cast out demons. Freely you have received, freely give. (Matthew 10:8)

Most assuredly, I say to you, he who believes in Me, the works that I do he will do also; and greater works than these he will do, because I go to My Father. (John 14:12)

For the weapons of our warfare are not carnal (of the flesh) but mighty in God for pulling down strongholds, casting down arguments and every high thing that exalts itself against the knowledge of God, bringing every thought into captivity to the obedience of Christ. (2 Corinthians 10:4–4)

For we do not wrestle against flesh and blood, but against principalities, against powers, against the rulers of the darkness of this age, against spiritual hosts of wickedness in the heavenly places. (Ephesians 6:12)

Saints of God, Satan knows whom we belong to. When he sees us, he sees the blood of Jesus Christ, and he's in fear. However, for us to be able to stand up and fight this spiritual war against Satan and his army of demonic spirits, we must take up and put on the whole armor of God, and we must wear it all the time. We must stay prayerful, pray in the Spirit, walk in the Spirit, be watchful, and fast often.

We must live a life that's pleasing to God. We must be baptized and filled with the Holy Spirit. We must know without a shadow of a doubt in whom we believe and have faith. We must have no fear, knowing that we stand in the faith and confidence of Jesus Christ and His name. We must at all times believe and trust Him, leaving no place for any doubt in our minds and hearts.

We are not on our own; we are not alone. For greater, mightier, and more powerful is the Holy Spirit who dwells in us than anyone in this world or Satan and his evil demonic forces. God our heavenly Father and Jesus Christ His Son, our Lord and Savior, wants us (and it's our responsibility) to stand and fight against the forces of evil. He has fully equipped us with His Holy Spirit living in us, granting us power and authority. By no means allow Satan to intimidate you, and believe nothing that he says or shows you. Always keep your mind, eyes, ears, and heart focused on Jesus Christ and the Word of God.

Stand therefore, having girded your waist with truth, having put on the breastplate of righteousness, and having shod your feet with the preparation of the gospel of peace; about all, taking the shield of faith with which, you will be able to quench all the fiery darts of the wicked one. And take the helmet of salvation, and the sword of the Spirit, which is the word of God; praying always with all prayer and supplication in the Spirit, being watchful to this end with all perseverance and supplication for all the saints [true Christians, believers in God, and Jesus Christ His Son]. (Ephesians 6:14–18)

Following is a prayer against suicidal demon spirits that we can pray together daily around the clock and around the world. Or you can pray it as God leads you. But please pray against these demonic spirits. They are on the rise and will get stronger because they know that they do not have much more time on earth to destroy young and old—but especially young people. Pray for your children, my children, and *all* children around the world. Satan is not interested in any special ethnicity, gender, or age, nor does he care about your religious beliefs. He hates all people, even those who serve him. If you're not sure what or how to pray in any situation, then ask the Holy Spirit for help.

Dear prayer warriors, people of God: before you pray and enter into the presence of God to fight against Satan and his demons, ask Jesus to forgive you of your sins and cleanse you in His blood of all unrighteousness. If you are harboring unforgiveness in your heart for anyone, then you need to get that solved with whomever it is and put it under the blood of Jesus. We want our prayers to be effective, powerful, and productive. We don't want any small cracks open where the adversary can sneak in. We don't want to give Satan or his demons any place in our lives or any cause to try to hinder our prayers.

Pray in the Spirit, for the Holy Spirit knows how to pray and intercede for the people. However, if you don't, that's okay too; just pray in love from your heart. For God looks deep into the hearts of people.

> Likewise, the Spirit also helps in our weaknesses. For we do not know what we should pray for as we ought, but the Spirit Himself makes intersession for us with groanings which cannot be uttered. Now He who searches the hearts knows what the mind of the Spirit is, because He makes intercession for the saints according to the will of God. (Romans 8:26–27)

> And the prayer of faith will save the sick, and the Lord will raise him up. And if he has committed sins, he will be forgiven. (James 5:15)

> For if I pray in a tongue [language], my spirit prays, but my understanding is unfruitful. (1 Corinthians 4:14)

However, God can reveal whatever He wants to whomever He wants. ... Pray for one another, that you may be healed. The effective, fervent prayer of a righteous man [person] avails much. (James 5:16)

Repent and let everyone of you be baptized in the name of Jesus Christ for the remissions [forgiveness] of sins; and you shall receive the gift of the Holy Spirit. For the promise is to you and to your children, and to all who are afar off, as many as the Lord our God will call. (Acts 2:38)

And whatever you ask in My name, that I will do, that the Father may be glorified in the Son. If you ask anything in My name, I will do it. (John 14:13–14)

People of God; fast, watch, stay sober, and pray so that you will not enter temptation. For the spirit indeed is willing, but the flesh is weak. (Matthew 26:41)

Keep your spirit fed with the Word of God, and fellowship with Him daily. Satan will challenge you as to in whom you believe and what you believe. But you know who you are in Jesus Christ, and you know whose you are. You know what He has done and is doing for you personally, and you know that your God is supreme and supernatural. He is the one and only true living Lord God Almighty.

Finally, family of God, my brothers and sisters in Jesus Christ: may God's Word richly dwell in you, and may you be strong in the Lord and in the power of His might. Put on the whole armor of God to stand and fight against Satan. Open your mouth and speak with boldness, authority, and power in the name of Jesus.

And may the love, peace, grace, and mercy (that endures forever) of God our Father and of Jesus Christ our Lord and Savior, who gave Himself for our sins so that He might deliver us from this present evil age according to the will and promise of our God and Father, to whom be the glory forever, be with us all, always and forever. In Jesus's name. Amen.

Prayer against Suicidal Demon Spirits

Father God, in the name of Jesus Christ, we, Your children, the saints of God, gather together from all over the world and come to You right now to the throne of grace on behalf of those who are contemplating suicide or who are about to end their lives here on earth. First of all, we ask that You forgive us of all sin, wash us in the blood of Jesus, and cleanse us of all unrighteousness and anything that is not pleasing to You or that will hinder this prayer.

Jesus said that where two or three are gathered together in His name, He is there in their midst (Matthew 18:20). We thank Him for that because without Him we can do nothing—we are powerless. But with Him we can do all things in His name—the name of Jesus.

Father, You told us to come boldly with confidence to the throne of grace and make our requests known to You so that we may obtain mercy and find grace to help us in our time of need (Hebrews 4:16). We know as Your Word tells us, "You are the Lord our God; You are righteous in all Your ways; gracious in all Your works; and You are near to all who call upon You in truth; You will fulfill the desire of those who fear You; and You will hear their cry and save them" (Psalm 145:17–19).

Oh, Lord God, hear us now; hear our cry for those who cannot (for whatever the reason) cry out for themselves right now. Let Your love, mercy, and amazing grace find them, rescue them, and deliver them right now from the grip of Satan and his demonic spirits, in the name of Jesus. As the demonic spirits come to attack them, let the devil and demon spirits see the blood of Jesus on your children and on the doorposts of their hearts. Let them see the blood of Jesus even on their doors to prevent demons from entering their house, in the almighty name of Jesus.

We, as the body of Jesus Christ, stand firm and come together as one in the power and authority that You have given us—and in the almighty name of Jesus. We rebuke and come against suicidal demon spirits globally and in all territories—in the name of Jesus. We plead the blood of Jesus against them in the name of Jesus. We pull down their strongholds and cast out all suicidal demon spirits from the people whom they have housed in or attacked, and we command them to go back to the pit of hell, where we bind them in the almighty name of Jesus until further notice from Him. Father, we put on the breastplate of righteousness and we take up the shield of faith to stand against the works of the devil (Satan) and his demons. We bind them and their demonic forces to the bottomless pit in the name of Jesus. We stand on Your word that You came to destroy the works of the devil (1 John 3:8).

Father, we ask that You forgive these Your people of their sins, save them, and cover them with the precious blood of Jesus Christ. If there is anything else that needs to be rooted out, then root out whatever is embedded in them that is still causing their souls to be cast down and giving them the desire to take their lives. Save their souls; make them whole; build them up in their spirits and in their faith in You. Reveal Yourself to those who don't know You; let them know that You are real, that You are God. Show Yourself strong in their life. Those who do believe in You and Your Son Jesus Christ. Surround them and fill them with your loving presence and let them know that You have not forgotten them; and You will never forsake them.

Embrace them with Your love, mercy, and grace. Let them know that they can cast all their troubles and concerns (no matter what they have done, or whatever it is that they feel is so terrible that the only way out is death, or whatever is causing them to think that they deserve death) upon You. Let them know that whatever they are going through right now is only temporary, is not permanent. Let them know that they do not have to make a permanent decision in their lives based on the temporary problem or situation that they are going through. Let them know that death isn't the way out. Let them know that You have a better way for them and that they can live and not die. You have the answer and solution to any problems they may have. Let them know that their lives on earth do not have to be over and that Satan is just trying to trick them and lure them into hell.

There is no problem that is too big or too small for You. Let them realize that the idea of suicide is from Satan; it is not from You. Let them know that Satan only wants to kill, steal from, and destroy them, but that Jesus Christ came to save them and give them an abundant and eternal life. Father, please do not let Satan and his demons cheat them and trick them out of their reward of eternal life that You have promised.

O Lord my God, You have power over all things. You created all things that are in heaven, on earth, and underneath the earth, visible and invisible. You are sovereign. You have supreme authority, control, and power over all things, every person, all thrones, all dominions, all principalities (rulers), Satan, all demons, and the powers of darkness. No one can do anything without You or unless You say so. You are the one and only almighty, all-powerful, true and living God.

You hold our breath in Your hand, and You own us and all our ways. You proved Your love for us by dying for us while we were still sinners. You love us so much that You sent Your Son Jesus Christ to redeem us and reconcile us into a right standing and relationship with You. Jesus took our sins in His body; He was wounded for our transgressions and bruised for our iniquities. He bore our griefs and pain, carried all our sorrows and sickness, suffered public humiliation, shed His precious blood for us, and died on the cross. Jesus went to hell, set captives free, and took the keys from Satan. You raised Him from the dead on the third day with all power and the keys of Hades (hell, the unseen realm) and death in His hands. Jesus Christ purchased our salvation, and oh what a price He paid.

Father God, You are omnipotent (You are all-powerful; You can do anything that You want to do), omnipresent (You are everywhere at the same time. There's no place where You're not already there), and omniscient (You know everything. There's nothing that You don't know, have not known, and will not know). You are an awesome God. You are the Almighty God, Creator of the universe and of everyone and everything in it. What a God! And we are so privileged to serve You. We give You praise, honor, and glory.

Father, let Your peace take rule right now in the hearts of those who are suicidal. Touch and change their mind as Your direct their hearts into Your love and to the patience of Jesus Christ. Let Your grace that brings salvation appear to them, and let them look to You for whatever the need, reason, or problem might be. Draw them close to You; hold them tight in Your loving arms; shelter them from the storms of this life and all they are going through. Spiritually open their eyes so that they can see You; their ears so that they can hear You; and their hearts so that they can believe and receive You and no longer be in darkness. Help them to believe, and help them with their unbelief.

Let them see a bright light, and let them see You standing at the end of the tunnel with outstretched arms. And if they can't see that far, O Father, I ask that You walk with them or carry them through that tunnel of darkness that horrifies them even to the point of death. Make their crooked places straight amid an evil and crooked generation. Let them know that You will never leave them or forsake them so long as they choose to have You in their lives. Let them feel your love and presence. Have mercy, oh Lord my God.

Father God, do not let Satan and his demons succeed or prosper at forming any weapons or schemes against these Your people. Hide them in Your secret place, under Your almighty wings, in the name of Jesus! We bind the hands of Satan, of suicidal demonic spirits, and of all evil spirits that try to destroy the people of God—in the name of Jesus. And we loose the angels of God to surround, minister to, and protect God's children—in the name of Jesus.

Shower them with Your love, mercy, grace, favor, and kindness. Heal their minds, bodies, souls, and hearts. Protect them and save them from the wiles and the hand of Satan, whose purpose and goal is to destroy them emotionally, mentally, physically, and spiritually and take them to spend their eternal life in hellfire with him.

Father, we speak the blessings of Abraham upon these Your people and ask that they will receive the promise of Your Spirit through faith. Supply and meet all their needs and those of their families, for they are Your creation, created in Your image for Your glory and good works. Please give them the mind and strength to think, or even whisper, Your name as they call upon and seek You for help and salvation in their moment of despair and hopelessness.

"For You have delivered us by the blood of Jesus from the power of darkness, and we have been transferred into the kingdom of Jesus Christ who You love; in whom we have redemption through His blood, and the forgiveness of sins, according to the riches of Your grace" (Colossians 1:13–14; Ephesians 1:7).

In the almighty name of Jesus, the name that is above all names, we pray. Amen.

Let Us Now Rebuke and Bind the Hand of Satan and His Suicidal Demonic Spirits

We the children of God, the saints of God, the body of believers in Jesus Christ, the church of God purchased by the blood of Jesus Christ our Lord and Savior, who made all things visible and invisible, the heavens, the earth, underneath the earth, and hell—we come together as one body in the almighty name of Jesus, and we speak to Satan and all suicidal demon spirits by the power and authority granted to us by God the Father and Jesus Christ His Son. We command you, rebuke you, cast you out, and bind you and your demonic works against God's creation and against His people in the name of Jesus.

We speak to all suicidal demonic spirits roaming all over the world seeking whom you can devour, kill, steal from, and destroy. In the almighty name of Jesus, by the blood of Jesus, and by the power and authority given to us by Jesus Christ, we command you right now to take your filthy hands off that man, woman, teenager, or child, leave them *now*, and never return again—in the name of Jesus. We also rebuke and command demonic spirits working in the area of depression, oppression, anxiety, loneliness, despair, sadness, and sickness (physical, mental, and emotional). We rebuke and come against demonic spirits that work in areas to bring and cause feelings of helplessness, sexual attacks, sex trafficking, domestic violence, child abuse, child sexual abuse, child pornography, verbal abuse, bullying, homelessness, death, failure, fear, feelings of inferiority, and poverty. Go—get out of the minds, hearts, and lives of those you afflict, and never return. We ask these things in the name of Jesus.

These are God's people who are made in His image. You have no right or place in their bodies, minds, hearts, or lives because they are God's property, purchased by and covered with the blood of Jesus Christ. Jesus, now that they have been delivered from the power, influence, and hand of Satan and his demon spirits, we ask that You protect and cover them and baptize them with the Holy Spirit. Encourage them. Lead and guide them to a church that preaches and teaches the full gospel of Jesus Christ so that they can grow in Your Word, grow nearer to You, and fellowship with other believers. Please send angels to encamp around them.

We the righteous, blood-washed, and sanctified of God intercede on behalf of our brothers, sisters, and children. They will live and not die! They will live and *not* die! In the name of Jesus. Hallelujah! And they will declare the goodness of the Lord and be ambassadors and witnesses for the gospel of Jesus Christ. For Jesus, God's holy Son, paid the price for us all on the cross. He died so that they could live, and He has set them free from the bondage of sin, guilt, and shame. He rose from the dead on the third day for us so that we could live and fellowship with Him forever. Greater is the Spirit of God who dwells in us than Satan and those who are in the world. Glory to God!

Any weapon you form against the body of believers in Jesus Christ, who intercedes on behalf of God's people who are tormented by you and demonic spirits and behalf of the souls whom you seek to steal and destroy, will *not* prosper. It will not work. Every tongue that revolts against us will be condemned, for this is our inheritance from God. And we stand on the promises and faith of God our Father and Jesus Christ our Lord and Savior.

Jesus told us that whatever we bind on earth would be bound in heaven. Satan, we rebuke you and command you to leave God's people *now*! In the name of Jesus, we cast you out and bind you in the bottomless pit of hell right now. *Go!* in the name of Jesus. We believe and call it done by faith in Jesus's name. Amen.

Note: Please email me at sarjon777 @gmail.com if you are willing to join this fight and stand with other warriors against Satan and his demonic suicidal demons. He cannot have our children, spouses, parents, siblings, relatives, or friends, or anyone else. We pray for *all* people regardless of who they are or where they are. Satan is no respecter of persons. We *must* bind the hand and works of Satan and all demon spirits in all territories all over God's world in the almighty name of Jesus! Time is short; we must get busy. We are stronger and more powerful in numbers. So please contact me soon and let me know the time that you will be praying. Thank you, and God bless you.

My Personal Prayers

Sarah's Prayers, in the following section, are my personal prayers that may feature some scriptures, psalms, songs, and words that God gave to me in dreams. I have made them part of my personal prayers, and I would like to share these prayers with you in the hope that you will be blessed. Make these prayers your own personal prayers. Put *your name* on them, as I have, and claim your blessings. For God is no respecter of persons; He is fair and just to all who call upon Him in faith.

God hears our prayers when we pray in faith with a sincere heart, and He always looks at our motives. We do not pray for show, to be seen or heard by others, but we pray to be seen and heard by our heavenly Father, who sees, hears, and knows our heart. God will also regard the prayer of the destitute and does not despise their sincere prayer. His mercies are new every morning, and He gives grace to the humble.

Whether your prayer is short or long, it has nothing to do with God's hearing or answering of it. It is your *faith*, *trust*, and *belief* in the Word of God the Father and in Jesus Christ our Lord and Savior, and your confidence that, without a shadow of doubt, He will answer you and that He is well able to do anything. Glory to God! After you prayer, begin to thank God for answering your prayer, whether it is for yourself or you're interceding for others. Believe that you have received from Him what you asked (according to His Word). Praise Him until you see the manifestation. For we walk and live by faith in His Word and who He is, not by what we see in the now in the natural.

Personally (I know that this is true for many other believers as well), I find that when I do not always know just how to pray for someone or certain situations, the Holy Spirit takes control and prays through me to our heavenly Father. When this happens, I yield myself to Him and begin speaking in a heavenly language or a tongue unknown to me. Now it is strictly between the Holy Spirit, Jesus Christ, and God our Father. It is an awesome time of communion, a holy time. I am so humbled and honored by His presence and by such an amazing gift.

> And they were all filled with the Holy Spirit and began to speak with other tongues [languages], as the Spirit gave them utterance. (Acts 2:4)

> Likewise, the Spirit also helps in our weaknesses. For we do not know what we should pray for as we ought, but the Spirit Himself makes intercession for us with groanings which cannot be uttered. Now He who searches the heart knows what the mind of the Spirit is, because He makes intercession for the saints according to the will of God. (Romans 8:26–27)

> For he who speaks in a tongue does not speak to men but to God, for no one understands him; however, in the spirit he speaks mysteries. (1 Corinthians 14:2)

> For if I pray in a tongue, my spirit prays, but my understanding is unfruitful. (1 Corinthians 14:14)

> If you can believe, you can receive—and you can depend on God! Believe and receive as you read in faith and expectation Sarah's prayers.

Sarah's Prayers

Goodness and Mercy Follow Me

Father God, hear my prayer.

You, O Lord, are my Shepherd, and I will not want, nor do I lack for anything, because You are my Source and my Waymaker, and You supply all my needs according to Your riches in glory by Jesus Christ Your Son. Thank You for making me to lie down in green pastures and leading me beside the calm waters. Thank You for restoring my soul and leading me in the path of righteousness for Your name's sake. Father God, when I walk through the valley of the shadow of death, I will not be afraid and will fear no evil, because I know that You are always with me.

Your rod and Your staff, Your Holy Spirit, they comfort me. I know that You will prepare a table before me in the presence of my enemies; for You anoint my head with oil, and my cup runs over. Surely, Your goodness and mercy will follow me all the days of my life, and I will live with You for eternity. So wherever You are, there I will be also.

Thank You for everlasting life in Your presence, in Your glory, and in Your kingdom.

In the name of Jesus, I pray. Amen.

(Psalm 23 was given to me in a dream, February 1980, September 18, 1989, and January 13, 1991. Also see Philippians 4:19.)

I Trust You, O Lord

Heavenly Father, to You I lift up my soul. I cry out to You. I trust You. Hear me, have mercy upon me, and answer me. Do not hide Your face from me. For You, my Lord, are my light and my salvation; therefore, I will fear no one. You are the strength of my life, and there is no one I am afraid of. You will protect me from the hands of my enemies and my foes, and as they come against me, no matter who they are or how many there are, my heart will not fear, for they will stumble and fall. Thank You for hiding me in times of trouble under Your almighty wings and in the secret place of Your tabernacle. Thank You for being my help, my strength, and my anchor. You have never let me down. Great is Your love, faithfulness, graciousness, and mercy toward me.

Father, You are the God of my salvation. Never leave me or forsake me. Teach me Your ways, and lead me on a smooth path, safe from my enemies. Often, I would have given up if I did not have You in my life and on my side, if I didn't have hope in Jesus's return to take me home to reign with You forever. If it were not for Your love, kindness, favor, graciousness, goodness, mercy, and grace, I don't know where or what I would be today. I will encourage others to wait on You and to be of good courage, knowing that Your Holy Spirit is with us and that You will strengthen our hearts. I will wait patiently on You.

For there is one thing that I desire of You that I want more than anything and that I will seek and pursue: that I may be where You are, dwelling in the house of the Lord, in Your holy temple, all the days of my life, which is forever, to behold Your beauty and Your glory. For You are my strength and my shield; I trust and rely totally on You. You have always helped me; You have always been there for me, even when I didn't realize it. My heart therefore rejoices, and I will forever praise and worship You. Father, save Your people, shepherd them, and bear them up. Bless and keep Israel safe. In Jesus's name I pray. Amen.

(Psalm 27 was given to me in a dream, January 13, 1991.)

Dwelling in the Secret Place
and Promises of God

Father and Most High God, thank You for allowing me to dwell in Your secret place and abide under the shadow of Your almighty wings. I will tell the world that You are my refuge and my fortress, my God, and in You will I forever trust. You will surely deliver me from the snare of the fowler, from the hand of Satan, and from the perilous pestilence. You will cover me with Your feathers, and under Your wings I will take refuge. Your truth will be my shield and buckler. I shall not be afraid of the terror by night or of the arrow that flies by day, for You will protect me and keep me safe from all dangers, all harm, and my enemies.

Father, because I have made You my refuge and Most High God, and my dwelling place, You said that no evil will befall or come upon me. Neither shall any plague come near my dwelling, for You will give Your angels charge over me to keep me in all my ways.

You said that when I am in the hands of Your angels they will bear me up; they will keep me from falling. I will trample underfoot all my enemies, for no weapon they form against me will prosper because it is my heritage as Your child. And because I have set my love upon You, You will deliver me. You said that You will set me on high because I have known Your name. Whenever I call upon You, You will answer me, and You will be with me when I'm in trouble. You will deliver me and honor me. You said that You will satisfy me with long life and show me Your salvation.

Father, thank You for Your Word and promises. Thank You for covering me (and my family) with the blood of Jesus. I will bless Your name and praise and worship You alone, both now and forever. In Jesus's name, I pray. Amen.

(Psalm 91 was given to me in a dream. See also Isaiah 54:17.)

Encouraging My Soul

There are times when the cares of this life become overwhelming. And whenever this happens, I must talk to myself, especially when I am feeling extremely tired, lonely, and sick, when I don't feel like praying or going to church, and when I am faced with financial and personal problems. There was a time when I even felt like giving up on being a Christian. Satan meets me on the battlefield of my mind and tries to invade and plant such thoughts. And even though I know that it is a trick of Satan (for he comes to steal from, kill, destroy, and discourage us), and even though I know that I have the victory through Jesus Christ, it still takes focus, energy, perseverance, strength, prayer, and faith to shake it off and get it out of my head, my mind, and my thoughts.

So, I began to encourage my soul, and myself, because I must stay rooted and grounded in whom and what I believe. I began to cloud my mind with God's Word and think on things that are true, noble, just, pure, and lovely—things that are of a good report. And if there is anything virtuous and praiseworthy, I will mediate on these things. I began to think about the goodness, mercy, and grace of God; all that God is doing for me (and my family); what He has done for me; what He has promised me that He will do; and what I believe that He's going to do for me. I began to pray in the Holy Spirit while building myself up in my most holy faith. I give God praise and call on the name of Jesus, and I say to Satan in a forceful voice of authority: "Satan, I resist, rebuke, and command you in the name of Jesus to stay away from me and stay out of my mind, for you have no right—and I give you no place—to be in my mind or any part of me. My mind, my body, and all of me belongs to God, for I am His child; I was purchased with the precious blood of Jesus Christ. Let it be known that you, Satan, have no bill of sale on me. I have been redeemed. I'm God's property bought and covered by the blood of Jesus, the precious and perfect Lamb of God. I rebuke you and bind you right now in the name of Jesus."

Then I began to encourage my soul, saying: "My soul, why are you cast down? Why do you feel unhappy and discouraged? Why are you troubled within me? Trust and rely on God, and praise Him for salvation and all that He has done and is doing for you. Soul, you are free in the name of Jesus, and you will bless your God. Listen and hear, my soul: we will bless our God with all that is within us. And we will magnify and exalt His holy name because He alone is worthy. He promised never to leave us or forsake us, and He has never failed us. We will never forget all His benefits. For He forgives all our sins and heals us of all sicknesses and diseases. He redeemed our life from destruction with His precious blood. He crowns us with His loving-kindness and tender mercies. He satisfies our mouth with good things, the very best, and our youth is renewed like the eagle's. He knows the secrets of our heart. God is our refuge and strength, a very present help when we are in trouble; therefore, do not fear or be afraid.

"Yes, my soul, we will bless the Lord whether we feel like it or not! For our God is more than worthy, and He has done and is doing great things for us. And we, O my soul, are so thankful and grateful, and we will worship and praise His almighty and awesome name. Be encouraged, my soul, and bless the Lord our God and Jesus Christ His Son, our Savior, for He deserves all the glory. Hope in the God of our salvation, for He is a marvelous God."

God, my heavenly Father, and Jesus Christ, my Lord and Savior, thank You for being my Rock and strong tower. Thank You for being so gracious, slow to anger, and always full of mercy. Thank You for not dealing with me according to my sins or punishing me according to my iniquities. Thank You for forgiving me of my sins. Thank You for looking far beyond my faults, hang-ups, selfishness, stubbornness, rebellion, and disobedience, and for seeing my needs—and my need for a Savior. Thank You for always being there for me, even when I didn't realize it or deserve it. For You know my frame. You understand me better than I understand myself, and better than anyone else understands me, because You made me and You remember that I am dust.

When I feel discouraged, You always encourage me and lift me up. You are always available when I call. I am so blessed, grateful, and privileged to know and have You as my God, Lord, and Savior. And I'm humbled, honored, full of joy, and thankful that You know and chose me. For You are the one and only true and living God. You are the great I Am! And I take joy and have confidence in knowing that You will never leave me or forsake me. As for humanity, Your creation, our days are like grass or as a flower of the field, so we flourish. Then the wind passes over it, and it is gone. So is our life here on this earth. But Your mercy, O Lord, is from everlasting to everlasting, forever and endlessness, on those who love and fear You, on Your righteous children. In Jesus's name I pray. Amen.

(See Psalm 103:1–5; 10; 14–17; 42:5; 46:1. Also see Philippians 4:8. Psalm 103 was given to me in a dream, March 11, 1983.)

May God's Blessings Be upon Me

Father God, I pray that You bless me and keep me; make
Your face shine upon me and be gracious to me; Lord God
lift up Your countenance upon me; and give me peace.
—Numbers 6:24–26

Father God, fill me with Your Holy Spirit and with the knowledge of Your
will for my life in all wisdom and spiritual understanding so that I may walk
worthy of my calling and of the Lord Jesus Christ, totally and fully pleasing
Him, being fruitful in every good work that I do for You, and increasing
in Your knowledge as You strengthen me with all might according to Your
glorious and awesome power. Fill me with patience and long-suffering, and
with cheer and joy, as I give thanks to You and You alone, who has qualified
me to be a partaker of the inheritance of the saints in Your marvelous light.

For You, Father, have delivered me from the power of darkness (of
Satan, of sin, and of death) and have transferred me into the kingdom of
Jesus Christ Your Son. Because of His love, He gave His life for me on the
cross over two thousand years ago. In Him I have redemption through
His blood; I have been bought with a great price, and I am not my own. I
belong to Him. In this I rejoice in You and glorify Your holy and righteous
name. (See Colossians 1:10–14; 1 Corinthians 6:19–20.)

Father, I also make this request for all my brothers and sisters who
love, believe, trust, and have faith in You. Let Your love, grace, and mercy,
and the peace of our Lord and Savior Jesus Christ, and the fellowship of
the Holy Spirit, be with us, Your children, until Christ comes to take us
to our eternal home. In the name of Jesus, the name that is above every
name, I pray. Amen.

You Know Me Better than I Know Myself

O Lord my God, You have searched me and You know me. You know my sitting and lying down, and my rising up. You see deep within my heart. You know and understand every one of my thoughts before I can even think of them. You know what I'm going to say even before I speak. For there is not a single word on my tongue that You do not altogether know before I say it. You know my path, the way that I will take, and You are acquainted with all my ways. You cover me and have a hedge of protection all around me and have laid Your almighty hand upon me. Such knowledge is too astonishing and amazing for me; it is so high, I cannot attain to it, for it is unreachable and is far beyond my understanding.

Where can I go from Your Spirit? Or where can I flee from Your presence? For if I ascend into heaven, You are there. If I were to make my bed in hell, behold, You are there. If I take the wings of the morning and dwell in the uttermost parts of the sea, even there Your almighty right hand will lead and hold me. If I say, "Surely the darkness shall fall on me," indeed, the darkness will not hide me from You, for the night shines as the day, and the darkness and the light are both alike to You. I want to stay in Your presence forever.

O Lord God, You made me in Your image; You formed my inward parts; You covered and wove me in my mother's womb. I'm most grateful, and I will praise You, for I am fearfully and wonderfully made. Your works are wonderful, marvelous, and glorious, and my soul knows them so very well. My frame and my bones were not hidden from You when I was made in secret and skillfully woven. Your eyes saw my substance before I was formed in my mother's womb. And in Your book of life all their names were written, the days fashioned for me, when yet there were none of them—there were no days. I existed in You before I existed, before there was a me. You gave me life—eternal life—and I am forever grateful. You know my beginning, my end, and everything in between. You are an awesome God!

How precious are Your thoughts to me! The sum of them is great. If I could count them, they would be more in number than the sand. I lie down and sleep as You watch over me; when I awake, I am still with You. Your enemies speak against You wickedly and take Your name in vain. Do I hate and loathe those who hate You and rise up against You? Yes, I do! I detest them completely and count them as my enemies too.

Examine me. You know my heart. Try me, and know my anxieties. Lord, look beyond my faults and see my needs; let Your mercy and grace rest upon me; cleanse and forgive me; and lead me in Your everlasting way that I should go, according to Your will.

In the name of Jesus, I pray. Amen.

(Based on Psalm 139)

Have Mercy upon Me;
Forgive Me of My Sins

Have mercy upon me, O God, according to Your loving-kindness. According to the multitude of Your tender mercies, blot out my transgressions. Forgive me and wash me thoroughly from my iniquity and cleanse me from my sin. I acknowledge my transgressions, and my sin is always before me. Against You, and You only, have I sinned, and done this evil in Your sight. That You may be found just when You speak, and blameless when You judge.

I was brought forth in iniquity, and in sin my mother conceived me. Behold, You desire truth in inward parts, and in the hidden part You will make me to know wisdom. Purge me with hyssop, and then I shall be clean. Wash me in the blood of Jesus, and I shall be whiter than snow. Hide Your face from my sins and blot out all my iniquities. Restore me spiritually and make me whole again. Make me hear joy and gladness; mend my brokenness.

Create in me a clean heart, O God, and renew a steadfast spirit within me. Do not cast me away from Your presence, and do not take Your Holy Spirit from me. Return to me the joy of Your salvation, and uphold and keep me by Your generous Spirit. Then I will teach transgressors and tell others of Your Word and ways, and sinners shall be converted to You and souls won for Your kingdom. I will tell the world of Your love, mercy, and grace and of what You and Jesus Christ, Your only begotten Son, have done for me and for the world.

Deliver me from all guilt and from the hand of my enemies, O God, the God of my salvation, and my tongue shall sing aloud of Your righteousness. Open my lips, and my mouth shall show forth your praise. For You do not desire sacrifice, or else I would give it. You do not delight in burnt offering.

The sacrifices that You desire are a broken spirit, a broken and contrite heart, inward worship in spirit and truth, and praise from the heart. You are also pleased with the sacrifices of righteousness and that we present our bodies as a living sacrifice, holy and acceptable to You. These, O God, You desire and will not despise. I confess my sins. Thank You for being faithful. Forgive me and cleanse me from all unrighteousness. Bless Jerusalem and all Your people in every nation. In the name of Jesus, I pray. Amen.

(See Psalm 51, given to me in a dream, June 11, 1988.)

God's Loving-Kindness and Mercy

Father God, in the name of Jesus, I pray that You will give ear to my words. Thank You for Your graciousness, loving-kindness, and mercy, for You are the God of my salvation. You are the one I love, trust, rely on, and have faith in. You are more than enough and everything that I want or need. I have trusted in Your mercy, and my heart shall rejoice of Your salvation.

Father, show Your loving-kindness by Your right hand; save Your children who trust in You; and keep Your covering over them. Your loving-kindness is better than life, and I will always praise your name and bless You while I live in this life and my eternal life. You withhold no good thing from me, and You take care of me and supply all my needs according to Your riches in Jesus Christ. You give me the desires of my heart. Keep me in perfect peace as I keep my mind focused on You. You give me unspeakable joy, and You give me Your perfect strength when I am weak. Your grace is amazing; Your mercy is great toward me, and I rejoice in You—and in You alone. I will forever praise, worship, exalt, and glorify Your holy name.

Bless Your people everywhere. Embrace them with Your love, save them, protect them, encourage their hearts, heal them, make them whole, and shower them with blessings. Let Your Holy Spirit draw them to You, and lead and guide them into Your truth. Reveal Yourself to those who are seeking You and those who are thirsty to know and learn of You. Let them know that You are real and that You love them so very much and want to give them eternal life.

Father, bless Israel and keep it safe from all those who wish to destroy it.

I pray that You are pleased with me and that You accept the words of my mouth and the meditation of my heart. Thank You for salvation and eternal life in Your kingdom.

In Jesus's name I pray. Amen.

Thank You

Father God, I come to You right now just to say thank You. I'm not asking for anything, nor am I complaining; I just want to give You thanks and praise for all that You have done for me and my family. For You have done so much for us. If I had ten trillion tongues, still I would not have enough to give You the praise that You deserve.

Thank You for my wonderful family. Thank You for watching over us all day and during the night as we sleep, and for waking us up each morning, and for letting us see another day with brand-new mercies. For You are our protector, shield, and buckler. You are our shelter from the storms of this life. You are so good to us. You are a faithful and gracious God. Thank You for food, clothes, shoes, and shelter. Thank You for my ability to walk and move my limbs, to talk and speak of Your goodness, and to praise Your name. Thank You for giving me wisdom, knowledge, and understanding. You are a loving and kind God.

Thank You for allowing the aches, pain, trials, and tests that I encounter from time to time. Because of them I have become stronger; my faith has increased. I know that You are a healer and a problem solver. I know that there's nothing too hard for You. You always make a way for me when there seems to be no way, and You have never left me alone. Thank You, Father. I know that nothing that I suffer on this earth can be compared to what You have prepared waiting for me in glory. You are a merciful God.

Thank You for loving me so much that even when I was yet in sin, You gave Your Son Jesus Christ, who was sinless, to die for my sins on a cross. Thank You for raising Him up from the grave on the third day for my justification. I thank Jesus Christ for loving me so much that He was willing to obey You even to the point of death and temporary separation from You. He loved me that much and wished to give me the gift of eternal life. You are a God of grace and mercy.

Thank You for canceling my appointment with hell, delivering my soul from the sting of death, and robbing the grave of its victory. Thank You for delivering me from spiritual death and separation from You. For the wages of sins is death, but the gift of God is eternal life. You are a just and righteous God. Thank You for this great gift that no one other than You could have given me and for Jesus Christ Your Son. What a loving, mighty, awesome, and remarkable God You are. There is no one like You. Thank You for always supplying my needs and the needs of my family. You are my source, and I depend totally on You. You are the God of more than enough. Everything on this earth, in heaven, and beneath the earth belongs to You.

Father, thank You for making it possible through Jesus Christ that I can now come boldly to Your throne of grace and tell you my request, obtain mercy, and find grace to help in my time of need. You already know my thoughts even before I speak. Thank You for such a great opportunity and for the honor and privilege to be in the presence of the almighty God, Creator of the heavens and the earth and all that is in it—the God who is all-seeing, all-knowing, and everywhere at once. Oh, what an honor! One cannot grasp such a thing unless they have a personal relationship with You and believe in and have faith in Jesus Christ Your Son. With my whole heart, I will forever worship, praise, and thank You. In the name of Jesus, I pray. Amen.

Lord, Your Word Says …

Father God, Creator of heaven and earth and everything and everyone that is in it, the one and only true almighty and awesome God who cannot lie and cannot fail, You keep your covenant and promises. You keep Your Word and fulfill it. You send Your Word out to perform whatever You send it to do, and it does not return to You void but accomplishes and fulfills Your purpose. You are a God of love, mercy, grace, forgiveness, and graciousness to all people. Please let Your ear be attentive to the prayer of Your child, and respond. I have confidence that You love me and that You do hear and will answer me.

I'm going through some things right now that threaten to overwhelm me. I sometimes feel like I can't breathe and that I'm drowning in my trials and tribulations. I'm finding it difficult to keep my head above water and hold on. Father, I feel as though I'm sinking. I need to hear from You right now; I need to feel Your embrace; I need You to rescue me from these troubled waters and storms that are endeavoring to overtake me. I need to see Your light at the end of this tunnel right now because darkness is trying to overshadow me. Father, save me!

Father God, Your Word says that I can cast my cares (anxiety, hurt, pain, problems) upon You because You care for me. It says that if I cast my burden on You, You will sustain me (1 Peter 5:7; Psalm 55:22). Your Word says that You will never leave me or forsake me (Hebrews 13:5) and that You will be with me until the end of this age.

Your Word says, "Come to Me, all who labor and are heavy laden, and I will give you rest. Take My yoke upon you and learn of Me, for I am gentle and lowly in heart, and you will find rest for your souls. For My yoke is easy and My burden is light" (Matthew 10:28–30). Your Word says that Your peace You will give me, not as the world gives, and that I must let not my heart be troubled or afraid (John 14:27).

Your Word says You will supply all my needs according to Your riches in glory by Christ Jesus (Philippians 4:19). Your Word says that no weapon formed against me will prosper and that every tongue that rise up against me, you will condemn. For this is my heritage as Your child (Isaiah 54:17).

Your Word says that You are full of compassion and that You show mercy (Psalm 78.38; Zechariah 7:9). Great are Your new mercies toward me every day, and great is Your faithfulness. For there is no one like You. Father, I believe, and I receive, Your Holy Word. I thank You for every promise and for working out everything that pertains to my life for my good.

Your Word says You will never leave me or forsake me (Deuteronomy 31:6). Thank You!

Thank You for Your strength, for Your sustaining and unconditional love, for my family, and for all You do for us. I will let nothing and no one separate me from You, and I will forever love and trust You.

In Jesus's name, I pray. Amen.

May You Be Blessed with God's Choice Blessings

May the Lord bless you and keep you and make His face shine upon you and be gracious to you. May He lift up His countenance upon you and give you peace.

May the Lord our God grant you your heart's desire according to His will for your life and fulfill His purpose for your life. May He be with you and answer you in times of trouble. May He never leave you or forsake you (so long as you don't forsake Him). May you remain rooted and grounded in your faith in Jesus Christ, God's Son, our Lord and Savior. May He abide in you as you abide in Him.

May you be filled with His Holy Spirit and with the knowledge of His will for your life in all wisdom and spiritual understanding so that you may walk worthy before our Lord Jesus Christ, totally and fully pleasing to Him, being fruitful in every good work that you do for Him, and increasing in His knowledge as He strengthens you with all might according to His glorious and awesome power. May you abide in all patience and long-suffering with joy unspeakable as you give thanks to God the Father, who has qualified you to be a partaker of the inheritance of the saints in the marvelous light. May you walk in the light as He is in the light and have true fellowship with Him.

For God has delivered you from the power of darkness, of Satan, sin, and death, and has transferred you into the light, the kingdom of Jesus Christ His Son and His love, in whom you have redemption through His blood. You have been bought with a great price, and you are not your own. You and I, and all who love, believe, have faith in and trust in Him, are now His children and belong to Him.

I pray that you will confess your sins to Jesus Christ, believing that He died on the cross for your sins, that God raised Him from the dead on the third day for your justification, and that He is faithful and just to forgive you and to cleanse you from all your evil and wicked ways. He loves you! My brothers and sisters: *nothing but the blood of our Lord Jesus can wash away our sins, make us whole, and give us a new life and eternal life with Him.*

May you (and your family) be blessed with God's choice blessings. May the love, grace, mercy, peace, hope, and favor of God the Father, our Lord Jesus Christ, and the fellowship of the Holy Spirit be with us all until His Second Coming, which is nearer than it was yesterday.

In the name of Jesus, I pray. Amen.

(Numbers 6:24–26; Colossians 1:10–14; 1 Corinthians 6:19–20; 1 John 1:7, 9, 2:25)

Hear My Prayer, O Lord My God

Hear my prayer, O Lord my God, and give ear to my supplications. I lift up my heart and my hands to You. In Your faithfulness and righteousness, please answer me. Stretch out Your hands from heaven above and rescue me and deliver from the hand of my enemies and from those who speak lying words against me. Protect me and preserve me from violent ones and those who have purposed to make my steps stumble. For in You I take shelter from the storms of life. You are my hiding place, my protector, and my deliverer.

Let my prayer be set before You as a sweet-smelling incense, and the lifting up of my hands as the evening sacrifice. I will give You the sacrifice of praise. I ask You to set a guard over my mouth and keep watch over the door of my lips. Lead and guide me by Your Holy Spirit in the way You will for me to go. I submit to Your purpose, will, and destiny for my life. You are my God, the strength of my salvation, and I trust in You.

I will praise You with my whole heart. I will honor, worship, and exalt Your holy name for Your mercy, grace, faithfulness, tender loving-kindness, and truth. You will perfect and complete all that concerns me. And even when I walk amid trouble, Father, You will revive me and stretch out Your mighty hand against the wrath (violent anger, fury) of my enemies. And You will save me.

Oh yes, I will extol You. I will bless Your name because You are worthy, You are great, and You deserve all the praise. Your greatness is unsearchable, beyond our understanding. O Lord my God, You are mighty in power, for You have all power, and Your understanding is infinite. Heal the sick. Mend broken hearts and make them whole. Open the eyes of the blind, and unstop the ears of the deaf. Cause the lame to walk and leap with joy. And the tongue of any who cannot speak, loose it so that they can sing and praise Your name. Strengthen the feeble and those who are weak. Encourage those who need to be encouraged, those who have no hope and have given up on life. Raise the dead spiritually and give them a heart of flesh.

Heal Your land, save Your children, and protect them from the hand and tricks of Satan. Cover with the blood of Jesus your children who face danger every day in other countries for proclaiming the gospel of Jesus Christ. Continue to protect them, encourage their hearts, and supply their needs according to Your riches in glory. For You are our refuge, our strength, and a present help in time of trouble. Lift up the humble and cast the evil and wicked down to the ground. For You are not a God who takes pleasure in wickedness, nor shall evil dwell with You (Psalm 5:4).

O Lord, my God, my Savior, You are faithful in all Your words and holy in all Your ways and works. Hear my prayer, and incline unto my cry. Remember that I am but flesh, but You, Father, are full of compassion, grace, and mercy that endures forever. You forgive my sins. And now, let the words of my mouth and the meditation of my heart be acceptable to You. For You are my strong tower and redeemer. In Jesus's name, I pray. Amen.

(Referenced scriptures: Psalm 143:1, 9, 144:11, 145:1–3, 8, 138:1, 7, 8, 19:14; Philippians 1:6)

Letter to My Heavenly Father, May 6, 1999

Dear Heavenly Father,

It's 2:04 Thursday morning. I just got up to read in the book of Daniel. However, I suddenly feel the need to inscribe this letter to You. I'm going through quite a few things right now—well, I have been for some time now—and I really, really need Your help. I want and need Your guidance. Some of these things I have already talked to You about, but I now realize that I have not totally trusted You to answer my prayers and solve my problems. Perhaps, I now wonder, if the reason why I didn't was because I wasn't fully ready to submit and surrender my whole heart, my whole life, and my whole being to You, Lord of Lords, God of heaven and earth.

Please forgive me of all my sins and cleanse me from all unrighteousness. Thank You for Your love, mercy, and grace. Please never forsake me or leave me, and do not take Your Holy Spirit away from me. For I confess that I have sinned against You, and You only. I admit that I have been hardheaded and disobedient. I have been slothful and lazy in reading Your Holy Word, going to Your house of worship, witnessing and winning souls for Your kingdom, performing church duties, and doing the work that You have called me to do. I have said things, done things, and gone places that were not appropriate for a Christian. I haven't always displayed love toward my neighbors, friends, and family. I even sometimes trusted and had faith in humankind more than in You. Father God, forgive me. Show Your mercy and loving-kindness toward me, Your friend, Your child, Your servant. Give me another chance to do Your will, to prove to You that I can be trusted and obedient to do the work that You have called me to do, and to bring Your message of love, grace, hope, and salvation to Your people and to a world where so many souls are dying without hope and without knowing You or experiencing Your love personally.

Father God, thank You for loving me, for saving my soul, and for making me whole. Thank You for Your Son Jesus Christ, who loves me so much that He gave His life on the cross. You raised Him on the third day so that I could have a right standing and relationship with You. Thank You for my family and for their salvation. Thank You for giving us the chance to have eternal life with You. And not just us, but everyone who loves You and who believes and has faith in Jesus Christ Your Son and our Lord and Savior.

I thought about sending this letter to You via express mail so it could reach You quickly. Then I remembered that You told me that I could come boldly to the throne of grace to obtain mercy and make my request known to You. My thanks to Jesus Christ, Lord and Savior, for making this possible; for being my Advocate, Mediator, and Intercessor; and for interceding on my behalf. Thank You for Your faithfulness, Your mercy, and Your amazing grace. My love for You is everlasting, and I'll never leave You, forsake You, or deny You or Your name. You are the Bishop of my soul. *You are the only true living God.*

Eternally Yours, Your daughter,
Sarah

Thank You for Healing Me

Abba, Father, first and foremost I thank You for forgiving me of my sins (known and unbeknown to me) and cleansing me from all unrighteousness. I come to You in the name of Jesus, asking You to heal me of this illness or disease [call it by name if you know it] that has attacked my body. I know that You are a healer and that You can heal me if You choose to and if I have faith enough to believe.

Father, I believe that You desire for me to be healed and be in good health. I do believe You and ask You to help me with my unbelief. I cry out to You, as so many others do who come to You, like a child comes to its father, for prayer in Your Word, saying, "Lord, I believe; help my unbelief" (Mark 9:24)! I know that You will give me the faith that I need to bring healing to my body.

Thank You for healing me. Your Word in Isaiah 53:5 says that Jesus Christ was wounded (pierced through His side) for my transgressions and was bruised for my iniquities. The chastisement for our peace was upon Him, and by His stripes, the blows that cut into His back and ripped out His flesh, I am already healed. Thank You for Your precious blood shed for me. I believe, and I receive, Your Word. Jesus Himself took my infirmities and bore my sicknesses (Matthew 8:17). Thank You for healing me. In Your Word (1 Peter 2:24), Jesus Himself bore my sins in His own body on the tree so that I, having died to sins, might live for righteousness. By His stripes (which He took for me) I *was* healed; therefore, I *am* healed. I will walk by faith, not by sight, nor by my five senses or the way that I feel.

Father, Jesus said (John 14:13) that whatever I ask You in His name, He will do so that You may be glorified in Him. Therefore, I ask for the healing of my whole body, and I receive it by faith in the name of Jesus.

Thank You for healing me and for never leaving me or forsaking me. Thank You for not giving up on me. Thank You for suffering and dying for my sins and for rising from the dead on the third day for my justification. I will love and trust You forever, and I will always look up to You for my help, knowing that it comes only from You. For You can do anything but fail. You are an awesome God! I will tell of Your graciousness, faithfulness, and mercy shown to me, and I will glorify Your name forevermore. In the name of Jesus, I pray. Amen.

Grant to Thy Servant, Your Child

Father, You are God. You made the heaven, the earth, the sea, all things, and everyone. You are Alpha and Omega. You know, hear, and see all. You are everywhere at the same time. You hold life and death in the palm of Your hand. In You I live, breathe, and have my being. I can't do anything without You, but with and through You, and Jesus Christ Your Son, my Savior, I can do all things that You have ordained me to do.

Thank You for Your mercy, Your grace, and the Holy Spirit, who enables me to live a holy life here on earth, to do the work You have assigned to me, and to have fellowship with You, Father, and Your Son Jesus Christ, our Savior and soon-coming King. Satan is trying to stop me from speaking Your Holy Word and doing the work You have called me and given me to do. He is trying to keep your people in bondage and darkness so that he can kill, steal from, and destroy them.

I realize that Satan is after my anointing because he knows that it is the anointing of God that will destroy his evil works. I resist him and give him no place in my life. No weapon he forms against me will prosper, and I know that You will condemn every tongue he causes to rise up against me. Father, I ask that You grant to me, Your servant, Your child, that I will speak Your Word in season and out of season, with boldness, with confidence, and in truth.

And with Your holy hand on my hands, as I stretch them out toward and lay them upon Your people, Father God, I pray that You will save their souls and give them eternal life; heal their bodies and spirits; deliver them out of bondage and darkness into Your marvelous light; and sanctify all of them who will believe with faith and accept Jesus Christ as Lord and Savior, along with the signs and wonders that will be done in and through the name of Jesus, who gave His life for us all so that we could have eternal life, as You raised Him up from the grave on the third day for our justification.

For we have been forgiven and accepted into a right standing and relationship with You as You desired in the beginning, from the foundation of the world. And for this, Father, I am eternally grateful. Hear my prayer, and grant my request to Your servant, Your child.

In the name of Jesus, I pray. Amen.

Hear Me, Oh Lord. Have Your Way

Father God, You said in Your Word (Jeremiah 33:3): "Call to Me, and I will answer you, and show you great and mighty things, which you do not know." So, here I am calling to You. I fully surrender and give myself totally to You. I am Your vessel and ready for my Master's use. Use me for Thy glory, not my glory (for You share Your glory with no one). Use me to help save the lost and to win souls for Thy kingdom. Use me to be a blessing to Your people. Mold me and make me the person You want and created me to be. Anoint me as You appoint me. I will give You all the glory and praise, and I will encourage other people to do the same.

> Let Your Holy Spirit lead and guide me into all truth. Your Word is truth. Let Your Word dwell in me richly. Order my steps, keep me on the right path, and keep me from going astray. Let Your will, not mine, be done in and through me, and let Your will be done here on earth as it is in heaven.

> Father, as a believer who has faith in You and in Jesus Christ Your Son, my Lord and Savior, I ask in the name of Jesus that You let these signs follow me according to Your Word in Mark 16:15–18. By Your authority and power, and by the power of the Holy Spirit that is in and upon me, in the name of Jesus (the name above every name), I will cast out demons, I will speak with new tongues, and I will tread on serpents. And if I drink (or ingest) anything deadly, it will by no means hurt or harm me. I will lay hands on the sick, and they will recover. And all who hear the gospel of Jesus Christ and believe will be saved, but all who do not believe will be condemned.

Hear me, O Lord. Have Your way in my life and in the lives of Your people. How excellent is Your name in all the earth! We give You glory.

In Jesus's name I pray. Amen.

Jesus, You Are My Everything!

Jesus, You are my everything! You are my light and my salvation. I will not fear what humankind can do to me, nor fear anything on earth or underneath the earth, because You are my God, Savior, and Lord. You made me in Your image; I am adopted into Your royal family, and I am Your child. You are my strength, shield, and buckler, and in You I live, move, and have my being. You are my light and my salvation.

You are my best friend. You supply all my needs. You lift me up when I am down. You make me smile when there is no smile. You make me happy when I am sad. In Your presence I am filled with so much joy. You are the only one who can put me in heaven or hell (literally). My whole desire—and I will seek after it—is to be wherever You are for eternity and to behold Your glory. Thank You for protecting me and my family and for hiding us in Your pavilion, in the secret place of Your tabernacle. Thank You for giving us victory over our enemies and foes.

There were times when I felt like giving up, but whenever I cried unto You, You had mercy on me and answered me. You comforted me like no other. You have always been my help and have come to my rescue. You have never failed me, and You have always been faithful to me. Thank You for welcoming me into Your sheepfold. I will wait on You, and I will be of good courage as I await Your return to this earth. Thank You for being my God, my Lord, my Savior, my King, my Judge, my Waymaker, and my Provider.

Jesus, You are my everything and all that I need. It is a great honor, pleasure, and privilege to know and serve You. Thank You for allowing me the opportunity to choose and have eternal life and live in Your presence forever. In Your name, I pray. Amen.

Praise the Lord Our God;
Serve Him with Gladness

I will make a joyful noise of praise to the Lord wherever I go! I will serve my God with gladness, and I will approach His presence with praise and singing, giving Him thanks, for He is worthy.

> I know that it is You, O God who made me; I did not make myself, nor did humankind make me. I am Your child and the sheep of Your pasture. I will therefore enter into Your gates with thanksgiving and into Your courts with praise and worship.

I am so thankful to You, and I will forever bless Your name. For You, Lord, my God, are good. Your mercy is everlasting, and Your truth endures to all generations.

In Jesus's name I pray. Amen.

(Psalm 100 was given to me in a dream on January 13, 1991.)

My Love Songs to Jesus

I'm waiting for You, Jesus, and I'll keep waiting for You. For You have been so good to me, and I will always give Your name the praise.

I love to sing songs for Jesus. I love to sing for You. When I feel like all hope is gone and I don't know which way to turn, I tell everyone what I'm going to do: "I will hold on to God's unchanging hand, hold on to His hand."

Jesus knows, and He cares. He knows about my hurt; He knows about my pain. Yes, Jesus knows, and He cares. O Lord, I shall not suffer to be removed from this place of love, peace, joy, strength, and safety.

If you can conceive, you can receive—and you can depend on God. Believe and trust Him with your whole heart.

Jesus, You said to me: "Just call on Me. I'll see you through. Just call on Me; I'll take care of you." Thank You, for I know that I can always count on You.

For You are my endlessness. You are my sole success. I don't know what I would do without You. Your love never ends, and Your mercy endures forever. Without You I am nothing, nor can I do anything. For in You, Jesus, I live, move, and have my being.

Hallelujah, praise the Lord! I give You thanks, O Lord my God. For 'tis so sweet to trust in Jesus, to believe in His Word and His promises.

When I pray, I will listen and wait for His answer. He's my lily of the valley. I know He's my bright shining star. What is His name? His name is Jesus. I know His name. His name is Jesus. And I know that God heard me (when I prayed).

I just want to say thank You, Lord, for all You have done for my family and me. Thank You for setting me free! Thank You for supplying all our needs; thank You for healing us; thank You for sealing us with Your Holy Spirit. Thank You for Your love, mercy, and grace. Thank You for everlasting life. I love You more than anyone or anything.

Jesus, I dance with no one. I'm waiting for You.

(God gave me these songs in my dreams.)

In the Word of God, There Is a Word

We are living in challenging and perilous times. We are living in the last days on this earth as we know it. There are countless Bible scriptures for every situation in life that we may face. No matter what we go through or what life throws at us, in the Word of God there is a word that will bring us comfort, joy, encouragement, confidence, strength, guidance, direction, and a peace that is beyond our understanding.

In the Word of God, there is a word that will lift up our hearts and tell us that God is with us and that He is more than those against us (Romans 8:31). Therefore, we should not fear our enemies.

In the Word of God, there is a word that tells us to cast our cares upon Him because He cares for us and He will carry our burdens and sustain us (1 Peter 5:7; Psalm 55:22).

In the Word of God, there is a word that tells us not to fear, because God has not given us a spirit of fear but one of power, of love, and of a sound mind (2 Timothy 1:7).

In the Word of God, there is a word that tells us to be strong and be of good courage (Deuteronomy 31:6). In the Word of God, there is a word that tells us that we can do all things through Christ, for it is He who gives us strength (Philippians 4:13).

In the Word of God, there is a word that ensures us that when we go through the fire, floods, deep waters, and the storms of life, God is right there by our side. He is either holding our hand as we walk through it or is carrying us in His loving arms (Isaiah 43:2).

In the Word of God, there is a word that assures us that we are healed from sicknesses and diseases because over two thousand years ago Jesus Christ was wounded for our transgressions and bruised for our iniquities.

The chastisement of our peace was upon Him, and by His stripes we were and are healed (Isaiah 53:4–5).

In the Word of God, there is a word that reassures us that if God is for us, He is more than the whole world against us, and no matter how difficult or fiery the trials and tests we may face, or the schemes and fiery darts that Satan throws at us, we are more than conquerors in Christ Jesus, for greater is He who lives inside of us than he that is in the world (Romans 8:31, 37).

In the Word of God, there is a word that lets us know our God will provide for us. He is our source, and He will supply all our needs according to His riches in glory by Jesus Christ (Philippians 4:19).

In the Word of God, there is a word that tells us that we may boldly say that God is our helper, that we can rely on Him and trust Him to be there for us in any situation. And then we will not fear what humankind can do to us (Hebrews 13:6).

In the Word of God, there is a word that assures us that God will never leave us or forsake us, so long as we believe and have faith in Him, so long as we trust Him, and so long as we don't leave or forsake Him (Hebrews 13:5).

In the Word of God, there is a word that promises us that we can now come boldly to the throne of grace (in faith and with confidence, making our request known to God), so we can obtain mercy and find grace to help in our time of need (Hebrews 4:16).

In the Word of God, there is a word that lets us know and assures us that Jesus Christ is alive and is seated in supreme honor at the right hand of God our Father as our High Priest, Advocate, Intercessor, and Mediator. And He is the propitiation for our sins (Acts 7:55–56; Ephesians 1:20; Hebrews 4:14; 7:25–26, 8:1, 6; 1 John 2:1).

In the Word of God, there is a word that tells us that if we do mess up, if we do fall down, we must get up quickly and confess our sins to Jesus, for we know that He is faithful and just to forgive us and cleanse us from all unrighteousness (1 John 1:9). In the Word of God, there is a word that promises and assures us of eternal life with God our Father and Jesus Christ our Lord, Savior, and soon-coming King (John 3:15; 6:47).

In the Word of God, there is a word that tells us that God comforts and encourages His children in all suffering, tests, trials, and tribulations.

He also chastens those whom He loves (2 Corinthians 1:3–7; Hebrews 12:6). In the Word of God, there is a word that lets us know that we do not have to live in fear because God is our protector, and we dwell in a secret place under His almighty wings (Psalm 91:1).

In the Word of God, there is a word that lets us know that we don't have to fear the darts and weapons that Satan throws at and uses against us. For God says that no weapon formed against us shall prosper, and every tongue that rises up against us shall be condemned, because as servants and children of God, this is our heritage, and our righteousness is from Him (Isaiah 54:17).

In the Word of God, there is a word that tells me that the Lord our God is gracious and full of compassion (Psalm 111:4). He is also loving, kind, and long-suffering. In the Word of God, there is a word that tells me that through the mercies of our God we are not consumed or destroyed because His compassions does not fail. For He grants us brand-new mercies every morning, and for this, great is His faithfulness (Lamentations 3:23).

In the Word of God, there is a word that when my finances are not looking too good and I still have bills to pay and personal problems that are weighting me down, "I will lift up my eyes to the hill from where my help comes from. For my help comes from the Lord our God who made the heavens, earth, and everyone and everything in it. I will trust Him" (Psalm 121:1–2).

In the Word of God, there is a word that tells me: "But when the kindness and the love of God our Savior toward humankind appeared, Not by works of righteousness which we have done, but according to His mercy He saved us, by the washing of regeneration, and renewing of the Holy Ghost; which He shed on us abundantly through Jesus Christ our Savior; that being justified by His grace, we should be made heirs according to the hope of eternal life" (Titus 3:4–7).

I hope and pray that you will be strengthened, comforted, encouraged, enriched, and enlightened as you read the Word of God (the Holy Bible). Allow Him to speak to you through His Holy Word. Talk to Him respectfully as you would talk to someone you love and trust. Jesus wants to have a personal relationship with us. He loves us with an everlasting love, and He wants to give us eternal life. What an awesome God we serve! There is none like Him.

I pray that God will guide you, prepare you, and direct your heart to His love and to the patience of Jesus Christ. May His amazing grace, plentiful mercy, and favor be with us all. And may we be found blameless and worthy to go back with Jesus on that great day when He returns, when we will reign with Him forever and forever. Prepare to meet the Creator of heaven, earth, and underneath the earth, the one and only true living almighty God.

Believe it or not, and whether you are prepared or not, Jesus Christ is coming soon. He wants us to be prepared for His arrival.

About the Author

Dr. Sarah A. Jones is a minister and ambassador for God the Father and Jesus Christ. She has a heart for all people. Several years ago, a voice spoke to her in a dream and said to her: "Let your testimony be: 'Jesus Christ is coming!' Tell the people so that they can be prepared upon His arrival." Therefore, she will cry out loud, will not hold back the truth, and will lift up her voice like a trumpet as she is commanded by God and as she is led, guided, and directed by the Holy Spirit.

God has been communicating with Sarah through dreams since she was sixteen years old. She has published two books about those dreams and her interpretations of them. Her focus and desire is to win souls for Jesus so that others may have eternal life in the kingdom of God. She also seeks to encourage, enlighten, and inspire others and to speak the truth based on the Word of God.

Sarah worked at one of the most prominent book publishing companies in New York for twenty-eight years. She advanced within the company, receiving promotions and positions based on her diverse abilities and superior performance. Her education, studies, and degrees are in business administration, religion, theology, and Christian education.

Sarah lives in New York with her family and frequently vacations in northern Virginia.

Also by the Author

God Revealing His Plan for You and Me through Dreams, volume 1 (covers dreams from 1966 to 1994)
Paperback: $17.95, ISBN 978-1-4497-1928-9
Hardcover: $33.95, ISBN 978-1-4497-1929-6

God Revealing His Plan for You and Me through Dreams, volume 2 (covers dreams from 1995 to 2008, with a preview of dreams from 2009 to April 2011)
Paperback: $17.95, ISBN 978-1-4497-3289-9
Hardcover: $33.95, ISBN 978-1-4497-3403-9
Also sold in Nook Book: $3.99

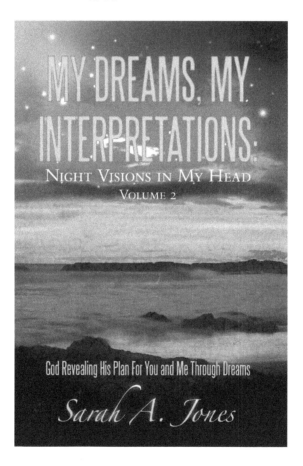

What has God told you to do through dreams and visions and in His Word that you haven't started doing yet? Well, now is the time to do all that He has told you to do because night is coming and then no one will be able to work. This book is for you. Find yourself in the pages; allow God, Jesus, and the Holy Spirit to speak to you and reveal Their plan and purpose for your life.

God has been showing me dreams and visions since I was sixteen years old. I was instructed by Him to write these books, and He told me that they would be a blessing to everyone who read them in faith with expectation to receive from God. All of my dreams and interpretations in these books are given, revealed, and inspired by God the Father, Jesus Christ, and the Holy Spirit. Volume 1 and 2 will inspire, encourage, and strengthen you, build your faith, and bless you. God loves you. He knows your situation and wants to minister to you personally—one-on-one.

To order, please contact the author, WestBow Press, your nearest bookstore, or order online.

We welcome your comments or questions concerning this book. For prayer requests and to book public engagements, please inquire by email or writing:

Sarah A. Jones
P.O. Box 260524
Brooklyn, NY 11226-0524
Email address: sarjon777@gmail.com

CPSIA information can be obtained
at www.ICGtesting.com
Printed in the USA
BVHW071217060919
557776BV00001B/58/P

9 781973 666653